Board Compass

Arthur D. Little Books

A series of books on management and other scientific and technical subjects by senior professional staff members of Arthur D. Little, Inc., the international consulting and research organization. The series also includes selected nonproprietary case studies.

Acquisition and Corporate Development
James W. Bradley and Donald H. Korn

Bankruptcy Risk in Financial Depository Intermediaries
Assessing Regulatory Effects
Michael F. Koehn

Board Compass
What It Means to Be a Director in a Changing World
Robert Kirk Mueller

Career Conflict
Management's Inelegant Dysfunction
Robert Kirk Mueller

Corporate Responsibilities and Opportunities to 1990
Ellen T. Curtiss and Philip A. Untersee

Board Compass

**What It Means to Be a Director in a
Changing World**

Robert Kirk Mueller

An Arthur D. Little Book

Lexington Books
D.C. Heath and Company
Lexington, Massachusetts
Toronto

Library of Congress Cataloging in Publication Data

Mueller, Robert Kirk.
   Board compass.

   Includes index.
   1. Directors of corporations. I. Title.
HD2745.M8   658.4'2   79-1539
ISBN 0-669-02903-3

Published simultaneously in Canada

Printed in the United States of America

International Standard Book Number: 0-669-02903-3

Library of Congress Catalog Card Number: 79-1539

Contents

List of Figures

List of Tables

Introduction

Count Axel Gustaffson Oxenstierna, a seventeenth-century Swedish chancellor-statesman during the reigns of Gustavus II, Adolphus, and Christina, was a great diplomat, administrator, and strategist. He organized conquered territories, skillfully managed financial affairs, and chalked up diplomatic victories. He would have made an ideal corporation director today. One of his most famous remarks is referred to as Oxenstierna's law: "If you knew, my son, with what little wisdom the world is governed!"[1]

The count could have been speaking to the inhabitants of our currently troubled boardrooms. Strangely, though, wisdom is all about us, but more directorates need to recognize it and tap its source. There is an understandable reluctance to go outside the boardroom on many sensitive issues. However, the very sensitivity more often than not concerns the interface of the institution with other institutions and domains in society. Corporations increasingly need to wire their governance intelligence network throughout global society. Such initiative will help sense in timely fashion the winds of change, the impending key events, the pendulum swings, and the trends in extrinsic affairs that have an impact on the governance of a modern corporation.

Directors are becoming increasingly conscious of their role in providing oversight, evaluation, and direction to the internal company organization. This awareness is clearly recognized as vital to fulfilling directors' legal and fiduciary responsibilities. However, the awakening seems relatively slow concerning the notion that the board has another equally vital role: the role of governing the corporation in and around external shoals, to seize opportunity, and to relate the organization outside the boundary of the corporation's self-generated plans. The aim of this book is to explore the boardroom boundaries in an effort to help directors fulfill the mounting obligations of good corporate governance outside the boardroom.

The problem and opportunity is that of Oxenstierna's law. Gaining knowledge of a broad range of affairs and activities enveloping a corporation calls for a *boardroom ecology*. Such ecology would search for the interrelationships of the institution with its social, economic, political, and cultural environment. The suggestions in this book show how to put this wisdom into better boardroom use.

Like Count Oxenstierna, and well before his famous remark, the wise men of Greece also dealt with this question when the Delphic oracle pronounced Socrates to be that wisest person. Socrates' modest rejoinder—"'Tis because I alone of all the Greeks know that I know nothing"'—predates Oxenstierna but highlights the same issue.

If we could transmogrify the Seven Sages of Greece and institutionalize them into an eight-member model board of directors, with Socrates as the chairman, would this provide the requisite wisdom to govern an institution appropriately today? I doubt it. We need not only more resident wisdom but better means to sense the global environment. What is required is a sophisticated modern board ecology.

Let us try to capture (and oversimplify) the wisdom of these wise men of Greece in their own time frame of about 638 to 548 B.C. to see what they would have had to offer as resident resources in a directorate.

Solon of Athens's major point of view was "know thyself."

Chilo of Sparta contributed "consider the end" before the phrase became banal.

Thales of Miletus opined, "Who hateth suretyship is sure," long before banks had so many vice-presidents that a meeting looks like a run on the bank.

Bias of Priene lived up to his name with "most men are bad."

Cleobulus of Lindos cautioned with the concept of "the golden mean" or "avoid extremes," which seemed to imply being moderate in all things.

Pittacus of Mitylene made a spur-of-the-moment contribution before his charge became a platitude in "seize time by the forelock."

Probably the most enduring capsule of Greek wisdom we can reincarnate for our hypothetical board of Wise Men was put forth by Periander of Corinth before he died in 585 B.C.: "Nothing is impossible to industry."

This book, however, is not so much about the lack of wisdom used in corporate governance. It is more about the means of getting existing wisdom put to use in the board process. The complexity of affairs and velocity of change call for governance concepts embracing multiple roles, multiple goals, plural executives, tiered legal structures, management of conflict, reduction of uncertainty to probalistic risk, redeployment of assets, work-place hygiene, central life interests, environmental assessment, and risk management. Such notions as corporate development, venturing and centering, social and stock-holder democracy, systems concepts, trade-off mechanisms, strategic planning, cooptation, organization, and motivation are among the host of other governance concepts around which buzzwords abound.[2]

One day recently, a dozen or so of my colleagues and I were sitting around a somewhat spartan-style conference room at Acorn Park in our headquarters in Cambridge, Massachusetts. The style is not a structured attempt at any philosophical Greek ambiance but rather a heritage of Dr. Arthur Dehon Little (1863-1935), who functioned very successfully in this laboratory-like milieu to make, inter alia, a silk purse out of a sow's ear. His purpose was to demonstrate dramatically the wonders of rayon in its early days. Our conference aim was more modest and in connection with an interesting environmental scanning case for a large multinational corporation.

One of the issues before the client was the matter of corporate governance requirements of the future. Occasionally it is customary for a case team working on a project "to play the Greek" to a limited extent after serious cerebration has taken place. The related creature comfort rule in Greek banquets was *E pithi e apithi* ("Quaff, or be off!"), and so rather than depart we opened the modest mobile bar briefly to hypothesize further and test our day's work. The subject concerned some of the corporate governance trends and force fields external to companies that will affect the future of institutional governance. The role of the board of directors in this matter is particularly interesting to hypothesize about.

To provide a backdrop for the chapters that follow, here is some of the nonproprietary fallout from the role-playing exercise . . . a moderate "playing of the Greek." Some of these hypotheses are my own and may be stretching the corporate environment of the future, but that was the purpose of the exercise. I am further indebted to my Arthur D. Little colleagues who shared this speculative exercise with me.

Given these trends and forces, and setting aside any catastrophic surprises, I believe that a board of directors should develop its own board ecology in an open system mode in order to be prepared to cope with the responsibilities of corporate governance in a changing world. Here are some of the hypotheses we might acknowledge in developing a boardroom scenario, say toward the beginning of the twenty-first century—or even before.

Hypothesis 1: The issues raised in 1959 by Adolf A. Berle, Jr., in his book *Power without Property* that corporations are controlled by management rather than shareholders may be redressed at the cost of present managerial autonomy.[3] The means may involve establishing cumulative voting rights for stockholders and/or limiting voting to beneficial owners; requiring that costs of proxy solicitation be borne by the parties at interest, including management, or requiring that the corporation bear the costs of proxy solicitation for all parties at interest, given an appropriate due-process procedure where the arbiter is an independent third party; or increasing the shareholder information flow and shareholder participation in director nomination processes.

Hypothesis 2: Means may be sought in the future to extend corporations' liability for certain actions considered antisocial, without the corporation's merely passing the economic impacts directly through to suppliers, customers, and society in general. These means may involve capital dilution, wherein governmental agencies are due and/or obtain a portion of a corporation's capital, which may be used for remedial action (for example, for rehabilitation of injured employees); beneficial stock dividends awarded to class-action suit damage recipients; or board-of-director term appointments where the appointee represents an agency or constituency to which a judgment of liability has been determined.

Hypothesis 3: Federal corporate chartering may be required for companies engaging in multinational operations. The quid pro quo could involve relaxations of various federal legal regulations and appropriate national or international regulatory support of key operations in special cases.

Hypothesis 4: Rapidly increasing abilities for full accounting for the societal costs of managerial hiring and firing prerogatives will result in sharp modifications of managerial freedom. Some of these costs are educational investments not resulting in employment; the ability to treat laborers and white-collar clerical workers as "fungible goods," to be hired and laid off as the corporation needs, which results in social dislocation, unemployment compensation, and mounting social service costs; the depletion of personnel mental and skill capital during much less than a working lifetime when educational and training reinvestments are not made; or the costs of alternative production means that reduce total labor and/or skill levels where this can be seen as a problem of the commons, resulting in lower corporate production costs but having higher social costs that do not affect the corporate financial situation. Thus, the drive for job tenure rights and worker representation on boards will be seen as rational least-cost developments in the mid- to late-1980s.

Hypothesis 5: Christopher D. Stone puts forth the notion that social incentives that effectively channel the behavior of individuals in a socially desirable direction are not effective in channeling the behavior of a corporation.[4] A future board model would change composition and responsibilities of directorates and provide the public with access to corporate information of public consequence with direct public monitoring of corporations in situations where there is likelihood of corporate misconduct.

Hypothesis 6: Rediscovery of organizational relativity at the board level, changing board structure, more diligent exercise of directors' duty of care, more sensing apparatus outside the corporation, and a radical change in the systems for a board's sensing of internal operations. This would indicate increased director participation and the board, assuming a change-agent role.

Hypothesis 7: Organizational value systems and individual value systems present a clash of paradigms. Resolving value dilemmas in the boardroom will require education and significant change in attitudes—even beliefs—of some directors who are loath to debate abstract concepts in a formal boardroom session. The one life-one company-one career concept is wearing thin with younger executives who have been brought up during a stage of corporate development where executive mobility was not confined to vertical rise in one company or industry. Switching to other careers in other domains of activity, with different reward systems and social horizons, can no longer be classed as defection by a corporation traditionally set in its concepts of company dedication and loyalty.

Hypothesis 8: Future-perfect-planning concepts. These permit back planning in a strategic sense from a desired position in the long-term future. The concept may be near its turning point in corporate governance techniques. Organizations act as though long-range planning is the only answer; future-perfect-planning is the ultimate good and nonplanning is irrational and bad. Consistency is always considered better than inconsistency and that "organizational history must not be interpreted" in Stanford professor James G. March's words.

Boards of directors and organizations in general need to respond to impulses, as well as to resident wisdom in the boardroom. A cognitive style of corporate governance with some intuitive directors on the boardroom seats may indicate an improved composition for the board of the future.

I will close this syllogistic introduction before it traps us into a deductive scheme on how to govern a corporation of the future. Such a scheme could prove specious in real time.

Let us turn back to the Swedish world of Count Oxenstierna and his observation about with what little wisdom the world is governed. The task in the following chapters is to set forth some notions, insights, concepts, mechanics, checklists, hypotheses, and observations from actual experience. A panorama of perspectives is offered on some different ways to view the topic of corporate governance.

A word is in order here to acknowledge what has been happening recently in the board world. All is not static by any means. There are motions and notions already at work. The fiduciary standards to which boards of directors in the United States are being held are expanding rather rapidly as interpreted by courts, by the Congress, and by the public. Originally the model for a board was a simplistic legal one, built around laws and bylaws that were not created to cope with the current problems or to serve as an adequate framework for characterizing a board which could deal with future issues.

The idea of directors serving as share-owner representatives is being supplanted by a concept of multiple board accountability. Constituencies and forces at work outside are significantly affecting the American corporation, as well as the corporate stockholders. One of the basic questions is how to ensure board independence from management bias without compromising board competence or expertise in corporate operations.

Many proposals have been made for changes in roles and responsibilities of corporate directors. They have been proposed recently by consulting firms, professors, the New York Stock Exchange, the Securities and Exchange

Commission (SEC), the American Management Associations (AMA), the Organization for Economic Co-operation and Development (OECD), the American Institute of Chartered Public Accountants (AICPA), consumer groups, and public-interest law organizations, among others. Many of these proposals are well on their way to becoming either law or regulation, or consensus. Some of these influences would require that board members be directly responsible for implementation and recite the number of board functions that cannot be delegated to management. The following are examples of some of these suggested changes on the United States scene:

Establishment by law of public-interest directors for all large corporations to monitor attention to public concerns such as those dealing with EEOC, EPA, OSHA, ERISA compliance.

Forced separation of chairman/chief operating executive positions and incumbents.

Independent staff and/or board advisory committees.

Audits of board performance by outside experts.

Mandatory rotation of audit firms.

Federal chartering of "corporate giants."

Formation of a national corporate ethics board.

Participative management, codetermination, and worker-directors.

Boards and/or board committees restricted to outsiders or outsiders predominating ("outsiders" exclude vendor-directors).

Increased prohibitions on interlocking directorates.

Extended definition of materiality for disclosure purposes, including a board evaluation of managerial integrity.

A commonplace model for a board assumes a rather limited role confined to somewhat routine, even perfunctory approval of management action. This model is entirely inadequate and unprepared to evaluate and respond to pressures or accept the initiative in certain board-level matters of corporate governance in the future.

The purpose of this book, then, is to help directors grasp the evolving nature of the directorate of the future. Such an awareness can provide different "compass" to the board process and can go a long way toward letting more of that outside wisdom get into boardroom use. Too often boardrooms are barricaded by tradition, past concepts, beliefs, prejudices, bias, some obsolete value judgments, and, occasionally, insensitivity.

I hope that the hopscotch perspectives offered in the following chapters help directors do something before the policeman-in-the-boardroom and the sunshine-in-the-boardroom movements are forced on our corporations. The already swift acceptance of these movements may be a vogue—like anagrams and bustles—but it is a result of the limited initiative in boardroom self-reform. The period ahead will surely be the most exciting phase of corporate governance yet to be offered to responsible corporate directors.

This book is not for experts in board practice, scholars focusing on corporate governance, legal counsel, or other experienced boardroom inhabitants who are already taking action or are aware of the need to increase the board's compass. Rather the book is a panorama of concepts from different perspectives. This variety is offered to worried directors who find themselves in a board situation where change and reform are needed but too little thought has been given to the matter. I expect that some of these perspectives will provide a basis for constructive controversy in an otherwise stilted, zestless, or insensitive boardroom.

Notes

1. Paul Tabori, *The Art of Folly* (Philadelphia: Chilton Book Company, 1961), pp. 222-225.

2. For an overview of some of these topics, see my *Metadevelopment: Beyond the Bottom Line* (Lexington: Lexington Books, D.C. Health Co., 1977).

3. Adolph A. Berle Jr., *Power without Property* (New York: Harcourt, Brace and Company, 1959).

4. Christopher D. Stone, *Where the Law Ends: The Social Control of Corporate Behavior* (New York: Harper and Row, 1975).

Board Compass

1 Credible Futures: A Boardroom Scan

You cannot fight against the future. Time is on our side.
Prime Minister William Ewart Gladstone, April 27, 1866

About a century before Gladstone acquiesced to the inexorability of future events, the French political philosopher, Baron de Montesquieu, defined an author as a fool who, not content with having bored those who have lived with him, insists on boring future generations.

Writing about the future, however, has since become a new industry. And from the boardroom vantage point, time is not on our side. A new perspective is required if directors are to fulfill their functions in corporate governance. Boardroom boundaries are expanding at an unprecedented rate and will continue to do so in the future.

The philosopher baron originally published his *Lettres personnes* anonymously in Amsterdam. This finessed, for a while, his own categorization of all authors as fools. It allowed his satirical call for reform to have an impact on the follies of his age in politics, society, religion, and literature. Later emerging as a literary lion along with Voltaire, Montesquieu took hold of the imagination of future thinking in Europe and the rejuvenation of France. His *Esprit des lois*, the most original book of its age, appeared in Geneva in 1748 published in two volumes, comprising 31 books in all. Montesquieu's fame continued long after his death in 1755, and for more than a century he was the authority on moderate reform in both France and other countries where the spirit of reform was abroad.

The spirit of reform is smoldering in most corporate boardrooms in the year 1979. Unfortunately this consciousness is mainly a response. The reaction comes from social, political, economic, and technological forces at work in the environment in which a board has to navigate its institution. Some exceptional companies have taken the initiative and stepped into the future by experimenting with the compass and role of the board. But others only grudgingly reform their practices and policies in a creeping mode when prodded by laws, regulations, and public sentiments.

Given the environmental turbulence ahead, there appears little merit to confining boardroom ponderings to the past. As Martin L. Ernst, vice-president of Arthur D. Little, Inc., opines, "There is no successful theory of history; hence there can be no models that are fully applicable, explanatory of futures events or capable of forecasting." This does not mean that a board of directors should

1

not seriously peer into the future as to probable trends, changes, discontinuities, force fields, surprises and the implications of certain potentials that are judged to be credible possibilities.

Futuristics

The future . . . seems to me no unified dream but a mince pie, long in the baking, never quite done.   E.B. White, 1944

The study of the future is a relatively new discipline. Contenders for the origin of futuristics have a list of names for the discipline. Among these are Jedrzewewski's *stoxology* (the science of conjecture), the anonymously minted *mellology* (the science of the future), Flechtheim's *futurology* (the study of the future), and Wescott's *alleotics* (the study of change).[1]

Roger William Wescott, professor of Linquistics at Drew University, offers an interesting discussion of the state of the art of the future. He points out that Bertrand de Jouvenel's *futuribles* or "possible futures" seem to have caught on in France and Italy but are less accepted in northern Europe and the United States. According to Wescott, "*futuristics* focuses on techniques of prediction: determinative, normative, and random. These types of predictions . . . correspond roughly to the three types of diachronic projection . . . forecasting, prophecy, and precognition. Forecasting is extrapolation of currently observable trends; prophecy, helping produce a preferred future by advocating it; and precognition, apprehension of the future by perceptual or conceptual means that are not yet elucidated." Futurology, the study of the future, is an effort to separate fantasy, wishful thinking, forecasting, and science fiction. Futurists' forecasts blend empirical trends with imagination. Doing this in a broadroom is not easy.

The pious perception of some established boards of directors about their institution's conduct, value and worth in the societal scheme of things is often outdated. The attitude that if unions, government, activists, and communities will only leave the corporation alone, everyone's welfare will be served does not work in our complex society. The future environment will be even more complicated. Oscar Wilde put it topically when he said that the only difference between a saint and a sinner is that every saint has a past and every sinner has a future.

We must venture to "sin" by posing some credible futures that could have an impact on the boardroom of the future. This precognition, to use Wescott's term, employs certain conceptual models that we have used in future environmental scans for various companies that Arthur D. Little, Inc., has recently served in North America, the Middle East, Europe, South America, and Japan. The environmental scans have generally been for the purpose of providing a datum plane. These are then used for strategic planning or for market potential purposes and in the process of acquisitions, mergers, divestments, and joint ventures either within a geographic region or transnationally.

Force Fields and Trends

The attraction phenomenon of a magnetic field was observed as early as 600 B.C. by the Greek philosopher Thales. This occurred as a force possessed by certain iron ores and also was created when amber, sulfur, sealing wax, glass resin, and precious stones were rubbed with suitable bodies. Electrical attraction was later separated from magnetism and its force fields by the physics experiments of Gilbert, Volta, and Oersted.

These natural physical force fields occupied man's interest persistently and more effectively for centuries than the similar force fields in the softer sciences of sociology, anthropology, political science and psychology. The creations of technology have pushed the institutional creatures of the developed world into a period where different governance systems are called on to navigate and rule our corporations more effectively amid the sociopsychological jungle in which the boardroom and top management find themselves.

A systems view of these force fields is helpful. It calls for an orderly arrangement of interdependent activities and related processes. They implement the performance of a major organization afloat in a sea of interacting and tangled force fields. The boardroom in idealized concept becomes an open subsystem in contact with the corporation's environment, external and internal. There is commerce between the board and its individual members with the other institutions and force fields in the environment. The task of the board is to identify the probable force fields and then to watch and assess them in an experimental frame of mind. The storm watch of the weather bureau comes to mind with the specially equipped aircraft and crews who seek and interact with impending storms, pierce hurricane vortices, and size up the forces at work for warning purposes. Anyone or anything in the path of the force field created by the storm then can be properly prepared.

In a corporate sense, the storm clouds that are on the horizon include many force fields, among them, political interests; ethics and morality questions; public perceptions of institutions; value and status hierarchies; risk tolerances; cost-benefit trade-offs on health, education, and welfare; cultural and religious beliefs; traditions; and abilities to deal with change. The major force fields that will have a long-range impact on the compass and role of the board of directors can be broadly grouped into technological-economic forces, regulatory forces, sociocultural forces, global interactivity and interdependence, and corporate governance concepts.

The various major forces and problem areas have been the subject of extended debate, study, and forcasting effort. The key concerns are involved with various specific matters. Some examples follow.

Resource related. Energy in its broadest context, oil dependency of various nations, investment costs of coal and nuclear power, world agriculture and food needs, forestry developments and tropical monocultures, alternate building materials and methods, natural resource extraction, the supply-demand balance of primary metals.

Technology related. Telecommunications boom, consumer electronics, pharmaceutical development, nonwoven fabric innovations, space technology applications, worldwide technology transfer, nuclear weapon proliferation.

Socioculturally related. Health-care systems and costs, environmental equipment and services, textile and garment industry markets, information industries growth.

Economic related. Telecommunications boom, textile and garment industry markets, environmental equipment and services, industrial growth of less developed countries, international trade relations, bulk shipping and containerized transport, balance-of-payments problems, stability of the International Monetary Fund system, exchange and inflation rates, nuclear weapon proliferation.

Services related. Information industries growth, telecommunications boom, mass transit development, consumer electronics, health-care systems and costs, bulk shipping and containerized transport.

Further development of such specific problem areas (and others) is beyond the scope of this discussion. However, with this cauldron of critical causes, more litigation and more government intrusion into the private sector can be anticipated. These trends appear relentless.

The sociocultural forces are particularly complex (and another subject beyond the scope of this book). To cite just two such trends, life-style changes and the strong egalitarian thrust are major ones that will affect the governance of many institutions. The range of perspectives offered in the following chapters should raise the level of consciousness in the boardroom regarding such pervasive trends in the future.

The belief in human equality, especially with respect to social, political, and economic rights and privileges, is a philosophy sweeping into most corners of the globe. This driving force of egalitarianism has fomented revolutions in the past. The current force is toward reducing the inequalities among peoples. It is causing a strong observable pattern of sociocultural unrest. These activities impact our institutions and pose new problems of governance for the board of directors. From a boardroom perspective these problems are focused around such topics as social responsibility, boardworthiness, public directorships, cumulative voting of shares, nonmanagement nominating procedures for directors, "sunshine" requirements for disclosure of more corporate information, whistle blowing, "policemen" in the boardroom, environmental and social audits, unaffiliated independence of directors, open-system concept of a board, corporate and stockholder democracy, and a few other issues. (Many of these are highlighted in chapter 14.)

Global interaction and interdependency is also an evolving phenomenon apparent to thinking directors. For example, the compass of multinational corporations makes clear that the function of an effective board of directors requires a better sense of this complex inter- and intra-activity with the resultant conflicts between private and public institutions. New rules of international business are evolving slowly to cope with the sociocultural, economic, and political influences impacting the corporation.

But corporate governance overall is our subject. The forces at work and evolving trends create an environment for corporate enterprise that is becoming increasingly socialized. The private sector corporation is being recognized more and more—despite some protest—as a form of social organization. As such there is material overlap and conflict with both individual and government rights, responsibilities, and liberties. Given this situation, let us look at the credible future potentials from various perspectives and a variety of viewpoints. The future environment is critically important to the institutions our directors serve. Reflection from different perspectives can help boards of directors be more effective in the future.

Panorama of Perspectives

Responsible directors will not quarrel with the position that the future is important to the welfare of the institutions that they serve. A problem arises, however, in the reluctance, sometimes refusal, and often, inability to acknowledge the realistic nature of conditions that can prevail in our complex, interactive future world. For example, short of catastrophe, policies of economic isolation among the industrial powers would entail a more cutthroat regime among multinational corporations. Voluntary codes of behavior for multinational corporations, from another perspective, could cope more effectively, I believe, with many of the problems that cause conflict in the world of business. This opposes the viewpoint that codes of behavior rammed through the respective national and regulatory bodies or the United Nations General Assembly, say by a hostile majority, provide the answer.

Another credible future condition can be postulated around the competition and conflicts of either an administered world or a market system type of world. In an administered environment, decisions concerning services and products are made from within the system or from above. Services and products are supplied to users or consumers for free or at a fee unrelated to economic considerations. Oversimplified administered systems provide what someone, or some group of persons in a hierarchy, think is proper for the users or consumers to have. In a market system, decisions concerning services or products tend to be made in response to perceived demand from outside the system. Market systems provide us with what we think is good for us, whether it is or not. Of course, this definition has some controversial ethical and moral overtones.

Some administered systems already extant include: the U.S. public education system; research and development in many corporations and government bodies; social welfare programs in most countries around the world; government postal service systems; the programs of the major radio and television networks and the publications industry; the health-care delivery system in the United Kingdom and some Scandanavian countries; and the Federal Reserve system. In general, administered systems tend to be oriented toward the producers' interests. They tend to seek their resources internally and survive and grow by internal political competition for resources. Boundaries or compass are well defined.

Administered systems pose particularly vexing governance problems in realistically measuring their effectiveness, in resource allocation, and in decentralization and delegation of decision making. The market system world tends to be less efficient in the short run but more effective in the long term. Economic, social, political, cultural, and technological factors interplay and trade off against the value systems, needs, and beliefs of those served by and serving with our institutions.

A series of equilibria are reached. Governing an institution in a somewhat continuously turbulent state is a demanding task. It calls for a strong board of directors willing to face up to the possibly adverse, constraining, debilitating, or changing forces at work in the environmental battleground of administered and market-oriented societal conditions of the future. The compass of such a governing board is a broad and searching one. It embraces the hypotheses listed in the introduction to this book, along with other possible characteristics of the future conditions to be faced. In essence, the compass of the effective boards of the future will have to heed Count Oxenstierna's law. This means that they will have to tap the wisdom available in the domains that border and surround the institution being governed.

One way to getting wisdom existing outside the boardroom put into use is to set forth some scenarios for governing an institution in future end states. This exercise will set various challenging backdrops against which alternative strategic plans can be developed. The examination of credible future end states may even raise challenges to the primary objectives and purpose of the corporation. Such issues are matters for the board of directors to ponder. (Chapter 3 sets forth a protocol to assist in scenario development.) The purpose of this book, however, is to offer some schemata. Some of these are united or related to one another and some are not, but each concept provides a perspective bearing on corporate governance for the future. The following array enables easy reference to the discussion of these distinctly different perspectives.

Perhaps such a galaxy of governance perspectives is best illustrated in chapter 6. Here it is depicted by the "spotted watermelon theory: a concept of board life-span development." The sweep from conception to maturity of the board of directors, the process it uses in various stages of corporate existence, and the "spots" of concerns that a board must face in its governance of the institution provide a useful paradigm and mental construct. The various viewpoints or perspectives on governance offered in the other chapters all can be placed in this abstract framework or prism to see the spectrum of perspectives.

The following viewpoints are, in effect, from both ends of the director telescope. They vary from being macro and micro; some are linear or orthographic; others are historical, impressionistic, or philosophical; some appear rational and others intuitive or subjective. In certain instances, the perspectives are biased and are based on limited knowledge or are derived from a shifting base. Their value, is in opening our thinking about corporate governance conditions for the future. This prismatic display of perspectives, of course, is not an exhaustive checklist of viewpoints and concepts, but it may suggest some new areas for directors to muse over as they become more conscious of their own boardroom ecology.

The widely varied issues and concepts of corporate governance are positioned throughout the book for discussion. For a prismatic boardroom view, with some symmetry in the nature of these different perspectives, the notions can be aggregated into four broad sectors, which allow these twenty-seven perspectives to be clustered: sector I, corporate governance; sector II, board environments; sector III, board evolution; and sector IV, board operations.

Sector I: Corporate Governance

Perspective	Viewpoint	Reference
Plural paradigm	Three interactive, interdependent patterns of corporate governance are coexistent	Chapter 2
Collect of concepts	Typology of boards; a collection of seventeen concepts of corporate governance	Chapter 2
Severity of concerns	Cognitive map of nine director functions with their different priorities	Chapter 6
Teleological	Six types of institutional ownership or purpose	Chapter 6
Corporate cabinet	Six roles performed by the board as adviser, monitor, and fiduciary	Chapter 2
Authority and power flows	Model business corporation law analyzed by source of power	Chapter 3
Independent stewardship	The current movement in corporate governance to ensure objectivity and disinterested oversight	Chapter 10
Hierarchy of governance concerns	The relevance tree concept, three zones of governance, governance as a system, and iconic scarabaeus structure of governance, an interdisciplinary system	Chapter 13

Sector II: Board Environments

Perspective	Viewpoint	Reference
Interdisciplinary and cognitive dimensions	Board boundaries and relations with society; cognition and competence of the directorate during evolutionary stages under conditions of increasing complexity	Chapter 2
Boardroom ecology	Philosophical mapping, hierarchical thinking, internal nature, interfacial zones, external domains, which comprise the compass of the board	Chapter 3
Corporate linkages	Permissive coalitions in the form of conventional legal, technical, commercial, and political links and more subtle psychological, cultural, social, familial, religious, and ethnic links; five processes of organizational linkage	Chapter 13
Regulated company issues	Directors of bank holding companies and similarly regulated institutions have a special stewardship encapsulation because of the statutory web surrounding them; some of this may creep into other boardroom domains in the future	Chapter 11
Opinion leader perceptions	A survey of attitudes that need to be considered before the social activists provoke boards to a defensive posture	Chapter 4
Alternative future	Use of scenarios in the longer-range planning as a framework for corporate governance; early warning systems	Chapter 3

Sector III: Board Evolution

Perspective	Viewpoint	Reference
Bipolar evolutionary process	Valence hierarchy and the process of board evolution	Chapter 2
Director diversity	Vance's model of director dimensions modified for various stages of board evolution	Chapter 2
Measures of maturity	Eighteen tests of board maturity	Chapter 6
Board life-span development	Stages of corporate existence from conception to maturity; the governance process; the concept of metadevelopment; the spotted-watermelon theory	Chapter 6

Sector IV: Board Operations

Perspective	Viewpoint	Reference
Specialists versus generalists	Boards as learning societies industry specific and company specific; perceptive-subjective and logical-rational mix of talents necessary for effectiveness	Chapter 5

Perspective	Viewpoint	Reference
Interiority concept	Becker's and Fechner's notions adapted to the future boardroom; omphaloskepsis, a hazardous obsession	Chapter 7
Internal imperatives	Board problems with concinnity bias; group-think phenomenon; pursuit of independence in director conduct	Chapter 10
Dissent role	Loyal opposition, devil's advocate processes in political, academic, and religious organizations point the way for improving institutional governance; pros and cons of such a process for economic institutions	Chapter 10
Trade-offs	The value of profiling conflicts in the decision-making zones of corporate governance; sorting out the accountabilities of the directors	Chapter 9
Advisory and peer directors	The resource value of advisory functions of the statutory board; advantages and role of separate advisory bodies; twelve inputs available from advisers; the council of peers	Chapter 12
Board mentors	Educators show the way in improving trustee effectiveness	Chapter 12
Boardroom-bathtub theory	Adaption of Van Cise's perception of government's theory of ultracorporate conspiracy; implications for directors	Chapter 8
Hidden agenda	Problems with the artless agenda; board insularity; neglected board issues	Chapter 14

Some changes are already underway, and some innovations are imminent. For example, some likely innovations are expected in the areas of stockholder democracy, possibly federal chartering, extension of liability limits for corporations, directors, and officers, reduction in corporate income taxes, and constituency representation on boards. Many other potential changes are discussed in chapters 2, 4, 6, 8 and 13. The purpose of this chapter's array of perspectives is to get the thinking opened up. Boards should then have a better chance to be more alert and effective in the future.

I began this discussion of credible futures with Gladstone's admonition about the inexorability of future events. These will provide no easing of the board of directors' condition. The condition of many boards is such that immediate concern and exploration of these credible futures is in order. Our institutions move slowly, and I hope that the following chapters will stimulate some notions and motions in and about the boardroom.

There is one discouraging aspect to getting any government action to facilitate the private sector's efforts in coping with the issues and opportunities of future. We can perhaps learn from a study for The Royal Institute of Public Administration in the United Kingdom. The study concerned the committees of inquiry, a conspicuous feature of British government. Over the years boards of inquiry have played a prominent role in the policy-making process.   Harold Laski's often quoted view of this process is a sobering note on which to consider institutional change to cope with the demands of the future. He Laski stated: "On the average in our system, it takes nineteen years for the recommendations of a unanimous report of a Royal Commission to assume statutory form; and if the Commission is divided in its opinion, it takes, again on the average, about thirty years for some of its recommendations to become statutes."[2]

Notes

1. Roger Williams Wescott, "Anthropology and Futuristics." Reprinted with permission from *Chemtech* (July 1973): 403-407. Copyright by the American Chemical Society.

2. H.J. Laski quoted in Gerald Rhodes, *Committees of Inquiry* (London: George Allen & Unwin, 1975).

2 The Board of Directors' Multiple Roles

The use of the word *compass* ("to take a circuit of, to encircle, to surround or to indicate the enclosing limit or boundary within which any power may be exerted or action effected") is the sense in which it is applied to the domain of the directorate.

> And the Lord said unto Joshua, See, I have given into thine hand Jericho. . . . And ye shall compass the city, all *ye* men of war, *and* go round about the city once. Thus shalt thou do six days.—Josh. 6: 2-3.

As an instrument of navigation, the compass derives its roots from the ancients. Traditionally claimed by the Chinese to have been invented by the Chinese Emperor Ho-ang-ti about 2364 B.C., the mariner's compass first recorded use-for-sea travel was set forth in A.D. 800, and it later emerged in the twelfth century in Europe.

Circumscribing or aiding the navigation of a board of directors takes more than six days. It requires an understanding of the nature of a modern board, its dynamic processes, and the territory of ferment in which it exists to lead its organizational system. Penetrating a board situation is more complex and uncertain than in the days when Jericho's walls came tumbling down on the seventh day of encirclement.

A Plural Paradigm

In the Bible a paradigm stood for a narrative passage in the Gospels that illustrated the sayings of Jesus and represented one of the literary patterns. In today's context, a compass of the board is a multipatterned paradigm. The following pattern of the domain of the directorate explains the plurality of this pattern.

A trinity of perspectives seems useful in ordering reality about the board of directors, its scheme, and the pattern of corporate governance. These three perspectives overlap somewhat and form a union of a three-in-one pattern for the directorate. The perspectives are interactive and interdependent. Sometimes they conflict; sometimes they reinforce one another; in some instances, the paradigm or pattern stands alone. Simply stated, this triad of patterns sets forth the compass of the board as being part of a complex system of corporate governance. The three board patterns in this context may be viewed in one or all of the three ways as a corporate cabinet, a collect of concepts, or a bipolar evolutionary process.

Looking at the board in each of these three patterned (or paradigmatic) ways allows us to develop three constructs or mental models that flow from the separate paradigmatic settings. Complicating the picture is the fact that these settings constantly change. The changes take place in various forms: ideology, philosophy, beliefs, articles of faith, traditions, norms, values, aspirations, and emotions. Furthermore our instincts and intuition tend to mutate with spiritual and intellectual growth or decay.

The models that flow from each of these paradigms set up categories that each individual develops in order to process information about the world. The following descriptions of such patterns for ordering realities of the board world are offered to assist our thinking and to develop our own constructs. These are useful as tools for improving the effectiveness of the board of directors.

The Mental Models

The Corporate Cabinet

In Great Britain the cabinet is comprised of those members of the government who hold the highest executive offices. Under the presidency of the prime minister, they decide national policy. The cabinet is collectively responsible to Parliament. In theory (and general practice) they stand or fall together, and their decisions are binding on all members of the government. Originally a cabinet consisted of advisers to the crown, and that form existed from pre-conquest times.

In the United States, the cabinet consists of the heads of the major departments of government who are nominated by the president and serve as his advisers. Stephen Hess of the Bookings Governmental Studies program played a prominent part in providing President Carter with ideas for reorganizing the White House staff. Many of his proposals were reflected in the White House reorganization plan sent to the Congress in July 1977.[1] The relevant part to this discussion was the concept of substantially reducing the White House staff as a source of presidential advice and invigorating the "Cabinet as the focal point of the White House machinery." The purpose was to give presidents better advice, reduce the cabinet's involvement in matters that are not properly presidential, and provide them with greater outreach than they would have had under the previous centralized system. Hess stressed that a more nearly collegial administration would have the president "relying on Cabinet officers as the principle sources of advice and hold them personally accountable . . . for the operations of the different segments of government." Hess argued that the president's main job is "to make choices—choices that are ultimately political."

Cabinet officers "collectively define what can be done in the executive branch, are responsible for implementing presidential policy and have power bases of their own to commit to the President's battles." Hess laid out seven strategies for the Carter cabinet:

1. Reconstitute the cabinet to reflect the president's need for advice.
2. Limit the size of the cabinet.
3. Hold cabinet meetings on a frequent, regular schedule.
4. Provide a skillful cabinet secretariate in the White House.
5. Identify cabinet members as the primary spokesmen for the administration.
6. Enable the cabinet to become the focal point of White House machinery.
7. Ensure that the president wants the cabinet to be an effective instrument of advice.

In the corporate context, the board of directors, created by law to perform certain functions, acts as adviser to the chief executive officer (CEO), but individual directors hold a fiduciary responsibility to the owners of the corporation. The exact role(s) of the board is a controversial topic because of changing attitudes about corporate conduct, calls for reform, and the increasing complexity and velocity of change in conducting a business. The following are various roles that a board may assume in its corporate cabinet sense:

Board Role	*Emphasis*
Statutory-Fiduciary	As required by law.
Evaluative	Formal criteria for corporate and CEO performance and corrective action necessary to ensure performance, compliance, and achievement.
Participative	Selective board committee roles.
Resource to management	Only when asked, to provide a wide range of advice and expertise from the board members, individually or in concert.
Change agent	Initiation of policies, strategic moves, or directions not necessarily originated by management.
Asset protection	Assurance of adequate management decision, information, and control systems. Wide distribution of share ownership and credibility of the accountability function at the board level.

A Collect of Concepts

The key issues about corporate governance are wrapped in a host of concepts, hypotheses, and philosophies. Most of them are generally acknowledged to some degree in the business community. However, some of these may exist only as a penumbra of abstract ideology, aspirations, or goals, even myths.

Some of the concepts have legal or sociocultural roots. Others rest on regulation, convention, experience, tradition, and precedent. Certain concepts are in experimental stages of acceptability and credibility.

A thorough consideration of the adoption of these optional concepts will often expose the implications to a corporation's culture, style, performance, liabilities (corporate and personal), nature of the business, risk, and growth potential. Trade-offs need to be employed to optimize the effectiveness of certain governance concepts. (These trade-off transactions are discussed further in chapter 9.)

Corporate Credibility and Accountability Function. The problem is who is in responsible charge. Ambiguity of board roles in federal and state statutes leaves uncertain whether the degree of power given to a board of directors is matched with an equal amount of accountability. Delegation of power by the board to management raises questions as to the extent to which it is possible to rely on the board to serve as a check and balance on the corporate decision making, usually focused in a single chief executive officer.

Board effectiveness, legitimacy, and credibility in governing the corporate system is the issue. The Securities and Exchange Commission (SEC) since the mid-1960s has imposed on outside directors the responsibility for auditing the performance of inside-director executives and the management. Court decisions are increasingly focusing the monitoring role and accountability of outside directors.

Plural versus Single Executive Role. Some large corporations are tending toward a plural CEO concept because of the complexity and velocity of changes and the demands on leadership. The plural role takes various forms, including the office of the president, with formal or informal division of responsibilities or spheres of interest. Such delegations by the board should identify both the degree of responsibility and authority and the accountability. Ambiguity exacerbates the credibility and accountability function.

Separation of Powers between Roles and Functions. Separation of powers is perhaps one of the most significant concepts in the constitutional form of corporate governance. One key legal advantage of a corporation over other business structures is this ability to delegate authority within the organization. Authority and responsibility may be delegated, but accountability usually cannot be.

Separation of Director Activity from Executive and Operating Activity. The three zones of governance—director, executive, and operating—overlap each other. (See the scarabaeus symbolic representation of this overlay in chapter 13.) Clear responsibility, authority, and accountability can be achieved by an understanding of the separations among these zones. Ideally in management practice, the zones are not violated by acts or interventions from one zone to another, except under established rules (such as the decision process, information process, and control processes).

Roles and Relationship of CEO and Operating-level Management. This concerns the interface between the corporate-level executive management and those in responsible charge of operating units. Normally these units have segregated profit and loss responsibilities as subelements of the corporate profit-and-loss account for the entire corporation. The problem of central staff overhead burden is the vexing one.

Board Organization and Extent of Committee Formation and Involvement in Affairs. This is a controversial issue that walks the narrow lines among interference, support, surveillance, assessment, evaluation, and audit. The public cry for reform of corporate conduct indicates that a more active, participative board is necessary. Organizing the board into active committees is one response to this need.

Balance of Achieving Success in Service to Customers with Success in the Investment Community. Two balancing acts vie with each other for the attention of the directors. The board cannot deal with the customer level achievement except to ensure a good CEO who realizes that this is a vital ingredient of success. The board can only ensure that the CEO and financial officer are qualified and effective in representing the corporation in relations with the investment community. Providing customer and investor satisfaction is the business game and neglect of either will cause long-term problems.

Role and Function of Central Staff. This depends on organizational structure, delegations of authority and responsibility, and stage of corporate development (start-up, rapid growth, maturity, decay). Companies operate successfully in highly centralized or decentralized modes or combinations of both.

Primary Role of the Board. A board needs to be able to shift gears in order to perform the most significant function—monitoring, leading, directing, or managing—at particular periods of corporate existence. The primary role may shift or stay settled in a mix of roles, depending on the success, a crisis, or the general situation faced by the company.

Separation of Legal Requirements from Policy Options in the Governance Structure and Management Process. A good corporate counsel will identify and communicate the legal requirements for a proper board. A good chairman and/or CEO will deal with the policy options in the right context.

Innovations for Future Development. Two types are normally encountered: garden variety, within-the-firm type of mutations, style changes, and promotional features of services and products; and breakthrough innovations, such as major advances in concept, technology, strategy, product, or service.

Use of Investment Company Structural Concept for High-risk Entrepreneurial Ventures. Such an investment approach subsidizes an innovative effort unidirectionally. It is eclectic, entrepreneurial, judicious, and kinetic (dedicated to change rather than resistance to change). By separately institutionalizing a new venture, by retaining its identity, the allocation of resources and flexibility of decision making are enhanced without jeopardy to the main business.

Property Rights. Optimize, long term, the distribution of share ownership in the corporation. The purpose, beyond estate considerations of major shareowners, is to provide some protection against unfriendly takeover or aggregations of stock in disruptive owner hands.

Power Structure: Official and Unofficial. Define the internal authority flow, impedances, barriers, gates, hurdles and criteria. Determine the policy framework and actual practice of exercising power. Both the formal and informal power structures and their political alliances need to be identified and acknowledged.

Expectations and Needs of Directors. Building a strong board with independent directors is increasingly difficult because of liability in exposure and more rigid criteria for director effectiveness. As a corporation renews and expands its board, some considerations are important. Not the least of these are what a director receives in return for service: intellectual stimulation, director time and task structuring, social relationships, identity and recognition, service opportunity and gratification, focused leadership, assurance of asset protection, indemnification and protection, and both monetary and psychic compensation.

Process Dynamics of the Board. The following elements are important in assessing an effective board:

Determination of corporate purpose and objectives and directions for growth.

Performance and other evaluations on a continuing basis.

Resource allocation.

Strategic decision making.

Board etiquette or ethical system (subjective) embracing established traditions and culture; group loyalty; hospitality and general ambiance; mutual interests of members; behavior patterns as directors; canons, dogma, and principles of the corporation; codes of conduct and ethics; values and beliefs of members; intellectual honesty; stability of the corporate climate; and emotional and political roles.

Board technical or rational culture, determined by members' educational background, experience, interests, sophistication and nous, independence, intellectual maturity, and delegated and withheld authority.

Separation of Chairman and CEO Roles. This is a controversial subject. The concept varies depending on the size, nature, complexity, and development state of a corporation. The rationale for the two roles is that the chairman functions as an agent of the board and the CEO functions as the executive person in responsible charge.

These seventeen concepts (undoubtedly there are more) make up what I have termed a board of directors *collect*. These concepts may be grouped to fashion a typology of boards. The models will vary and mutate as the sophistication of members of the board changes and as the nature of the institution governed evolves.

For purposes of examining how this collect polarizes to form a particular board type, it is useful to cluster these concepts into five board types: benign, sovereign, system, dominant, and adaptive. Table 2-1 displays the organizational concept, comparative strengths, and weaknesses of these five models.

Bipolar Evolutionary Process

According to historic symbolism the number two symbolizes conflict, counter-space, or countraposition—a momentary stillness of forces in equilibrium. In such esoteric thought, two also stands for the passage of time. For our use its bipolar sense, two has value in conceptualizing the board as a process in various stages of evolution.

First are the two polarizations. One relates to the plane of knowledge about our sociocultural system. The second, parallel plane of knowledge relates to our technoeconomic system. These parallel planes visualized as flowing from left to right lead the state of knowledge about the board domain directly into a what is called a *valence hierarchy*. In this hierarchy we can cognitively map a corporation's state of development and concern over its existence. Such a hierarchy of values is actually a set of rising concerns of a corporation. These occur as it moves from its creative and entrepreneurial beginning to become an institution of economic and social prominence. The levels in this valence hierarchy and the degree of power existing between activities cause them to unite or to produce a specific effect on each other. The fourteen levels of this valence hierarchy leading to a state of metadevelopment follows:

Table 2-1
Types of Boards of Directors

Model	Organizational Concept	Strengths	Weaknesses	Remarks
Benign	Minimum activity, reactive only, probably captive to the CEO; may well be owner representation; classical and historical type	Harmony with management; board is led by the CEO	No checks and balance; questionable legal validity	Patrimonial type of class of director
Sovereign	Autarchic, ritualized responses to highly limited precedented stimuli set; essentially an automatic function	In face of invariant set of environmental conditions, automatically copes with problems	Tendency to revert to primitive type reaction; system remains rigid even in the face of major environmental alteration	Patrimonial or political class of directors
System	Consistently maintained throughout the entire system domain even though dissimilar elements exist in a symbiotic organizational environment; operates logically rather than intuitively or subjectively	Maximum internal efficiency and operative control in the face of routine but often critical performance demand	Tendency to become obsolete; system maintains internal consistency at the expense of environmental congruence	
Dominant	Makes most efficient use of resources on a short-run basis; quickly mobilizes forces to take advantage of innovation and emerging opportunities; tightly controlled, run by strong executive, either chairman or CEO	Effective over the long run in exercising continual trade-offs between versatility and ordered existence; trade-offs exist between external congruence and internal efficiency; board and entire institution are managed as a common system	May misallocate resources due to time lag between recognition of new opportunity and internal readjustment; some adverse innovation or strategic change may upset the dominant force of the board	Patrimonial or political class of directors
Adaptive	Fluid organization to provide effective response to unprecedented situations; tends to instill creativity rather than systematic and orderly process	Adaptivity in the face of nonroutine and unpredictable forces from outside; has a flexibility on structural and functional aspects of the board	Tends to have largely autonomous parts, which may be only weakly cohered, causing dissolution or nonviability of parts of the organization or functions of the board; constant quest for innovational responses entails a high probability of error or commission	Professional class of directors

1. Creation.
2. Discovery.
3. Shaping of the concept.
4. Innovation.
5. Survival.
6. Security or defense.
7. Growth or change.
8. Organization.
9. Identity.
10. Value exchange.
11. Sociocultural aspects.
12. Environmental responsibility.
13. Teleological dimensions.
14. Extraorganizational forces (such as scientific and technological, physical and environmental, ethical, moral, and legal, economic, and sociocultural forces).[2]

Given this valence hierarchy, the process of board evolution takes place within two planes of knowledge. To complicate further, there are several stages as far as the life cycle of a board is concerned. Stanley C. Vance has identified an evolution of dimensions in the boardroom that captures certain stages of evolution operating between these two planes of knowledge, which I refer to as the bipolar process of the board of directors.[3] The following stages are paraphrased from Vance's model of director diversity needed to cope with institutional problems and are related to phases of maturity of a corporation and its industry. In our context, these stages can be set forth as follows:

Stage I: Entrepreneurial. The start-up stage of an enterprise in which, normally, the directorate is organizationally internalized. The primary determinant for corporate governance is owner's equity. The owner-operators, the inventor, the entrepreneur, the investor—perhaps family and friends—pool their assets and talents to govern the budding enterprise cooperatively. Product or service technology, product concept, the technical feasibility of the business, the design of the enterprise and, its development are at stake.

Stage II: Technical expertise. The demands of the enterprise call for more talent than the creators and entrepreneurs possess. The board membership is often changed to provide resources needed for this stage of development. Consulting assistance is often utilized.

Stage III: Managerial experience. New ingredients are required as the enterprise moves from a state of development beyond creation, discovery, concept shaping, and survival to the levels of security and defense, growth, and change. Management becomes a vital component. It requires selection of competent management by the board and willingness and ability to delegate to it and then evaluate it.

Stage IV: Special economic services. As the scale of the enterprise expands, external financing becomes essential. As competitive pressures intensify, the need for board members with special business and financial acumen increases. Acquisition and application of capital resources are vital in order to convert the product or services offered into a viable economic business.

Stage V: Interlock and linkages. Vital business intelligence becomes available to the board by adding members with connections (nonconflicting) in other domains of business and social activity. As the business grows, the phases of production, distribution, marketing (with the problems of quality), market penetration, and response to competitive forces require a perspective of the competitive world.

Stage VI: Asset impact. The epitome of the use of elitism. Boards tend to seek well-known directors who serve on large corporations or have governmental or social organizational experience. Appointments of this sort add apparent strength to the balance sheet by the impressive roster of directors with integrity, experience, wisdom, and status. Such intangible assets are important in financial matters, contracting for business or supplies and often in trade relations and customer situations.

Stage VII: Image and identity. The importance of financial community and marketplace identity calls for activity from those directors who can enhance this level of development. Public, government, and industry relations are furthered by an impressive board of directors.

Stage VIII: Board economic sophistication. Educational background, professional eminence, and publications become important attributes of directors as a corporation increases its position in business competition. Knowledge of government trends and policies becomes important to strategic planning. Diversification of business technology, markets, and capital structure for further growth requires experience and judgement in economic affairs.

Stage IX: International expertise. Given a transnational canvas on which to paint a corporate record, the need for international knowhow is obvious. Board members with such experience are hard to find. Foreign nationals are difficult to engage in a realistic role for the board. Corporate conduct of a multinational firm requires responsible and careful governance from the directors.

Stage X: Representativeness (corporate democracy). Social activists are putting increasing pressures on boards to admit minorities, representatives of constituent groups, consumers, and public directors. The legal and moral imperatives are there. Dealing with them is an unstable and uncertain area at this time. Some arguments for stockholder democracy—the opportunity for owners to have a more effective role—are becoming fashionable.

Stage XI: Social responsibility. Rather an emphemeral boardroom dimension, as Vance points out, the increasing call for boardroom reform and the general topic of corporate social responsibility call for serious board deliberations and decisions. The sociopolitical aspects of this stage involve confrontation

with threats to and opportunities for the firm's goals, resources, and prerogatives. These confrontations arise from constraints and incentives imposed to
protect or advance the general welfare.

Stage XII: Public Directors. We lack a good formula to deal with the proposal
for a representative of the public on the boards. The professional director may be
one answer. The wisdom and rationale for this proposed specie is under debate.

Stage XIII: Comanagement. This concerns the topic of worker members
on the board. Variations of such codetermination are being experimented with
throughout the world. It is a concept to be acknowledged and cannot be ignored
in future planning.

These thirteen stages of board development can be clustered into the following phases of evolution for a board:

Phase		*Stage of Board Development*	
A.	Entrepreneurial-innovation.	I.	Entrepreneurial.
		II.	Technical expertise.
		III.	Managerial experience.
		IV.	Special economic services.
B.	Growth	V.	Interlock and linkages.
		VI.	Asset impact.
		VII.	Image and identity.
C.	Complex system	VIII.	Broad economic sophistication.
		IX.	International expertise.
		X.	Representativeness.
D.	System of systems	XI.	Social responsibility.
		XII.	Public directors.
		XIII.	Comanagement.

Figure 2-1 is a portrait map of the bipolar process of board evolution. It
displays the process of a board's evolution through the four phases. They lead
to a hierarchy of values relevant to the developed phase of the board, which
are listed in order of decreasing concern of a board, that has reached the system-
of-systems phase of development.

Interdisciplinary Dimensions

A rationale is needed for the interdisciplinary dimensions of a board of directors.
The rationale should support a board structure that fully articulates both disciplinary and interdisciplinary dimensions of the board as it changes and evolves
with the development of the corporation that it serves. Rustum Roy has applied
these concepts to interdisciplinary science on campus.[4] Drawing on his approach,
we can develop some concepts for the board of directors.

First, the board's relation to society is such that it must reflect the major
concerns of the society that sanctions the corporation. These sanctions have

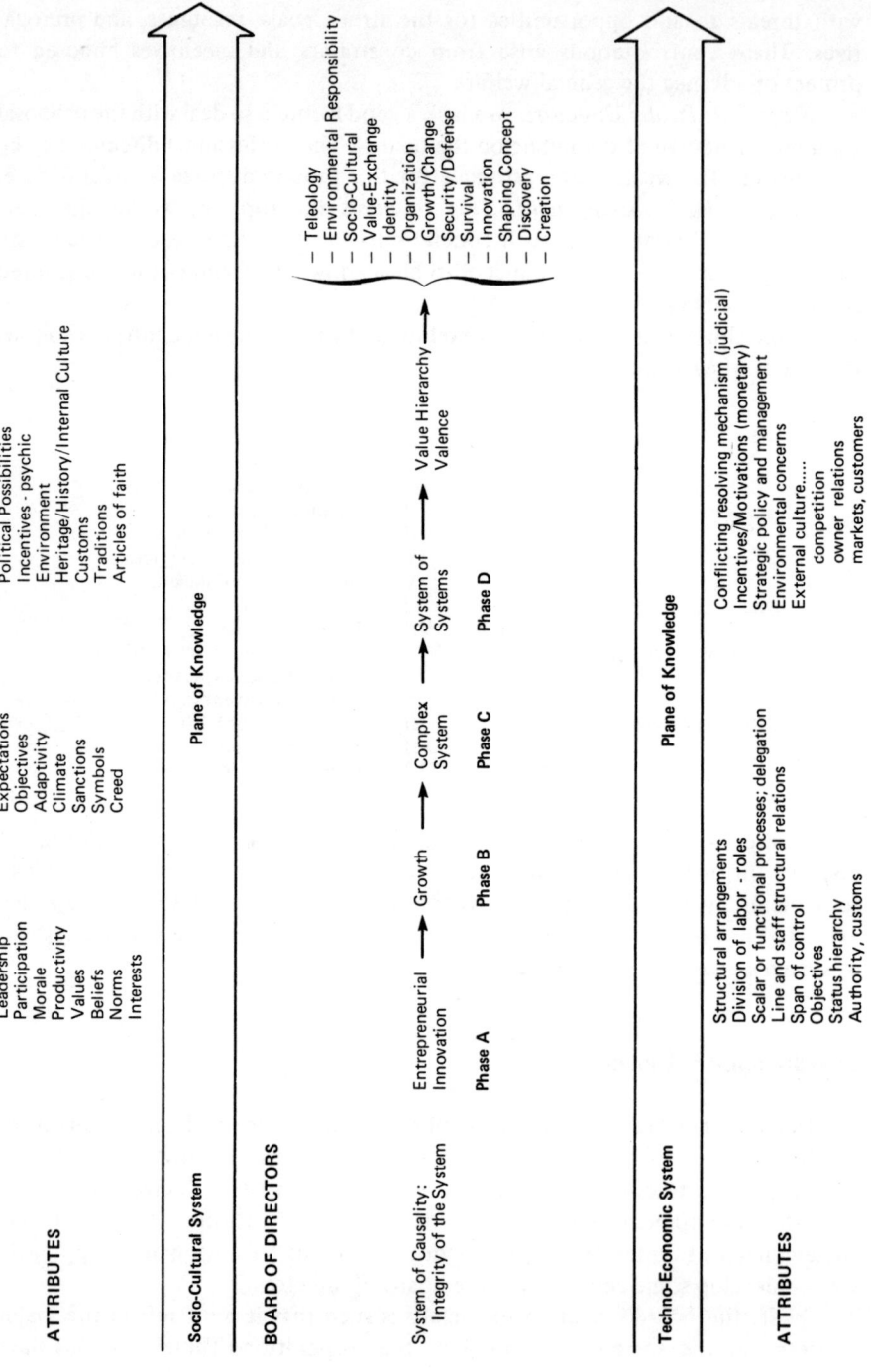

Figure 2-1. Portrait Map: Bipolar Process of Board Evolution

become more important with the growth of corporations, the interdependency of institutions, and the increased complexity in human affairs.

There is a second relationship: the capacity and competence of the directorate during its evolution. These notions can be displayed in a series of simple figures that follow. Figure 2-2 shows the cognitive capacity of the board members. This capacity has been relatively constant since the turn of the century when most boards were dominated by the founders, owners, entrepreneurs, and operators (entrepreneurial-innovation, phase A). The scale of enterprise then expanded and a growth phase B took place, followed by a complex system (phase C), and then the system of systems (phase D). The problem is that the directors as individuals and the board as an entity have not kept pace in their cognitive capacity with the increase in the complexity of the institutions that the directors serve and the increase in complexity and interdependence with the environment.

The outer circle in figure 2-2 represents a turn-of-the-century board's capacity to organize raw data and information without the knowledge, understanding, and wisdom needed for the board role in corporate governance today. In the early phases, the directors were able to embrace intellectually the necessary scope of the institution's affairs and the environmental aspects of it. Within this relatively fixed cognitive board scope is superimposed varying estimates

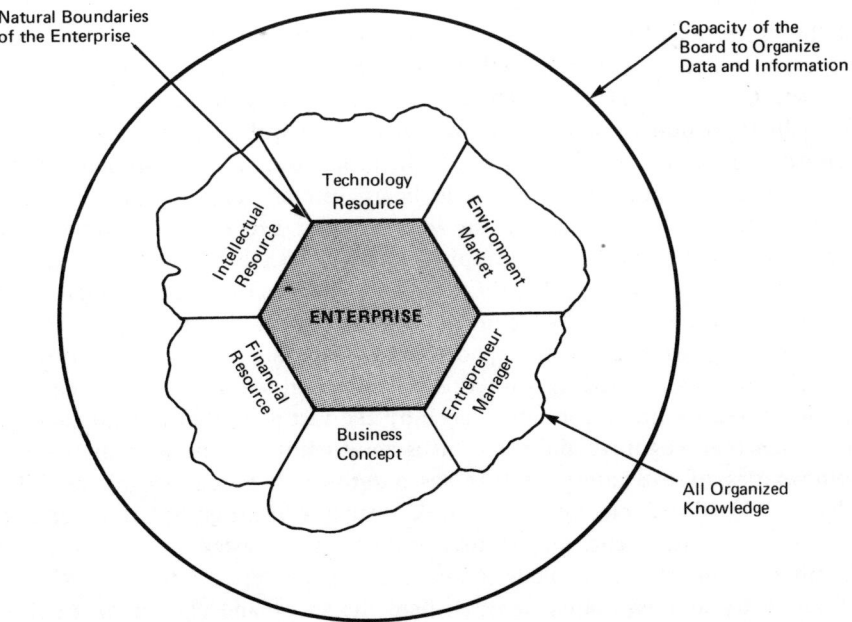

Figure 2-2. Cognitive Capacity of Directors at the Turn of the Century

of the range of total volume of human information and knowledge at a particular time in corporation growth and development in our societies. Directors were able to comprehend, keep on top of, and use essentially all of the knowledge in a specific domain in which they were expert. Someone on the board either had an idea of or knew where to get in reasonably short order the necessary organized knowledge about any corporate matter before the board.

The enterprise as a hexagon symbolizes six key ingredients of a business: the business concept, the entrepreneur and the management, the market and environment, the intellectual resources, technological resources, and financial resources. The members of a business board of directors usually are drawn initially from any or all of the provinces represented by these six ingredients of necessary components for a successful enterprise. Often the inventor, owner, entrepreneur, and/or his family or friends are the source of directors. The knowledge of the directors extends beyond the indicated hexagonal boundary of the particular enterprise at the early stages but is still within the cognitive circle of the entire board's compass.

As business becomes more complex, so does the span of organized knowledge within the directorate about human, technological, economic, environmental, and social affairs. At the same time, the enterprise expands. But with a few distinguished exceptions, this radius of board cognition generally does not keep pace. In fact, with some of the larger and more complicated enterprises, the board's composite ken is unable to cope with the scope of affairs of the institutions for which the directors serve. As a result, some corporations get into trouble with conduct, ethics, profit-making ability, and environmental and social impacts. Directors are fast realizing this problem and are calling for help from outside sources or for a reduction in the strategic scope of the company in order to be able to provide the proper overview of corporate affairs.

In many companies an old-style board can no longer contain virtually all codified knowledge bearing on its corporate existence and governance. Disciplines as disparate as philosophy, ecology, sociology, high technologies, legal concepts, psychology, political science, and others begin to relate more directly as separate force fields impact on corporate governance. The ordinary board often finds itself ill equipped to deal with these fields (see figure 2-3).

The options for dealing with this phenomenon seem to be two. The first is represented by the unconscious move by the vast majority of board members to stretch their cognitive abilities. This is an attempt to cope with the growing complexities of the enterprise that has outgrown its board's cognitive ability (figure 2-4). Board members may seek further education or the criteria for director nomination and service may become more specific and demanding. Another technique is to explode the corporate architecture into a constellation of subsidiary and associated boards where the scope and charter of a unit of the institution can be adequately comprehended and governed by a board (figure 2-5).

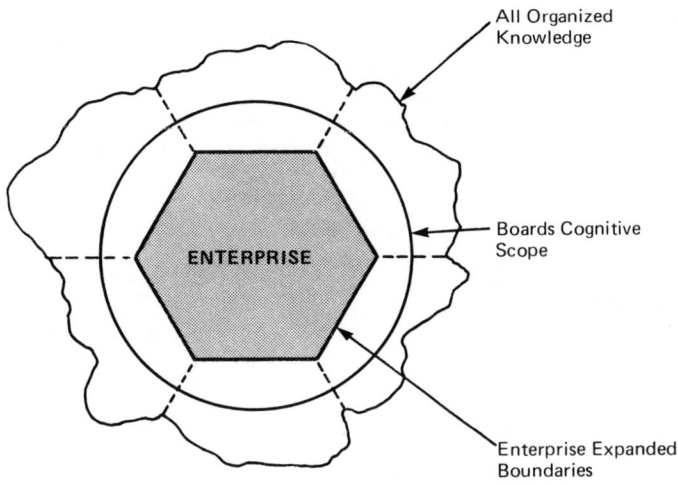

Figure 2-3. Force Fields Impacts: Twentieth-Century Knowledge Expansion

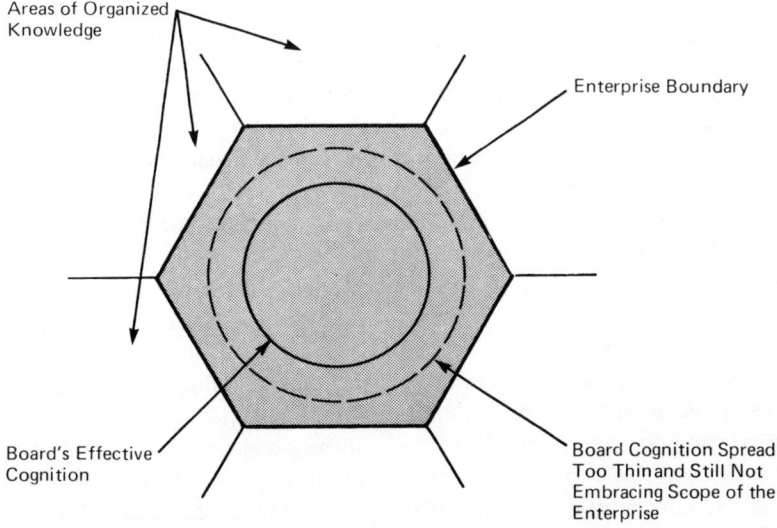

Figure 2-4. Growing Complexity: Twenty-first Century Potential with Conventional Corporate Structure

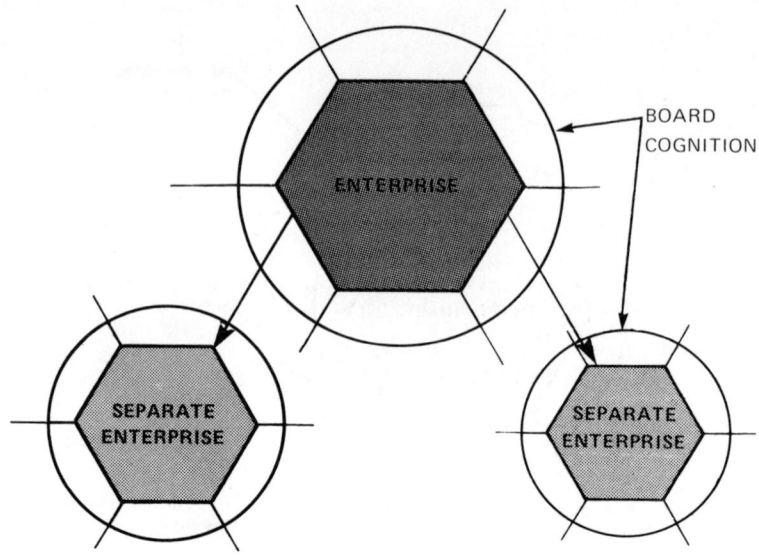

Figure 2-5. The Constellation Concept: Corporate Architectural Options

There is hardly any way, however, that most boards' cognitive capacity can realistically compass the exploding areas of organized knowledge relevant to a large corporation. Thus, use of the board as a resource for all problems and decisions has practical limitations. The management organization and outside resources must be called upon to deal with the force fields at work. Few large and complex corporations can risk their future based entirely on internal resources. The fracturing into manageable entities is necessary for many situations.

The board that stretches its ken too thin is likely to get into trouble—legal, social, environmental, or economic. An alternative option for coping with the cognitive demands of a board is sketched in figure 2-6.

Figure 2-6 is an interdisciplinary model. Certain board members are encouraged to include a major disciplinary or functional area of competence and awareness of one or two such areas. The gain to the board is a different mix of talent, which is more appropriate for understanding the complex society and velocity of change encountered by an enterprise as it moves toward maturity. Board member dynamics and interpersonal relationships are the key to the successful use of this device.[5] Symbolically, this type of board, fully extended to cope with a wide-ranging purview, is indicated in figure 2-7.

The role of the chairman in shaping the composite wisdom of these spheres of knowledge into the board deliberations and decision making is a formidable challenge. Effectiveness in this regard calls for an office of the chairman separate from the CEO who is managing the enterprise when the institution is a large and complex one.

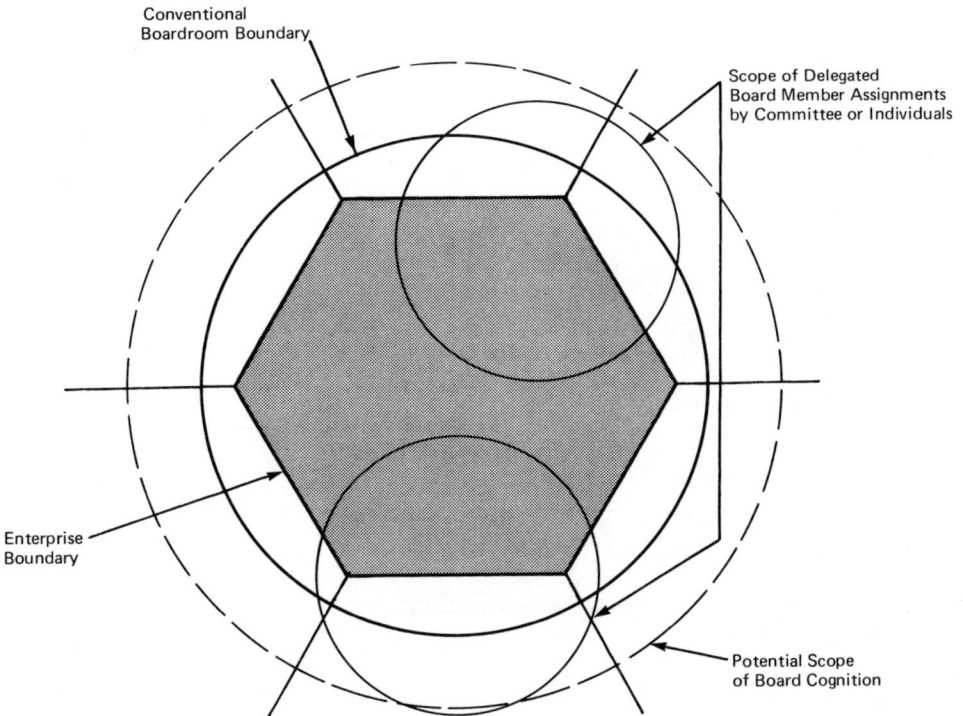

Conventional
Boardroom Boundary

Scope of Delegated
Board Member Assignments
by Committee or Individuals

Enterprise
Boundary

Potential Scope
of Board Cognition

Figure 2-6. Extending Boardroom Cognition

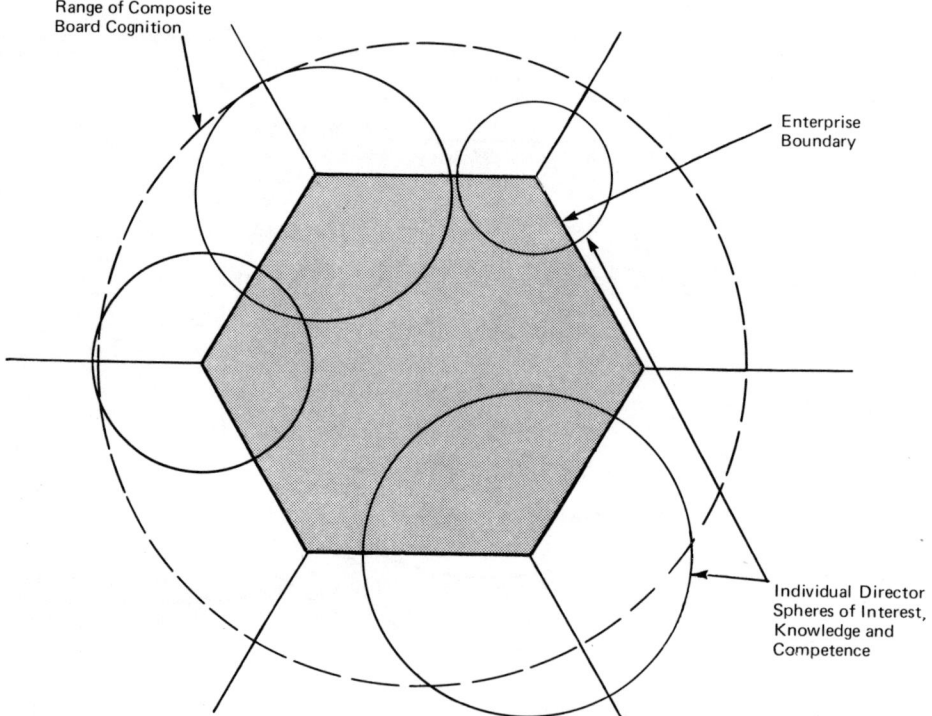

Range of Composite
Board Cognition

Enterprise
Boundary

Individual Director
Spheres of Interest,
Knowledge and
Competence

Figure 2-7. Broad-ranging Boardroom Boundaries

Notes

1. Stephen Hess, *Organizing the Presidency* (Washington, D.C.: Brookings Institute, 1976).

2. For more on this perspective, see my *Metadevelopment: Beyond the Bottom Line* (Lexington, Lexington Books, D.C. Heath, 1977).

3. Stanley C. Vance, *Director Diversity: New Dimensions in the Boardroom* (McLean, Va.: Directors and Boards, 1977), pp. 40-50.

4. Rustum Roy, "Interdisciplinary Science on Campus: The Elusive Dream," *C&E News*, August 29, 1977, pp. 28-40.

5. For more on this, see my *New Directions for Directors: Beyond the Bylaws* (Lexington: Lexington Books, D.C. Heath, 1977).

3 Boardroom Ecology

Many men ... have not a compass of soul to take an interest in anything great.
—1822, Hazlitt, Table t., II, VII, 163

The late Dr. E.F. Schumacher, the author of *Small Is Beautiful*, was taught that knowledge of the past was considered interesting and occasionally thrilling but of no particular value for learning to cope with the problems of the present. The first principle of the philosophical mapmakers seemed to be, "If in doubt, leave it out," or put it in a museum. Contrary to this school of thought, St. Thomas Aquinas in his *Summa Theologica* thought that the "slenderest knowledge that may be obtained of the highest things is more desirable than the most certain knowledge obtained of lesser things." The uncertainties of the boardroom future are indicated by certain wisps of "slender" knowledge. Thus, the future corporate environment is a domain where members of a knowledgeable board of directors can prove most effective in helping to chart a corporate course beyond the management's perception of the problems of the present, albeit with slender knowledge at times.

An economist turned into a high priest of ecology, Dr. Schumacher viewed the world by resorting to some philosophical mapping of his own. It was focused around four great truths, or levels of being, as he labeled them. He attempted to reconcile the scientific world with that of poetry, feeling, and the spirit and to plea for a radical turn toward self-awareness. Schumacher's attempt to repudiate scientism, reinstate the hierarchical mode of thinking, and reclaim some perennial philosophy, however, failed to impress many reviewers. The criticism of his last book, *A Guide for the Perplexed*, does not eliminate from the director's domain some thinking about a hierarchy of traditional wisdom and the value of self-knowledge for directors.[1] As Hazlitt said, too few men "take an interest in anything great." It is time for directors to "think great."

The hierarchical mode of thinking is not unique to Schumacher by any means. The analogue in consulting work is a straightforward four-step drill labeled as follows when mapping an institutional client situation: situational analysis; realistic assessment of situation uniqueness, if any; governance process (functioning of the enterprise); and scenario presentation of alternative future potential(s).

In looking at the domain of the directorate, it is helpful to use these four steps to compass the situation as it appears today. Board ecological considerations require examining the value of this hierarchical mode of thinking for corporate governance in the future.

Situational Analysis

Boardroom ecology is concerned with the internal nature of the board organization, the interfaces of the board, the individual directors, and those other domains of activity impinging on the directors. Such a compass includes the management organization, competitors, clients and customers, suppliers, the financial community, regulatory agencies, trade and professional associations, and the media.

The board organization, with its committees and officers, is a subject of great interest to those of us who are directors. Particularly important are the concepts, architecture, board process, and criteria and nominating process for directors. Judgment of board effectiveness and terms of service of directors is a touchy—often sacrosanct—area, which has been given much study elsewhere.[2]

The role(s) of the board can be a controversial subject in itself. Board role varies around the world. In the United Kingdom, for example, the role of a board is focused on four functions given the concept that a company director is a human agent of the company, which in turn is an artificial person in the eyes of the law. The four roles generally accepted in the United Kingdom are that of an agent acting on behalf of the company, trusteeship with the corporate assets held in directors' hands on trust for the company (delegated powers are used to benefit the company by the director in his fiduciary role), master and servant (referring to the distinct difference between a nonexecutive director and an employee director and the need to keep these two capacities separate), and independent contractor role of the director who renders service for a reward.

Business International's Public Policy Research Unit recently published a summary of developments, trends, and functional issues in corporate governance based on on-site investigations of about a hundred companies in seventeen countries. The global climate on social and regional trends in the European Common Market, Scandinavia, and Asia, the legislative and regulatory trends, and corporate response were summarized as of the end of 1977. Functional issues concerning board management, composition, board orientation and information, board role, meetings, director recruitment and compensation were identified in each of the countries.[3] The study found that more social responsibility, more liability, and more involvement by employees, shareowners, government, and the general public in corporate affairs were distinctly evident. The typical corporate response is a search for accommodation and balance. Certain companies are innovating new concepts at the board level regarding commitment and compensation of directors, organization of the board, constituency directorships, employee participation, linkage mechanisms for the board with outside institutions, communications, and other governance systems. Corporate adaptation is truly multifaceted, and innovation is predicted "to continue for the foreseeable future."

Another way of viewing board roles, at least in the United States, is in five separate role perspectives:

1. Statutory and fiduciary role.
2. Evaluative role: Judging corporate and chief executive performance on behalf of the shareowners.
3. Participative role: Providing advice, counsel, and aid in governance through service on standing or ad hoc committees of the board.
4. Resource role: Providing special expertise to management and the board when needed and assistance when requested.
5. Change agent or catalyst role: Referring to actions initiated by the board in its own right rather than reactions of the board to proposals from management. Such a role is important in crisis situations, takeover threats, new strategic ventures, divestments, management succession, or shake-ups.[4]

Situation Uniqueness

Each board tends to think its situation is different. How realistic such an assessment is becomes the true issue in assessing a corporate setting, particularly a board of directors' uniqueness and effectiveness in governing a corporation. In the long run, a company is no stronger than its individual board members. Ultimately at some point in a company's life cycle, determinative decisions must be made. Often these are made by the management, by competition, by the government, or by some factor other than the board of directors. When such changes are beyond the control of the boardroom, the directors' wisdom in coping with the consequences will identify the weak and strong boards. Where the impact or changes are management initiated, the board's ratification or benign tolerance of a significant determinative event or shift exposes the better board by the consequences of the action or inaction.

The importance of capable independent directors is obvious in assessing a corporation's uniqueness and potential for coping with normal business risks. Much has been written about the independent nonaffiliated director—loosely referred as the outside director—and regulatory and legal trends are sharpening this role.[5] A modified version of Phillips Petroleum Company's definition of an independent director is a good example of director uniqueness. The statement was derived from the settlement of suits based on illegal political contributions in which Northrup Corporation and Phillips Petroleum Company agreed that a clear majority (ultimately 60 percent) of each board and the entirety of each audit committee must consist of independent outside directors. (see chapter 10.) The role of the independent director in assessing a company's unique attributes for surviving and prospering in a competitive climate is one of the most important functions of such a director.

Consulting firms assess uniqueness of a firm against the competitive environment. The value of a professional, objective look at the present situation, strategic plans, corporate objectives, director effectiveness, and company policies is one way to assess corporate uniqueness.

The cold shower question to boardroom clients who are examining the institution they serve as directors is, What is so different about your company? This question should appear in every board report to emphasize that in the private enterprise system, uniqueness is what counts with respect to survival, innovation, expansion-growth or diversification-growth. Companies that are not unique can last only so long before profit margins become unsatisfactory to the investors or owners. My experience is that too few boards call for a realistic assessment of their corporate uniqueness. Instead, business as usual and short-term operating problems or crisis tend to fill up the boardroom agenda.

Even some sophisticated companies that are committed to formal strategic planning often fail to explore in sufficient depth or with adequate objectivity the uniqueness of present and planned future business in respect to its differentiation and the implications of uniqueness. Often it is only after margin squeeze and unsatisfactory return on investment are experienced that a critical objective appraisal of this key factor is considered. Often that is too late; investment and other commitments are frequently irreversible.

Governance Process

In engineering, a governor is a device for regulating the speed of a prime mover (such as an engine or turbine) irrespective of the variations in load. The governing of a business device such as a corporation, partnership, joint venture, or association places this regulatory function as the centerpiece of the boardroom table. The directors govern the corporation in its broadest sense and under all sorts of loading. True, they delegate certain executive functions and powers, but they also withhold certain functions and powers by law or by policy. The conventional corporation and delegation of powers in U.S. corporations are displayed in figure 3-1. Note the subtleties in power discrimination on this idealized array. Smaller firms frequently include all of these legal and policy type power separations into one big governing process dominated by the CEO, who deals at will with a malleable and tractable board. The role of a board to "direct and not be led" has been explored long ago in the courts and is a subject of separate discussion.[6]

The elements of a partnership form of governance are shown in figure 3-2. The advantages and disadvantages of these alternate forms of governance are shown in figures 3-3 and 3-4.[7] Some public companies are run as partnerships with the CEO and board members cast in a collegial mode, which does not fulfill the constitutional type of relationship or the check and balance of a properly functioning corporation.

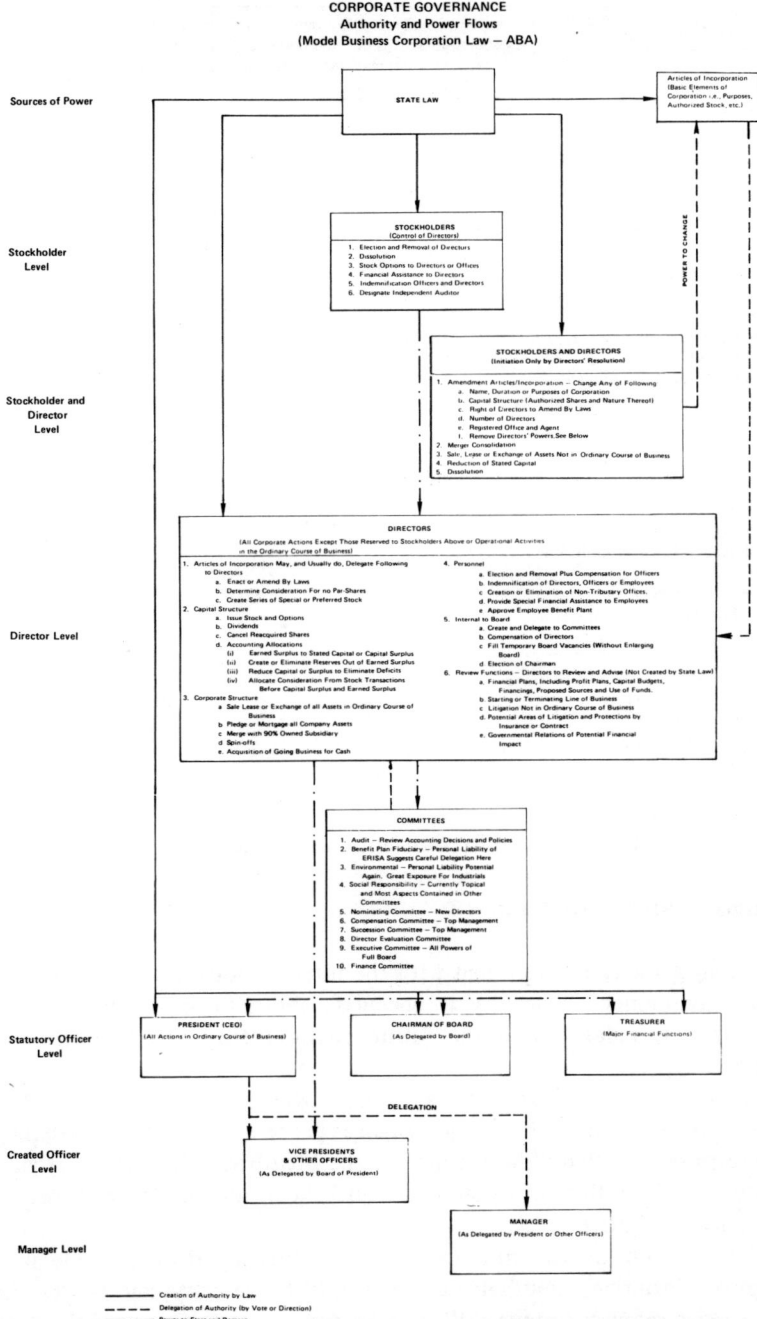

Figure 3-1. Corporate Governance: Authority and Power Flows

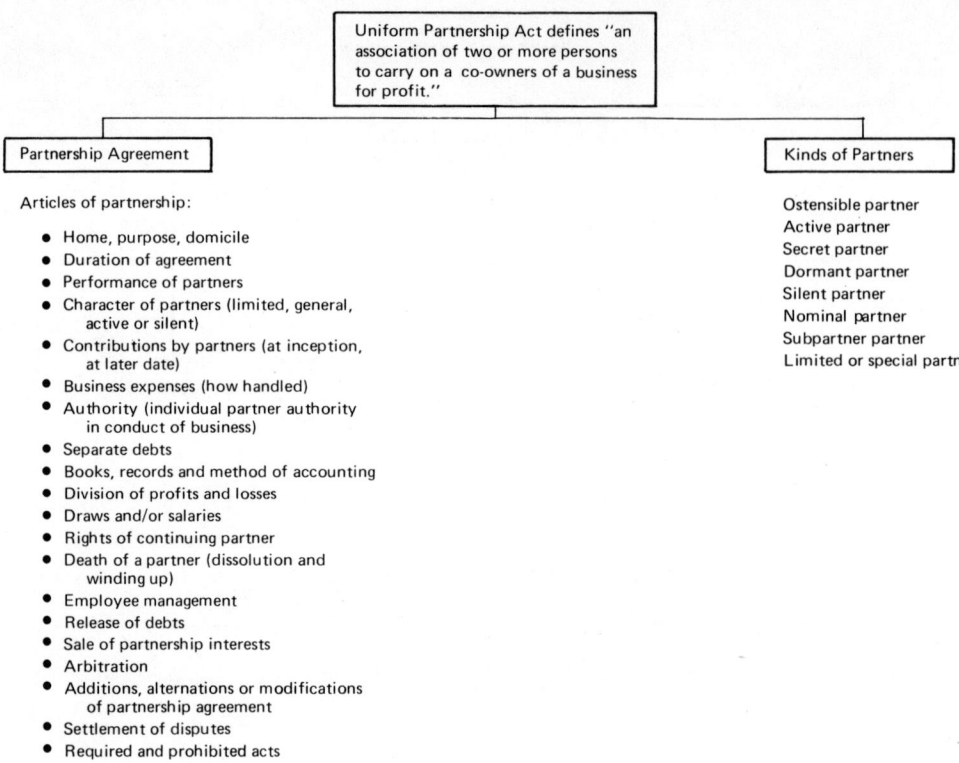

Figure 3-2. Partnership: Conventional Elements of Agreement

Scenarios of Alternative Futures

Boardroom ecology is concerned with the interrelationships of the corporation and its environment. One way to speculate about future governance requirements is to speculate about the future environments in which the corporation may find itself.

Given a situational analysis, a realistic assessment of uniqueness, if any, and an understanding of the governance process currently appropriate for the enterprise completes the setting for the boardroom to make its significant contribution. The first three steps are analytical, logical, rational, sequential, and mainly qualitative.

The creation of scenarios departs from this algorithmic mode into the perceptive, intuitive, simultaneous, and qualitative mapping of the future. This exercise requires unique skills and an appropriate amount of thinking and debating time. Alas, too few board meetings permit or encourage such. Time

Advantages of the Corporation

- Limitation of the stockholders liability to a fixed amount, usually the amount of investment (not to be confused with appropriate liabllity insurance considerations.)
- Ownership is readily transferable
- Separate legal existence
- Stability and relative permanence of existence
- Relative ease of securing capital in large amounts and from many investors
- Delegated authority
- The ability of the corporation to draw on the expertise and skills of more than one individual

Disadvantages of the Corporation

- Activities limited by charter and by various laws
- Manipulation (minority shareholders are sometimes exploited)
- Extensive government regualtions and burdensome local, state and federal reports
- Indirect reward (less incentive) if manager does not share in profits
- Considerable expense in formation of corporation
- Numerous and sometimes excessive taxes

Figure 3-3. Legal Structure: Business Corporation

Advantages of the Partnership

- Ease of formation
- Direct rewards
- Growth and performance facilitated
- Flexibility
- Relative freedom from government control and taxation

Disadvantages of a Partnership

- Unlimited liability of at least one partner
- Unstable life
- Relative difficulty in obtaining large sums of capital
- Firm bound by the acts of just one partner as agent
- Difficult of disposing of partnership interests

Figure 3-4. Legal Structure: Business Partnership

is taken on the ceremonial, statutory, and fiduciary chores and on the performance evaluative measures but all too little is devoted to exchanging tentative judgments or perspectives, tossing out speculative thoughts prior to critical plenary evaluation, and engaging in plain mental vamping. Many chairmen and CEOs are nervous with any unstructured, undisciplined period of a board meeting for fear of losing control and prematurely polarizing opinion and political alliances among board members. There is this hazard, but good chairmanship tactics can orchestrate such free-wheeling interchanges. Learning to govern a board meeting and director committee sessions in a fashion that will draw upon the wisdom, intuition, and impulses of sophisticated directors is in its elementary stages of evaluation. One school even rejects this role of directors. The boardroom of the future will undoubtedly encompass the protocol of drawing on directors to critique and speculate on future scenarios of performance.

Scenario building is a relatively recently adapted tool of business management. It can be simple and direct or complicated, indirect, and complex. It is essentially a methodological attempt to view and combine various trends in a systematic way. A clear distinction can be made between opportunity-oriented forecasting, which is normally labeled as exploratory, and need-oriented forecasting, which is normative in nature or responsive to what should occur. Forecasting is further classified as integrative or systemic, in which economic, technological, and market forecasts are composited for the shorter-term implications, which in turn are affected by longer-term human and social perspectives and trends. The state of mind from which forecasting springs has been analyzed formally as objective, subjective, and systemic, scenario writing fits as one technique.[8]

The systemic approach to forecast exploration uses static techniques such as input/output matrices, morphological analysis, and time-independent contextual mapping. It also uses so-called dynamic techniques, such as scenario writing, cross-impact analysis, interactive system projection, and others.[9]

Scenario writing is particularly valuable for identifying forthcoming decision nodes, focusing on causal processes, and lessening carry-over thinking.[10] The technique answers single dimensionally, step-by-step, how a hypothetical situation might come about and what alternatives exist at each step for each actor to prevent, divert, or facilitate the process. The changes implied in the scenario are mapped, and decisions are considered and systematically explored. The term *alternative futures* is used for generating additional scenarios, criteria, and systematic comparison of various alternative policies. It can be meaningless to consider only one scenario. Alternate courses need to be mapped to test different decisions. By constructing a specific series of credible futures and treating all of the factors involved in an internally consistent fashion to form a simulation of outcomes, the interactions and interdependencies can be better perceived and consequences determined that might not surface in a more general, abstract analysis.

Herman Kahn and Anthony J. Wiener cite the six advantages of scenarios:

1. They dramatically alert attention to think the unthinkable and lessen carry-over thinking from past experience.
2. They force attention to details and dynamics.
3. They illuminate interactions of psychological, social, economic, cultural, political, and military factors.
4. They forcefully illustrate issues or principles that might be missed in examining real-world examples.
5. They make good artificial case histories and historical anecdotes to fill in for a lack of real examples.[11]

Scenario writing has been termed science fiction, paranoidal and unrealistic by various critics. But it can indicate plausible or credible futures, which the board of directors should contemplate if they are to fill their role in determining strategic directions for the enterprise they serve. (Chapter 1 dealt with some of the perceivable events that merit being on a boardroom agenda.)

A simple approach used by Arthur D. Little in scenario writing has been employed very effectively in peering into the future for the benefit of share-owners who read the 1976 and 1977 Arthur D. Little annual reports. This speculation replaced the usual rear-view mirror of company operations not with a forecast of the future but with an examination of the impacts of some of the events that could affect operations in coming years. The scenarios were prepared by the professional staff as a basis for planning in areas of national health insurance, a satellite solar power station, no corporate income tax, banning of major pesticides, farming for energy, workfare versus welfare, recycling waste products, microprocessor applications, health-care costs, contingency planning for government planning, and solar heating and cooling for new construction.

The use of scenarios in longer-range planning can be illustrated in the following eight steps developed by Martin L. Ernst, vice-president of Arthur D. Little, Inc.

1. Analyze the company or activity concerned to determine the most critical variables (such as inflation level or energy costs) that will influence the success of its future operations.
2. Select a reasonable number of end states illustrative of a wide band of alternative future combinations of values or conditions of these variables.
3. List (sequentially where possible) the types of events that would favor or be necessary for reaching each of these respective end states. Each event should be credible. They should be derived from observed trends that are expected to continue or from analyses or analogies with actual events. The events themselves can serve later to develop indicators that a particular end state is likely to arise.

4. Examine the events and relate them where possible to longer-term forces at work (social or demographic ones, for example). Reexamine the forces at work to search for other trends and events that are logically consistent and that may contribute to—or against—reaching the individual end states. This step can lead to an expansion and a consistency check of the events.
5. Develop a full set of plausible characteristics of the end states. This step requires some sophisticated imagination, brainstorming, and inhibition lifting by persons knowledgeable in various domains and disciplines.
6. Determine the implications of the end-state characteristics, again using experts in various fields to create an array of the impacts of the alternative end states on specific company operating or planning policies or practices. In effect, ask questions of the end states, such as the type of management skills most desirable or the organization structure most viable, given that a particular end state arises.
7. Perform a cross-futures analysis to determine which business needs or practices are relatively invariant, no matter what future arises, and which needs and practices will vary in what way across the futures.
8. Employ the cross-futures material to establish a general plan posture, using the invariant characteristics to start structuring the basic plan, the variable characteristics to develop contingency plans, and the indicators derived earlier to develop a monitoring system to help determine when particular contingency plans should be called upon.

The introduction and chapter 1 offer hypotheses and some forces at work that should be useful to a board interested in experimenting with scenario writing.

The future of broadroom ecology depends on whether directors can shed the traditions and patterns of the past sufficiently to open up the boardroom. This will allow its compass to embrace the ecological factors that should nest with the activities and concerns of the directors. Some force fields come from within the organization at the board-executive interface, and some come from outside the corporation. The social, cultural, political, and economic forces work along with other institutions, which function for their own purposes coetaneously with each other. This open board concept requires more sophistication than an isolated board does. An open board functions more organically because of the complexity and uncertainties of matters that are often outside the control of the directors.

To close on a confusing yet interesting note, an ancient but sophisticated conceptual transformation of past and future times is found among the Quechua Indians of Peru. They use *past* where we use *future*, and *future* where we use the word *past*. The Quechuans believe that since past events can be recalled and visualized, they lie in front of them, before their very eyes; hence they are called future events. Events yet to come, being neither known or capable of envisioning, lurk invisibly behind them; hence are called past.[12] Directors—like

Quechuans—need to let their imaginations run a bit and conceptualize what is behind the future of their activities. At the same time they must be aware of what is obviously in front of every directorate: the need to reform its character to match the times and improve effectiveness.

Notes

1. E.F. Schumacher, *A Guide for the Perplexed* (London: Jonathan Cape, 1977).

2. For more on this subject and a bibliography, see my *New Directions for Directors: Behind the Bylaws* (Lexington: Lexington Books, D.C. Heath, 1977), chaps. 6-7.

3. *New Trends in Directorships and Corporate Governance* (New York: Business International Corporation, 1977).

4. Robert Kirk Mueller, *Board Life: Realities of Being a Corporate Director* (New York: Amacom, 1974).

5. For an analysis of this prominent factor, see the excellent summary statement of Bryan Smith before the Securities and Exchange Commission, November 1, 1977.

6. Mueller, *New Directions*, pp. 153-154.

7. For further information, see U.S. Small Business Administration, *Selecting the Legal Structure for Your Firm*, Management Aids for Small Manufacturers, MA231 (Washington, D.C.: Government Printing Office, 1973).

8. Erich Jantsch, *Technological Planning and Social Futures* (London: Cassell/Associated Business Programmes, 1972), pp. 70-75.

9. Ibid., p. 71.

10. Herman Kahn and J. Anthony Wiener, *The Year 2000: A Framework for Speculation on the next Thirty-three Years* (New York: Macmillan, 1967), pp. 262-264, 357.

11. Ibid., p. 263

12. Leo Rosten, *The Power of Positive Nonsense* (New York: McGraw-Hill, 1977), pp. 234-235.

4 Notions and Motions about the Boardroom

There is a question regarding whether the board of directors performs as an echo chamber, an engine room, or a control tower. An obvious answer is, of course, some of all three. But the problem is how to be responsible and effective in this plural role and when to do which. The performance and compass of an alert board will reach out into the public opinion area to see how better to conduct the affairs of the corporation in the social interest.

Until a few years ago, the general public took little interest in corporate governance or in the sacrosanct area of the boardroom. On the other side, most businessmen do not listen to the public until too late and the social activists call attention to the evolving problem areas. More recently, individual directors are finding themselves in the spotlight of considerable public concern. This public attitude is a by-product of the increasing complexity of human affairs, the economic and institutional growth patterns, and the recoil from corporate misconduct on top of the recent financial crisis in the banking industry. Demands on the time and energy of company directors has expanded considerably. Board membership is no longer the rather quiet, reserved endeavor that it was in the past. Directors need to heed the numerous evaluations of public attitudes now regularly portrayed by the survey researchers in the area of corporate social responsiblity.

Opinion Research Corporation, a subsidiary of Arthur D. Little, Inc., recently completed a study of public attitudes with respect to directors.[1] Its interviews with 173 social activists, including environmentalists, consumers, feminists, civil-rights leaders, church-affiliated activists, labor leaders, educators, and corporate social responsibility activists, reflect a critical evaluation of the performance of boards of directors. Only 40 percent praised the way in which the average board of directors lives up to its economic responsibilities. About 20 percent approved of the way that boards fulfill managerial responsibilities, and only 5 percent perceived boards as fulfilling their corporate social responsibilities. (See figure 4-1.)

Activists criticize boards quite heavily for putting too much emphasis on short-range profits and growth rather than on the long-range impact of the corporation in society. They also criticize boards for being too elitist, secretive, insensitive, and isolated.

Very few activists believe that corporate boards of directors adequately represent the interests of the public or of important subgroups. (See figure 4-2.)

43

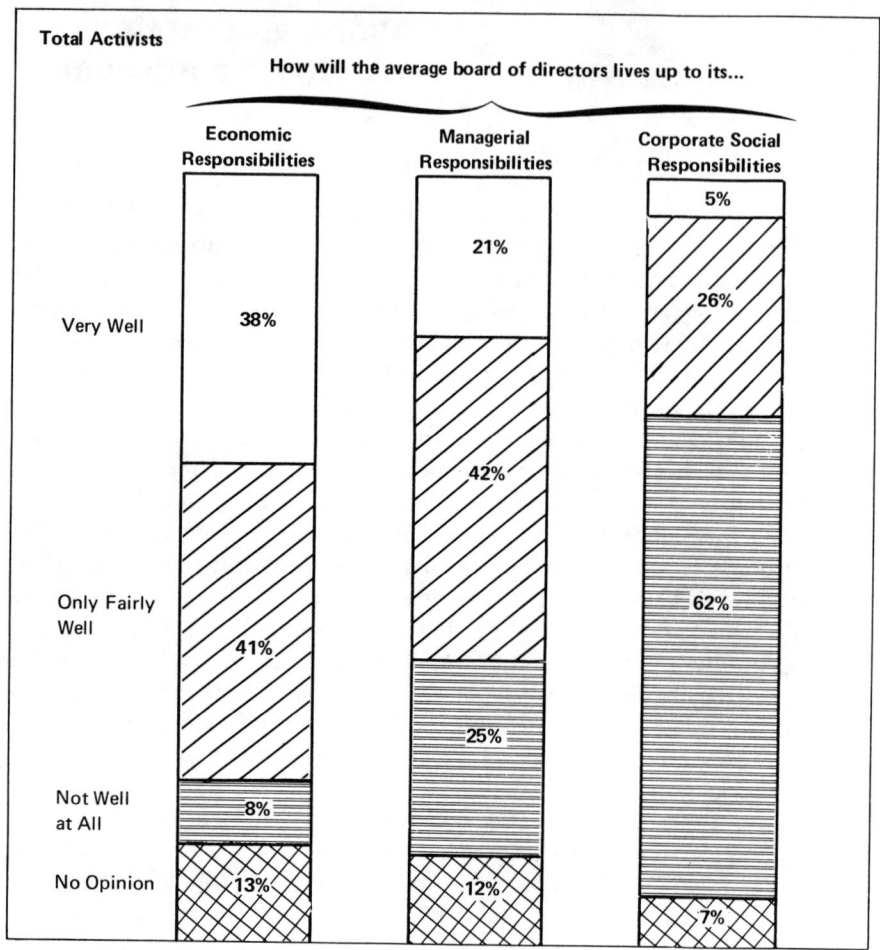

Figure 4-1. How Well Corporate Bodies Fulfill Their Responsibilities

Activists are aware that some of the larger companies have established public policy committees and appointed special-interest representatives to corporate boards (figure 4-3), but they seem skeptical about the effectiveness of the establishment of such committees or of such appointments (figure 4-4). There is real question in their minds whether this activity is tokenism for public relations purposes.

The importance that activists attach to special-interest representatives is underscored by how they view the composition of an ideal board. (See figure 4-5.)

Notions and Motions about the Boardroom   45

GROUPS WHOSE INTERESTS ARE OVERLOOKED
BY CORPORATE BOARDS

"In your opinion
are there any groups
whose interests are
overlooked by today's
board of directors?
Which ones?"

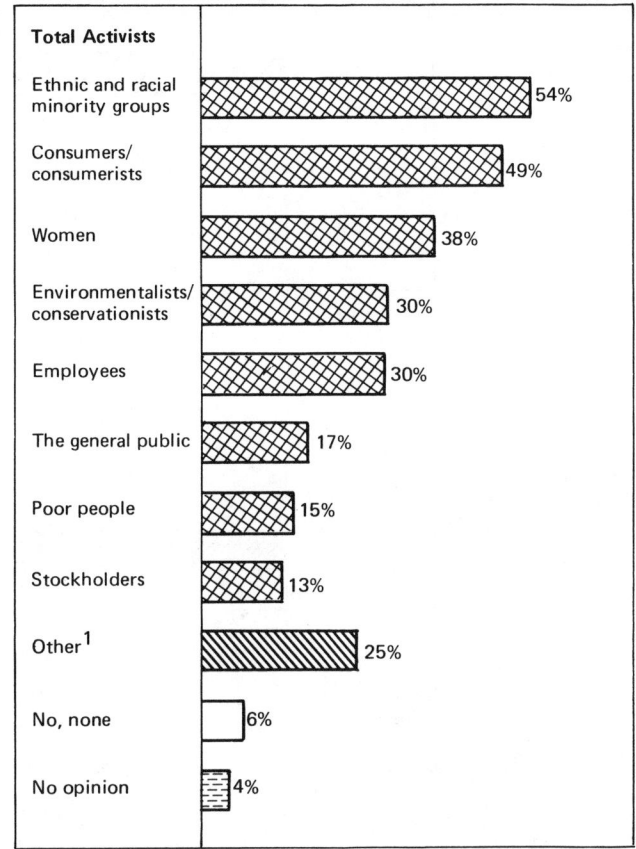

Multiple mentions
[1]Included in the "Other" category are mentions of "the plant
community" (9%); "labor" (7%); "old people" (6%); and "youth"(5%)

Figure 4-2. Groups Whose Interests Are Overlooked by Corporate Boards

Many activists would like boards to be held legally accountable for corporate actions that affect the public interest. There is a general feeling among them that boards should have their own staff and adequate resources to carry out their functions independently of management. Cumulative voting, full-time directorships, more public disclosure, and federal chartering are matters being urged by some activists.

Activists overwhelmingly believe that boards should provide more information to stockholders. (See figure 4-6.)

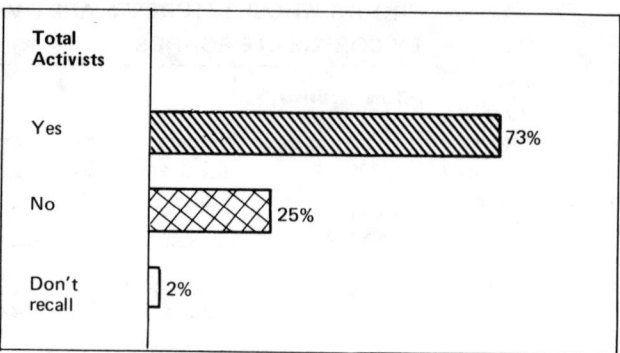

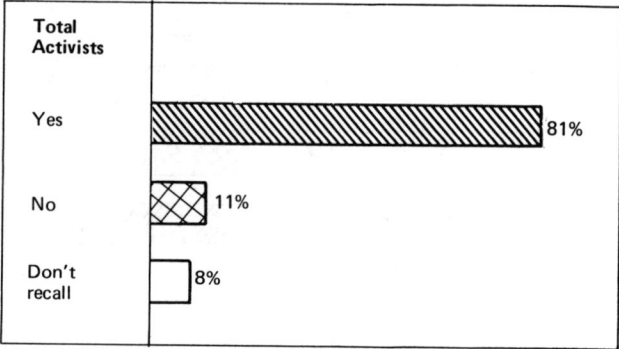

Figure 4-3. Awareness of Board Efforts Regarding the Public and
Special Subgroups

Activists are divided over whether legislative or regulatory changes are needed. (See figure 4-7.)

Activists want to limit the number of directorships per person and impose additional restrictions on membership. (See figure 4-8.)

On a related question, there is every indication that thought leaders believe that boards of directors should be more evenly balanced than they are today. Public thinking would have equal representation from outside as well as inside the corporation. Figure 4-9 reveals the ideal composition of a board of directors. These data are from a 1976 survey.

Many thoughtleaders also support the idea of a greater representation on corporate boards by spokesmen for the many groups affected by large corporations.

*"Overall, how effective
do you feel that these
committees have been
to date- very effective,
only somewhat effective,
or very ineffective ?"*

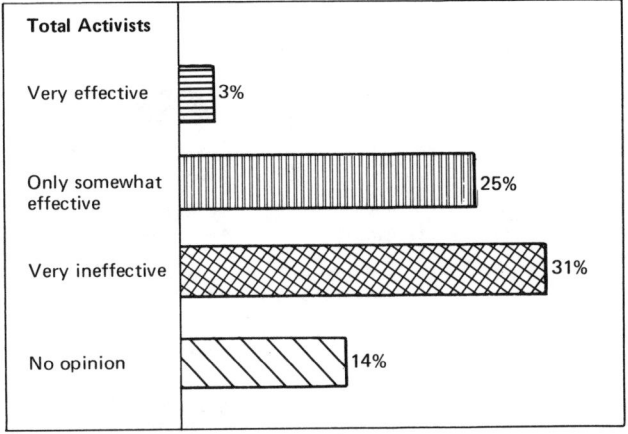

[1]Percentages above add to the 73% who say they have heard of the establishment of the committees and who were therefore asked this question.

*"In general, how
effective do you think
the board members
who represent special
interests have been to
date—very effective,
only somewhat
effective, or very
ineffective?"*[2]

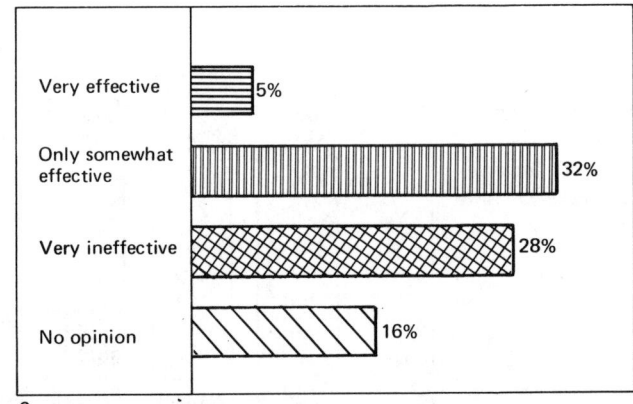

[2]Percentages above add to the 81% who say they are aware of the appointment of special interest representatives and who were therefore asked this question.

Figure 4-4. Awareness of Effectiveness of Special Committees and Appointments

"Should [an 'ideal' board] include certain numbers of [these groups]?"

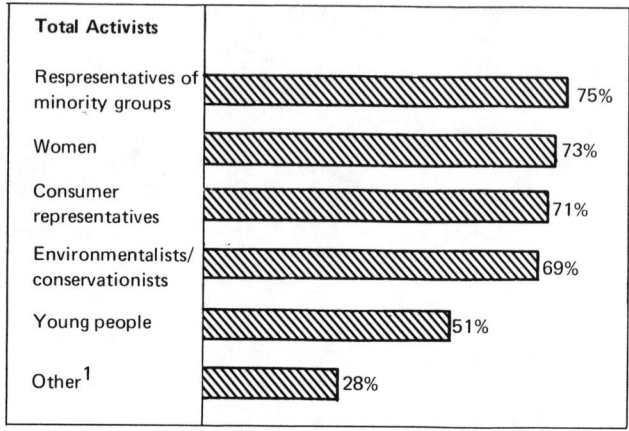

"No opinion" omitted
Multiple mentions from a list

[1]Included in the "Other" category are mentions of "employees/labor" (16%); "old people" (6%); "business people" and "stockholders" (3% each).

"In your opinion, what would be the 'ideal' board of directors? Should it be made up primarily of outsiders?"

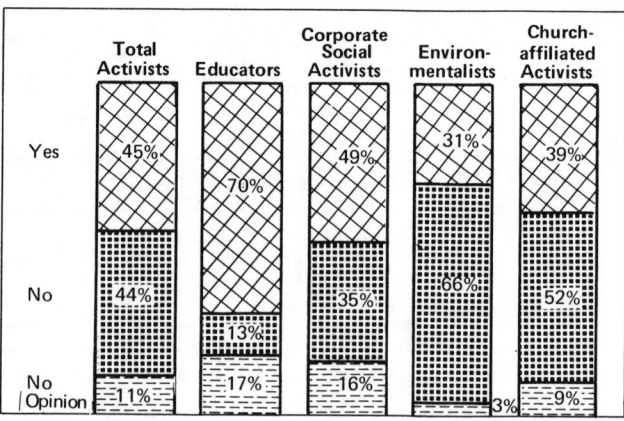

Figure 4-5. Ideal Board Composition

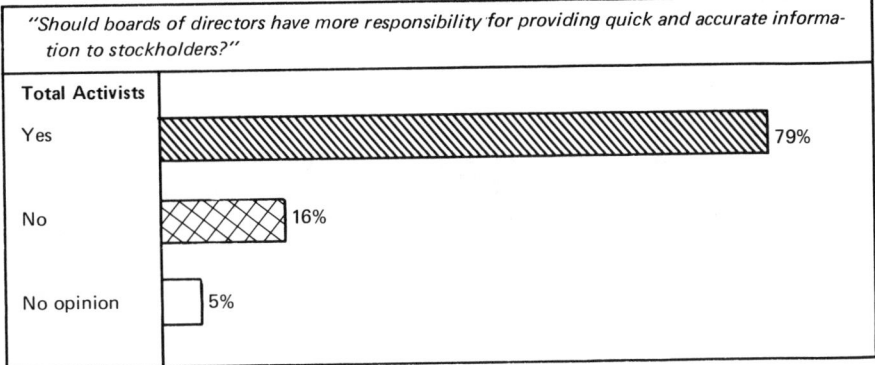

Figure 4-6. Information for Stockholders

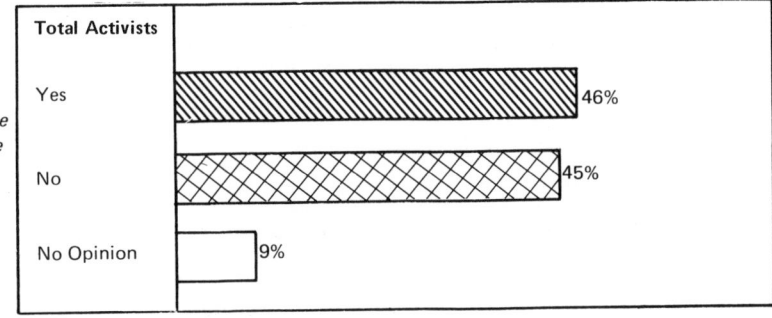

Figure 4-7. Legislation/Regulation of Boards

The social responsiveness—or lack of it—is an outgrowth of thought leaders' desire for broader public representation in the boardroom. Figure 4-10 charts the thinking on this issue as of 1976.

These notions in the public mind are causing motions in the boardroom, which are reflected in many ways, one of which is increasing concern over the conduct of corporations and of individual directors. Chapter 8 sets forth some implications of this concern in the legal context.

In an even broader context, the public attitudes reflected in the ORC survey focus the problem of the board of directors as one with some confusion as to actual responsibilities and roles (figure 4-11). The corporate and social environment and stage of development or maturity of the enterprise on which directors serve in their boardroom capacities change with the times.

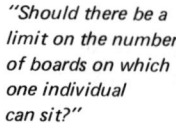

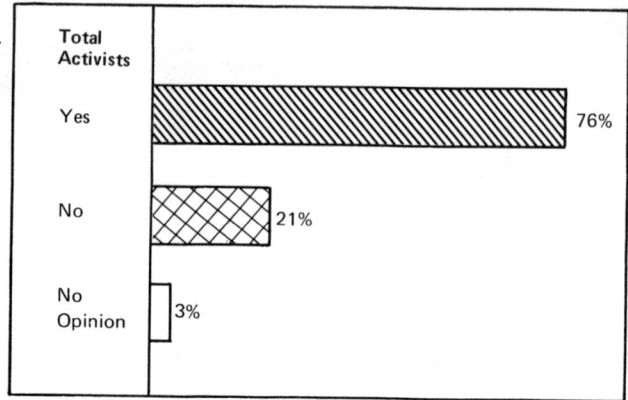

Figure 4-8. Limits on Directorships

Latest Survey	Total Thought Leaders (105)	Legislators (47)	Executive/ Regulatory Officials (23)	Union Leaders (12)	Public Interest Group Leaders (14)	Press/ Media Reps. (9)
Mainly Outside Directors	22%	13%	35%	25%	64%	22%
Mainly Inside Directors	13%	19%				
Evenly Balanced	61%	64%	65%	58%	36%	78%
No Opinion	4%	4%		17%		

[1] "Do you think that a corporate board of directors should consist mainly of outside directors, mainly inside directors, or do you think it should be evenly balanced?"

Figure 4-9. Ideal Board Composition of Board of Directors[1]

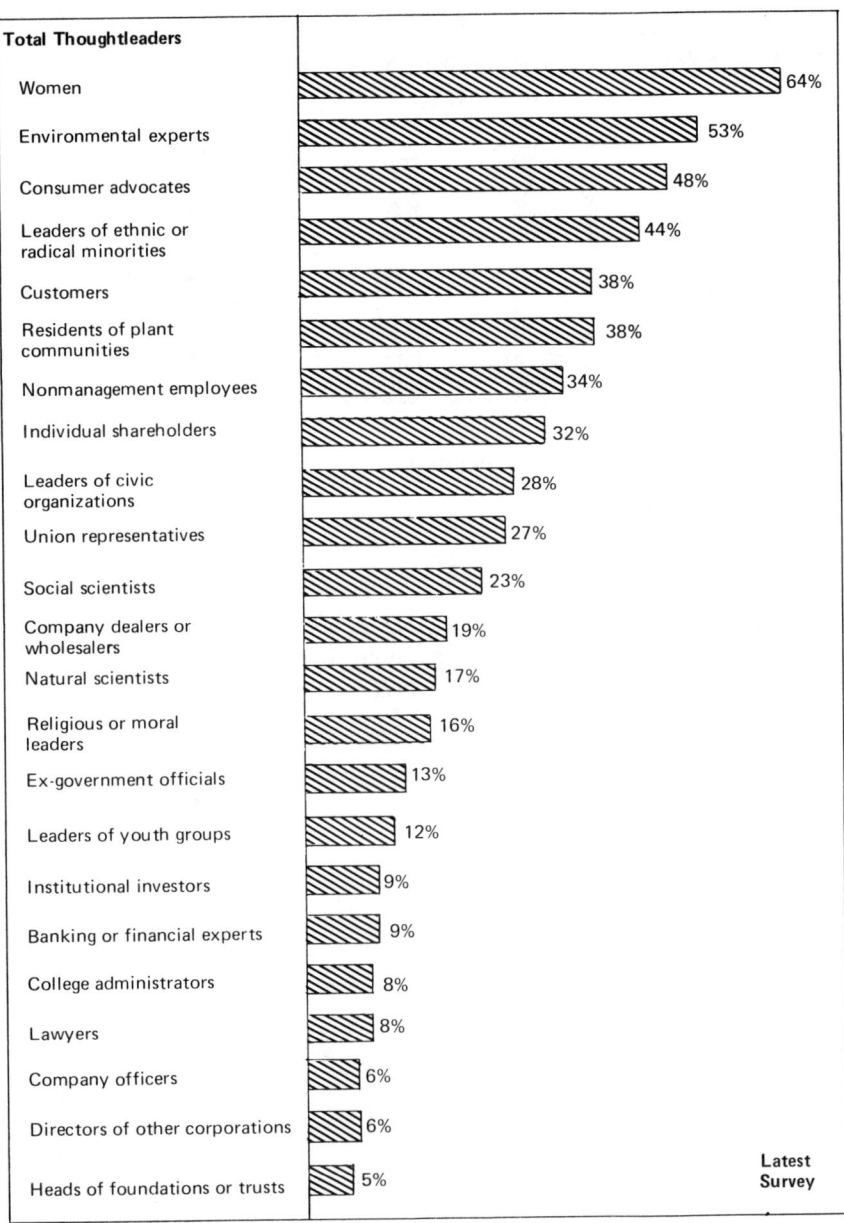

Total Thoughtleaders

Women	64%
Environmental experts	53%
Consumer advocates	48%
Leaders of ethnic or radical minorities	44%
Customers	38%
Residents of plant communities	38%
Nonmanagement employees	34%
Individual shareholders	32%
Leaders of civic organizations	28%
Union representatives	27%
Social scientists	23%
Company dealers or wholesalers	19%
Natural scientists	17%
Religious or moral leaders	16%
Ex-government officials	13%
Leaders of youth groups	12%
Institutional investors	9%
Banking or financial experts	9%
College administrators	8%
Lawyers	8%
Company officers	6%
Directors of other corporations	6%
Heads of foundations or trusts	5%

Latest Survey

Multiple mentions from a list

[1] *"Which of the various kinds of people on this list should be represented in greater numbers on corporate boards of directors than they are today?"*

Figure 4-10. Kinds of People Who Should Have Greater Representation on Corporate Boards[1]

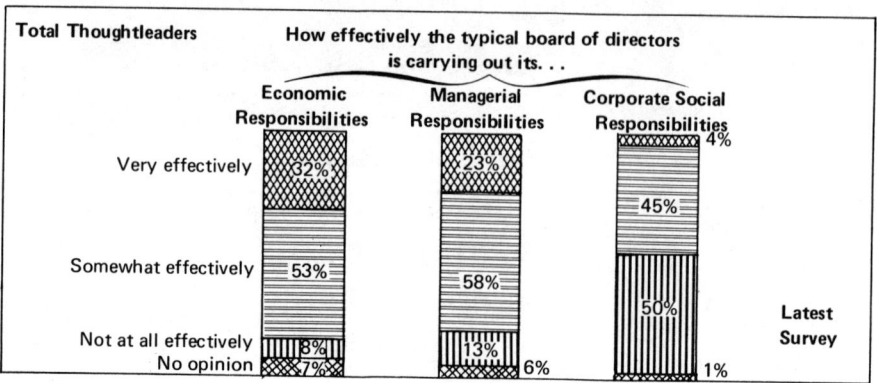

Figure 4-11. How Effectively Corporate Boards Carry Out Their Responsibilities

Notes

1. *ORC Public Opinion Index: Report to Management, Corporate Social Responsibility April 1974,* Washington Thoughtleader Survey (Princeton, New Jersey: Opinion Research Corp., August 1976.).

5 Bringing Up Boards

In his greeting to the Harvard and Radcliffe College class of 1980, Dean Henry Rosovsky of the Faculty of Arts and Sciences told the freshmen what they should have gained at the end of four years when they would be welcomed into "the company of educated men and women." An educated person, said the dean: has to be able to read and write the English language; should have a critical appreciation of the ways we gain knowledge and understanding of the universe, and an informed acquaintance with the results of scientific inquiry and the literary and artistic achievements of the ancient, medieval, and modern world; cannot be provincial . . . must understand events outside his or her own geographic and historical place and time; must have some understanding of the moral issues facing our society; should have taste, standards, and manners; should have achieved a depth of learning in a field of knowledge—"here we call this an area of concentration."[1]

In similar fashion, we might ask, What is a proper director? They should have most, if not all, of the attributes described for an educated person. The problem is that many directors are yet on a steep learning curve as they become better educated in board affairs. Perhaps an equal number of directors, however, fail to appreciate that being on a board of directors is not membership in a learned society; rather it is membership in a learning society. There is a great deal for members to learn as boards are challenged to improve the effectiveness of their changing role in corporate governance. Bringing up boards and board members may take more than the four years that Harvard requires to turn freshmen into educated men and women. It is time for this education to begin if boards are to be truly learning societies of the future.

Before I suggest any dogma for altering a board's role in such time of change and diversity, it may be fun, and perhaps helpful, to examine one unusual taxonomy of director practice. Directors as "top dogs" in the corporate governance hierarchy can be classified in two categories according to a friend of mine. Recognition of these categories is important if we are to bring our boards up to speed in learning to be both industry specific and company specific in the economic-social environment of the future. He refers to them as sighters and sniffers. The analogy is between the boardroom practice of some directors and the hunting characteristics of dogs.

Depending upon the breed, dogs hunt primarily by sight or smell. A sight hunter moves briskly through the field, pausing occasionally to survey the immediate surroundings with an acute vision that can identify his prey from afar. When he sights his quarry, he moves quickly and efficiently by the shortest possible route to it. He is limited, however, by range and poor visibility conditions and is often frustrated by prey that does not move, possesses good camouflage, or doubles back.

The smell hunter, or sniffer, is less affected by distance and visibility. He pokes about seeking clues. Once he detects a scent, he follows it until close upon his prey, where he uses his limited sight for the final pursuit. He is less rapid than the sighter in finding within the latter's visibility range. He is often misled by strange and curious smells that do not emanate from the desired quarry.

Directors are not bred for specialized hunting characteristics as are dogs, but good directors' natural aptitudes, schooling, and experiences tend to characterize many of them as either sighters or sniffers regarding their boardroom behavior. Sighter-directors are often specialists efficient and proficient in their job or profession. They handle facts and details quickly, arriving at the right answers. They generally come from within the ranks of R&D engineers and scientists, computer science specialists, market researchers, accountants, and financial analysts. Medical and legal specialists also belong to this class.

Sniffer-directors are not as specialized and are more people oriented than fact oriented. They may be trained in a particular area of management or business problem solving but are not expert within this area. They are often intuitive. Sniffer-directors are generally found within the ranks of marketing executives, general managers, and, occasionally, investment bankers, clergymen, artists, and most educators.

Since sighter-directors are more efficient directors when the issues are well defined and apparent, they are often the more successful when these situational characteristics exist. Sniffer-directors are generally more successful where the issues are murky, more difficult to define, and the facts are not clear. They can filter out the various nuances and pheromones until the proper direction or strategy is found. However, this process is uncertain and time-consuming since many interesting but unproductive paths must be explored. Sniffer-directors often point out the right course to take; sighter-directors deal better with its execution.

In a structured and defined business environment, filters are often constructed to replace sniffer-directors and identify the issues so that the effective talents of sighter-directors can be applied more rapidly. An example in the boardroom is in the formation of board committees. The success of these subsystem organizational units varies depending upon their internal communications and ability to comprehend the scope of the territory assigned.

In high-technology fields, the role of the specialist is enhanced by the increased usage of tests that screen and reduce the options to be explored. However, chemistry, physics, and instrumentation have little relevant application in the board world of business or government. Some scholars have looked to the computer to serve a similar function for corporate governance. One such current application is a study underway of director interlocks among corporations. The computer does provide a powerful instrument for such an analysis; however, its success depends upon the scope of the program and the capabilities of the model makers. Given problems that fall within the limits of the model, it can be a useful tool. When conditions change, however, the model itself may have to be changed. The sighter-director is often limited during a period of change, waiting for the dust to settle so he can get the facts straight.

Not only individual directors but board organizations themselves often have the characteristics of sighters and sniffers. Specialized firms that evolved during the past two decades to serve the specific needs of the military, aerospace, and data-processing industries were able to govern the corporation by the logical, rational, sequential, quantitative model. In the changing economic and political climate, however, many such firms find survival difficult. Witness the inability of many Department of Defense-oriented firms to diversify into commercial markets. They have become so proficient at focusing on limited and clearly identified markets that they are unable to function effectively in a different environment. The ability to cope with perceptive, intuitive, simultaneous, and qualitative issues is nonexistent in these boardrooms.

Another example is the technical specialists in the Pentagon. They continued to predict victory in Vietnam without really understanding the complexities of the situation, including the enemy or our allies. The actual situational framework did not coincide with their predictive framework, and subjective talent was missing at the level of governance.

In established markets, success is dependent upon efficiency, and the sighters often make a firm successful. However, when conditions change, sniffer-directors can help lead the firm in another strategic direction. Many boards try to combine the best of both of these types. For example, a board may have an engineering company president with a professor of philosophy or psychology as outside director. Either of these two directors may prove to be a sniffer or a sighter. Occasionally, a talented director is adept at both roles. Generally, sniffers are found in evolving growth industry companies and sighters in companies working in the established marketplace.

When some of these types of persons are independent, unaffiliated directors, the board tends to be more effective. Board meetings must provide for great interaction for the organization to be both stimulating and effective. The difficulty is establishing and maintaining such a board without friction among the directors. The CEO requires unusual management and director talent plus a good chairman to orchestrate the group.

Contemporary Force Fields

The original corporate form was common in Rome, under the Normans in England, and especially in medieval towns. The modern corporate form was brought along more directly in response to the needs of European commerce in the sixteenth and seventeenth centuries' trade expansion overseas. Associates in such ventures bought shares in a ship and divided profits accordingly. The Stuarts created the doctrine that corporations are legal persons distinct from their members and, arguing thus, extended their control over all corporations, municipal and trading. The existence and role of the board as we know it today had no similar function in these past times.

This heritage of control by owners was replaced in large degree with the advent of professional management hired by the owners and exercising "power without property" in a society that recently has rebelled at the abuse by and the unsensitivity of power wielders. The corporate governance system that has evolved often lacks relevance to society particularly at the board level. It also often lacks flexibility, integration with the environment, and ability to cope with multiple objectives in a diverse setting under rapidly changing conditions.

Arthur D. Little, Inc., has been in the corporate strategy consulting business almost since its founding in 1886. At least thirty issues have surfaced recently, and more are in the offing, regarding the credibility, adequacy, and accountability of corporate governance. These issues emanate from a series of force fields of regulation, legislation, public opinion, special-interest initiatives, self-reform, and changing value systems. Treatment of these issues can be grouped in clusters of contextual, teleological, ontological, practice, and process issues at the board level.[2] These issues are all relevant to the task of "bringing up a board" to the speed and cognition required for the future.

Four contextual issues are typical of the contemporary force fields that have an impact on corporate governance at the board level:

1. Social responsibility (the outside world consciousness).
2. Overbreadth of public and owner interests (whose interests are served?).
3. Corporate activism (environmentalists, consumerists, and special-interest initiatives).
4. Business and public conflicts of interest (interdependence of economic and social interests).

There are other forces at work, both from inside and outside the corporation. This chapter, however, will not catalog all of these drives, energy shifts, persuasions, influences, powers, threats, vacuums, and pressures, which all have an impact on or draw on corporate governance. The purpose of the chapter is to set forth the argument for organizational relevance, particularly at the level of the board of directors. This relevance can change the architectural concept of the board by changing the participating groups and the organization of the board itself. Further, a change in organizational relevance will be a dynamic process to fit the board's maturity with the corporation's life cycle in a changing environment.

Strategic planners generally agree that industries can be grouped into four stages of maturity. First is an embryonic industry, normally characterized by rapid growth in technology, active pursuit of new customers, and fragmented and changing shares of the market. Second, a growth industry is one that is still growing rapidly. However, customers, shares, and technology are better known. Because of competition, entry into the industry is more difficult than in the embryonic stage. The computer business is an example. Third, a mature industry is characterized by stability in known customers, technology, and shares of market, although the industries may still be market competitive. Fourth, aging industries are best characterized by falling market demand, declining number of competitors, and often a narrowing of product lines.

These stages, which have been well chronicled by many consulting firms and authors, have been likened to sweepstakes; stock, bond, and mortgage classifications; spring, summer, fall, and winter; and so on. The stage of maturity is a negative factor only if the role of the corporation and its type of corporate governance are at odds with what should be reasonably expected for success in such a milieu.

Directorate Relevance

In chapter 2, the bipolar evolutionary process was used to characterize the board in one of its three important contexts. Thirteen levels of corporate development were ranked in ascending order toward a state of metadevelopment. These different stages of evolution depict a board's functions during these sequential development levels. The stages of board development were clustered into phases that can be related to stages of corporate maturity:

Board Development Phases	*Board Stages of Maturity*
Entrepreneurial-innovation	Embryonic
Growth	Growth
Complex system	Mature
System of systems	Aging

The way to be successful is not to allow the board to age too much at a time of its existence when corporate governance requirements become so complicated and change so fast that either a complex system or system-of-systems situation exists.

Bringing a board up to adulthood and then keeping it young is an interesting challenge for the chairman of the board. It is often like Oscar Wilde observed: "The old believe everything, the middle-aged suspect everything, the young know everything."

Notes

1. Henry Rosovsky, "What Is an Educated Person?" *Harvard Magazine* 79 (November 1976). Copyright © 1976, Harvard Magazine, Inc. Reprinted by permission.

2. I have set forth this clustering more extensively in my *New Directions for Directors: Behind the Bylaws* (Lexington: Lexington Books, D.C. Heath, 1977).

6 Boardroom Maturity

Boardroom behavior can be characterized by several modes: sustained activity, growth, retrenchment, crisis, or moribund state. The concept of growth contrasts with a state of maturity in a biological context. As a result, we tend to think of maturity negatively as nongrowth or degrowth, such as cutting back, retrenching, or retreating. Maturity also connotes nearing old age, with all the negative aspects of that state.

The three phases of growth are the lag phase, the log phase, and the stationary phase. The lag period represents little or no growth and the adjustment of the individual directors to a new environment. The log phase is an increase in the maximum rate of growth at an exponential rate. The stationary phase is a plateau or slowdown rate that includes negative decline in board activity. The lag and stationary phases imply a biological type of maturation.[1] If, however, we define maturity in a social rather than a biological sense, there is more flexibility in the concept. There is no evidence that old age is relevant to a society or a microsociety such as those that inhabit a boardroom.

Adlai Stevenson once defined maturity in the political sense as "voting the same way I do." This rather imperious viewpoint is, unfortunately, manifest by some boards that proceed with their corporate affairs without adequate consideration of the impact of corporate actions on the economy, environment, or society. As a result, the public is aroused and, through government intervention, places more and more constraints on corporate and boardroom behavior.

Measures of Maturity

We tend to view boardroom phenomena most often in monetary terms: earnings per share, dollars invested per employee, and a host of financial ratios. But such monetary measures are relatively useless in gauging a board as immature or mature. Proxy statements, disclosure documents, SEC forms 10K, 10Q, 8K; annual reports, comfort letters, and other corporate forms of communications are heavily oriented toward numbers. Comments on corporate conduct or individual contributions by directors are limited in most instances. The following guidelines are suggested as a list of items reflecting maturity of the directorate.

A board can be considered mature when it has satisfied the legal requirements and individual directors involved with regard to:

1. Basic statutory and fiduciary compliance, including performance of principal duties to the corporation served of obedience, diligence, and loyalty.
2. An established code of ethics for the corporation.
3. Appropriate degree of independent, disinterested components of the board membership to ensure objective check and balance on corporate decisions, particularly in audit, compensation, director nomination (and criteria), indemnification provisions, and management succession matters.
4. The board's existential nature, including clear corporate objective(s) and strategic plans.
5. Recognition of responsibilities to the society, which sanctions the existence of the corporation.
6. Understanding the environmental hazards and obligations inherent in the type of business the company chooses to engage in and the taking of appropriate and responsible safeguard actions.
7. Establishment of board processes and organization to monitor corporate conduct and integrity of the corporate systems.
8. Delegation and retention of powers, responsibility, and authority necessary to conduct the affairs of the company effectively.
9. Explicit policy and procedures for evaluating corporate and management performance.
10. Adequate and reliable information system to keep directors informed on company matters. Directors have a responsibility to maintain a current understanding of developments in the industry, the securities laws, and the liabilities of directors.
11. An effective, constructive, mutually trustful interface between the board and the executive management, particularly the CEO.
12. Programmed replacement of directors lost by retirement or otherwise, with a "woodbox" of potential candidates who have been screened and investigated regarding their qualifications to ensure that they represent the experience and wisdom needed by the board.
13. Separate roles and incumbents for the chairman as an agent of the board and the CEO. Exceptions to this pattern are often sound and important.
14. Stock ownership by the individual directors is at least nominal and not dominating.
15. Faithful attendance at board and committee meetings and devotion of a substantial amount of time to directorship.
16. Directors' contributions in the form of corporate ambassadorial roles in the community and marketplace.
17. Stimulating trustful and respectful peer relationships within the board.
18. Disaster and emergency plans formulated for management of the corporation and for handling the consequences of such a major interruption.

Given a good rating on these eighteen characteristics of a mature board—there are undoubtedly a few more—there can be further growth not in an economic or biological sense but in a social or cultural sense. The board can improve its flexibility, its initiative, its resources, and its participative roles.

Social Growth

The social growth or further development of maturity of the board can be in terms of:

Improvement in quality of decision making (outlined in chapter 10).

Strengthening of the rapport of the directors with each other and with executive ranks.

Enhancement of corporate climate for executive recognition and development by increased exposure of the directors to personnel, plant sites, offices, and laboratories.

Extension of the perceived boundaries of director concern to environmental, social, and political domains surrounding and impacting on the corporation (discussed in chapter 2).

Increased but carefully controlled participation by directors on board committees and as expert resources when qualified and requested by management.

Change agent or catalytic role on the part of the board by introducing new concepts, new directions, new objectives, and a constant reexamination of the long-term viability and integrity of the business in which the corporation is engaged. When new thinking is introduced in the form of suggestions for the company to explore, the board can stimulate the management. The imperative form of this change agent role may be called upon in crisis situations or when management fails to carry out its proper functions.

Upgrading of the talent and resources of the board by adding distinguished individuals to the membership, subject to shareholder approval, for the purpose of broadening the base of representation on the board.

The latent capacity of most boards to improve is tremendous, and many companies have made great strides to tap such unutilized capacity for improved corporate governance. Spreading this movement to more directorates requires raising the consciousness of the potential and emotional acceptance of the merit of maturing or fully developing the board. It also requires enlightened leadership of the board, most properly the chairman's role. It may also come from other effective or psychological leaders among the board members. The priority of concerns of a board varies considerably with its state of maturity and the nature of the institution being served. Nonprofit institutions, by their very nature, place social and noneconomic objectives ahead of profitability and return on investment measures of a business corporation. This different emphasis does not diminish the social responsibilities of shareowners and directors of a profit-making enterprise, but it defines certain boundaries of social responsibility for the profit-oriented corporation.

Director Concerns

I looked through the list of diseases and couldn't find worry and melancholy thoughts among them: this is quite wrong.   —G.C. Lichtenberg

Figure 6-1 cognitively maps the wide range and variations of functional concerns of directors serving different types of institutions. The differences are apparent in both nature of ownership and institutional purpose. The descriptive ratings given are purely subjective and subject to change depending on a particular situation.

The map shows that the role of a director in a privately owned institution has significant level of concerns in four of the nine functions. Further it is rated of optional concern in two roles and minimal in two of the nine director roles. Some further indications of this mapping can be approximated by assigning numerical values from 1 through 8 to the priorities of concern, as shown in the legend.

The role of a director in a publicly held institution shows half of the four significant ratings. They are not only placed differently from the privately held institutions, but the rating total is numerically more "severe" in the weighing of the significant and important composited ratings.

Quasi-public institutions, like COMSTAT, AMTRAK, the U.S. Postal Corporation, and the Port of New York Authority, have multiple interests to serve in carrying out their functions. Directors on COMSTAT's board, for example, have the problem of fiduciary responsibilities to both communications common carriers, who purchased half of the $200 million stock issue, and to the general public, who purchased the other half. Their functional roles become quite complex. The severity-of-concern ratings given these quasi-public institutions is graded even higher than the composite rating for the publicly held institutions. This rating, arrived at by adding the numerical priority values of each role, provides a first, albeit subjective (and challengeable), attempt to give some severity significance to these three ownership classes of institutions.

—— OWNERSHIP —————————— PURPOSE ——

Director-Trustee Steward Role (Function)	Privately Held Institution	Publicly Held Institution	Quasi-Public Institution	Not-for-Profit Institution	Professional Institution	Conventional Service/Mfg. Institution
Statutory	Minimal	Consequential	Consequential	Minimal	Optional	Consequential
Supervisory	Optional	Optional	Optional	Optional	Optional	Optional
Evaluative (Performance of Mge and Corporation)	Significant	Significant	Significant	Minimal to Reactive	Reactive to Important	Significant
Participative	Reactive to Active	Reactive to Minimal	Reactive to Minimal	Minimal to Reactive	Minimal to Optional	Minimal to Active
Determinative (Strategic)	Significant	Important	Important	Reactive to Important	Reactive to Minimal	Important to Significant
Change Agent (Self-Actualizing)	Significant	Reactive to Optional	Important to Significant	Minimal to Optional	Minimal	Minimal to Active
Identity	Qualified to Minimal	Influential to Significant	Influential to Significant	Influential to Significant	Significant to Important	Minimal to Significant
Institutional Linkage	Optional	Significant & Important	Significant & Important	Significant & Important	Significant & Important	Minimal to Important
Constituent Representation	Significant & Important	Significant & Important	Significant & Important	Significant & Important	Minimal	Optional

PRIORITY OF CONCERN

Keyboard:
1. Significant   5. Consequential
2. Important   6. Reactive
3. Active   7. Optional
4. Influential   8. Minimal

Figure 6-1. Severity of Director Concerns

The differences in level of concern for the three types of institutions can
be compared roughly as follows (a lower point total implies a greater concern
for the director's functions):

Institution	Total Weight of Priority Ratings in the Nine Director Roles	Severity of Concerns
Privately held	46-50 points (avg. 48)	Least severe
Publicly held	30-48 points (avg. 34)	Average severity
Quasi-public	25-33 points (avg. 29)	Most severe

This attempt to compare the influence of ownership on the role of directors would imply that the directors on a quasi-public institution board have
the most worries. The directors on privately held company boards presumably
have the least number of worries about fulfilling their stewardship. Intuitively
this conclusion seems correct, although to indicate that directors on any board
are free of any of the concerns is, of course, misleading.

The difference in concerns over director roles in institutions whose primary
purposes are focused in three separate directions, shown in figure 6-1, has some
possible and interesting, if controversial, implications. The validity of ascribing
a numerical weighting to these abstractions can be challenged—or the data even
discarded—by the methodologist experts in cluster, cross-impact factor, or
parametric analysis. However for the purposes of a lively discussion, the three
types of institutions tally up their director concern ratings in the following index:

Institutional Purpose	Total Weight of Priority Ratings in the Nine Director Roles	Severity of Concerns
Not-for-profit	39-53 points (avg. 46)	Moderate severity
Professional	47-56 points (avg. 52)	Least severe
Services/manufacture	30-54 points (avg. 42)	Most severe

This display indicates that directors on a corporate services or manufacturing type of company have the hardest roles to play. Certainly the public
cross-fire would support that in these times for the publicly held company.

The director on an eleemosynary institution board; on a hospital, college,
or university board of trustees; or on a foundation directorate has an indicated
position of less worry about director functions. While this may not hold up
under the theory of trustee-stewardship-directorship responsibilities, it appears
true for the real world. This worry level, however, is rapidly rising.

The director of a professional organization has a unique role, perhaps because of the nature of the professional activities. These organizations are supposed to have technical and ethical standards that have separate social sanction, government charter, or license to operate in the public and professional society interests. Stewardship rests with the entire professional organization.

I began this chapter by reciting five modes of boardroom behavior that parallel various states of maturity. The concern of directors shifts its focus constantly depending on the state of the enterprise and of the culture and environment. The time is well past when directors or trustees can rest easy in their role. Responsibilities increase with opportunities, they become electrifying cogent in time of crisis, and they bubble ominously when there is a drift in performance compared to expectations.

All of these problems could frighten a timid candidate for director into asking whether board service is worth the psychic and other rewards that accompany the position. Those of us who enjoy the challenge can take limited comfort in Winston Churchill's remarks: "When I look back on all these worries I remember the story of the old man who said on his deathbed that he had had a lot of trouble in his life, most of which never happened."[2]

The Spotted Watermelon Theory

In 1977, the *Saturday Review* reported an exciting, innovative scientific discipline that is claiming as its province the study of the entire human life span from the moment of conception to the moment of death. It examines all of the psychosocial and biomedical aspects of human development in the context of a person's total environment. Robert A. Aldrich composed a diagram expressing the nature of the life-span continuum.[3] Buckminister Fuller dubbed it the "watermelon model" because of its gourd-like appearance.

There appears to be a correlation of the concept with the life-span development of a corporate enterprise. With acknowledgment to Aldrich and Fuller for the idea and characterization, let us look at the concept of life-span development of a board of directors as it governs an enterprise through the four stages of corporate existence and development. This concept affords us a conceptual framework in which to place the panorama of perspectives set forth in chapter 1 and offered in more detail throughout this book.

The spotted watermelon theory draws heavily on my previous work that outlines the concept of metadevelopment with thirteen levels in its continuum.[4] This abstract conception of metadevelopment is positioned into evolutionary stages on the "watermelon concept" of life-span development in figure 6-2. The various schemata proposed for different perspectives can be focused or anchored at different spots along the evolutionary stages of corporate maturity.

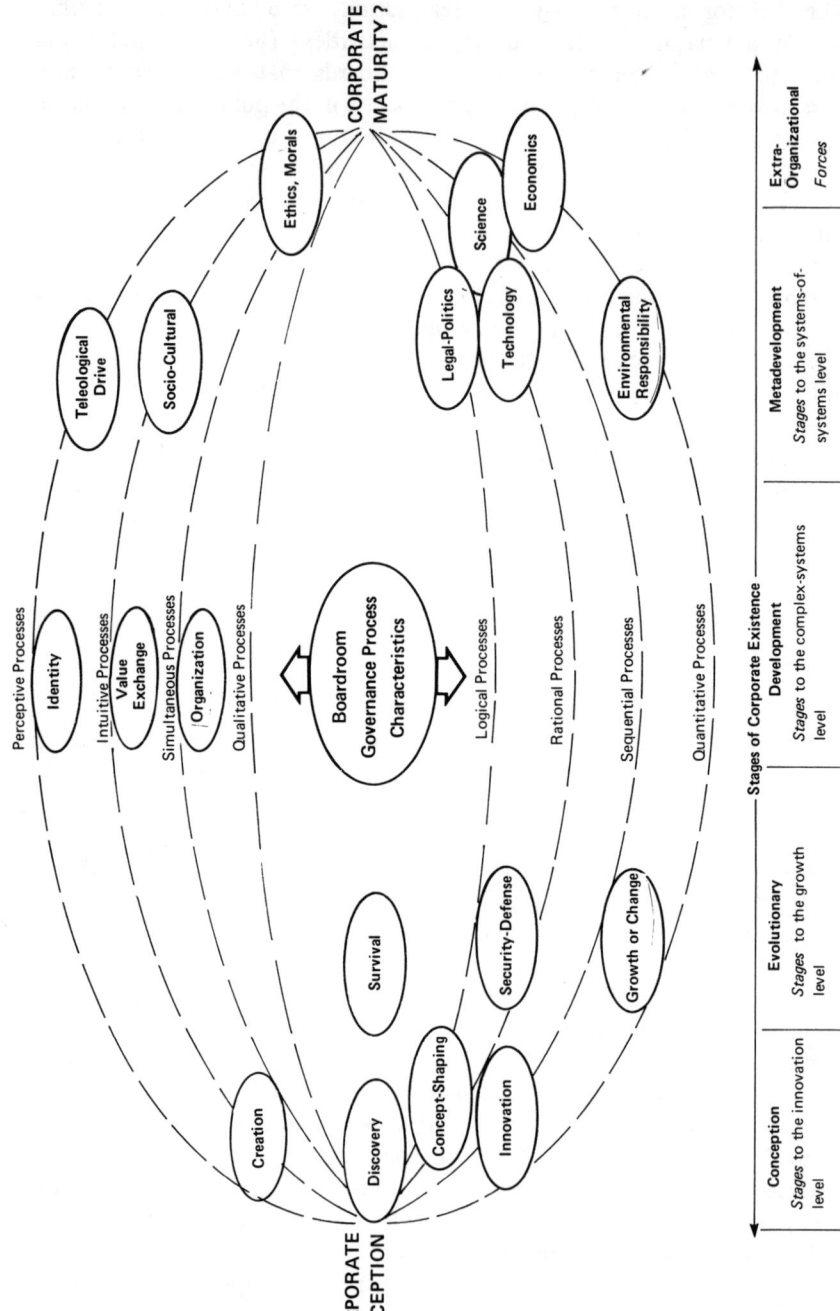

Figure 6-2. The Spotted Watermelon Theory: A Concept of Board Life-Span Development

The spotted watermelon model starts at the left with corporate conception and ends at the right of the figure with corporate maturity. The question mark beyond indicates the uncertainty of the future. The top half of the model represents the soft value-laden thought processes that are part of the governance process of a board of directors functioning in overall corporate guidance, monitoring, and direction. These processes are qualitative, simultaneous, intuitive, and perceptive. The lower half represents the other stream of thought that takes place in a boardroom as the directors address the more definable elements of corporate governance. These thought processes are logical, rational, sequential, and quantitative. The combination of the two halves makes up the melon model of the boardroom governance process.

Four stages of corporate existence are characterized over the time axis of the spotted watermelon, with extraorganizational forces particularly affecting stages of maturity and beyond. First, the conception stage moves the enterprise from birth to the innovation level. Innovation in this context means the stage of market or social acceptance of the enterprise's service or product. During this stage, "spots" on the watermelon may form to identify and track the evolution. The creation and discovery spots obviously occur in the intuitive-simultaneous-qualitative half of the model because they are imaginative and entrepreneurial. The concept-shaping stage spots itself in the logical and rational side of the model, as does the innovation phenomenon, which tends to be more of a sequential and quantitative bound stage.

The second stage, reaching the rapid-growth level of existence, spots the survival phase in the melon middle; the security-defense reactions tend to be focused in the rational zone; and the growth or change stages occur sequentially and, often, quantitatively. This does not mean to say there are no qualitative changes in nature too.

The third development stage involves a complex system of governance. Three stages are spotted on the melon model. The organizational phase is mainly a human-relations-oriented, behavioral stage—a continuing one, in fact—so it positions itself on the soft side of the model somewhere in the qualitative and simultaneous process areas. Corporate identity is the next concern in normal corporate development. This is primarily a perceptive issue from within and without the corporation. This creates the institution's own character which is unique from other institutions. This is an important stage, fraught with emotional and psychological overtones. Value exchange comes to the fore also in this third stage. This is the trade-off of the objectives to the growth and impact of the enterprise with all of the opposing forces. Some of these forces may be economic, social (or lack of social) sanction, political, or environmental. Uncertainty is another one. Value exchange is often an inductive, intuitive process and is so placed on the model.

The fourth stage of corporate development is the system-of-systems level. The interaction and interfacing of one complex system in equilibrium with other systems in equilibrium or disequilibrium can best be comprehended by resorting to the concept of a metasystem that embrases all concerned.[5]

Occurring in this metadevelopment stage are spots of director concern that have great long-range significance. The sociocultural level of social responsibility is positioned in the simultaneous-intuitive process area (it could also lap over into the perceptive zone). The environmental-responsibility concern is essentially a quantitative one with environmental impact studies defining its parameters. Teleological drive is an esoteric level of concern over philosophy, purpose, design and destiny of the enterprise. This, rightly, is situated on the soft side of the melon and is governed by instinct, tradition, intuition, and perception.

Beyond the metadevelopment stage of maturity, the enterprise is free-floating in a welter of opposing extraorganizational forces: political and governmental; ethical, moral, and legal; scientific and technological; sociocultural; physical and environmental; and economic, all from external sources.

This completes the description of figure 6-2 depicting the spotted watermelon theory as adapted for the board of directors' processes of corporate governance. It can be viewed from either a "melancholy" or an enlightened perspective. If boards are to be learning societies, the framework provides some guides to areas of concern for better governance. If the complexity and obtrusiveness is depressing, then realistic acceptance of the future compass of the board is the root issue to be addressed.

Farfetched? Intriguing? Irrational? If this exposition does not spark some thought about the challenge and dynamic nature of director's responsibilities, then the effort stands in vain. I believe the road ahead will always be challenging. As soon as one problem or issue is resolved, a more complex one will arise.

A Georgia farmer put this sign in front of his watermelon patch: One watermelon in this patch has been poisoned. The next morning the sign had been changed to read: Two watermelons in this patch have been poisoned.

Notes

1. For a further exposition of this phenomenon, see my *Metadevelopment: Beyond the Bottom Line* (Lexington: Lexington Books, D.C. Heath, 1977).

2. Laurence J. Peter, *Peter's Quotations: Ideas for Our Time* (New York: William Morrow and Company, Inc., 1977) pg. 510.

3. Albert Rosenfeld, "The New LSD: Life Span Development," *Saturday Review*, October 1, 1977, pp. 32-34.

4. Mueller, *Metadevelopment*, chap. 6.

5. Ibid., p. 81.

7 The Interiority Complex

The Nobel people have never rewarded the great innovators in the study of human character, and perhaps rightly so: so far there is no proof that this has anything to do with the progress of man on this planet; and if most people knew those things about themselves it would probably throw whole nations into chaos. —Ernest Becker, Pulitzer Prize winner[1]

The cosmography of the inner worlds of man places self-esteem as a dominant motive. With what cultural anthropologist Ernest Becker calls an "inner newsreel," we pass in review the symbols that give self-esteem and make us feel important and good. Becker's general theory of human nature as part of an emerging appreciation of social science taps this and other recent discoveries in the fields of anthropology, sociology, psychology, and psychiatry.

The fact that all objects, animate and inanimate, all individuals, and all organized units have both an inside and an outside is hardly a recent scientific breakthrough. However, the inside story is the side of this vital dualism that has been neglected for both individuals and for groups. The board of directors is no exception.

The Concept of Interiority

Gustav Fechner, one of the fathers of psychophysics and experimental psychology, introduced the notion of interiority over a hundred years ago in an attempt to prove that there is an equal part of soul for every particle of matter. Fechner believed that all objects, even trees, have "interiority": "A tree leans on a fence because it feels weak. It soaks up water because it is thirsty or bends to stretch toward the sun." The recent fad of being kind to plants undoubtedly had its root thinking in Fechner's hypothesis. At the bottom of Fechner's scale, the objects possessing the least interiority were rocks. Their inner life is the "idling of their atomic structures, but in these as physicists have taught us, there is nothing but repose."[2]

Whether or not one accepts Fechner's animistic theory, it is plausible to believe that man's distinctive interiority presents a poignant problem. He learns very quickly to cultivate his private self, which puts a barrier between him and the world and thus shields him from the demands of the world.

For most individuals, our existence consists of only the joining of exteriors. Like a marriage that is never consummated or a merger that never gets fully integrated in spirit or in fact, this tendency to cultivate a self that others cannot probe is often a tragedy. It turns people away and fosters existence in an unreal world. Becker claims that we tend to become "masters at dissimulation" in this regard, to a point of hopeless separation from everyone else. Evan Esar said it more simply, perhaps, in describing egocentricity as the vanity that makes you wonder what people are thinking about you when they are really wondering what you are thinking about them.

This phenomenon of interiority is also characteristic of what sociologists term *social aggregations*. Boards of directors fall into this classification, as do more simplistic social structures that have an external boundary and at least one internal boundary. The internal boundary of this social form—the board of directors—separates the leadership region (the chairman) from the membership region (the directors). Both of these regions are contained in a so-called group space (the physical analogy is the boardroom), which has an external boundary or barrier to the outside world.[3]

Boards, like individuals, tend to emphasize interiority, often to a vulnerable point of ignoring competition, society, the environment, or the interface with the institution, owners, or consumers that they serve. One inside-dominated board of a medium-sized manufacturing firm, with which I worked recently, was so oblivious to its competitors' inroads into its traditional business that the outside directors finally forced the hiring of a consulting firm to assess the drifting performance and to recommend changes. The management had failed to be realistic about the trend of lost market position due, in large part, to their interiority complex. The outcome, among other things, was a new CEO and a *revamping* of the board membership to balance the dominant group of management directors whose interiority clouded over a realistic acceptance of the company's situation.

The 1976-1977 series of payoff scandals rocked scores of major corporations and focused concern in the boardroom on a board's responsibility in overseeing and monitoring the ethics and performance of the management and, in particular, any interiority complex. Examples of the board's new clout in evaluating all aspects of the chief executive officer's performance have been highlighted in newspapers. The easing out of such chief executives as chairman Franklin Harman of Genesco, Inc., two successive executives, chairman Robert W. Sarnoff and president A.L. Conrad of RCA Corp., and president William Goodwin of Johns-Manville support the awakening of boards of directors to one of their prime responsibilities.

Another instance of excessive interiority was exposed when the Environmental Protection Agency recently moved in on a well-known multinational industrial firm to stop it from polluting a major inland body of water. The management and the board were so engaged in their own inner newsreel that they failed to recognize the severity of the adverse impact of the company's operations on the environment surrounding one of its major plant sites. A $5000-per-day fine until clean-up was complete got the company's attention. When a board of directors lives in a world all its own, the whole corporation tends to develop a carapace-like shield that insulates it from the exterior real world.

Bridges to Exteriority

This tendency to carry interiority of the directorate too far is the reason for the hubbub over board reform and a pro-active view of the function of a board. The closed-system concept of a board is passé (if it ever truly had any integrity).

Demands for a greater number of nonmanagement, unaffiliated directors seek to provide credible objectivity and perspective in the boardroom. Perhaps an equally important function is to combat excessive interiority and to open up the boundary of the board. One way to permeate the boundary is to provide human linkages with other nonconflicting organizations and domains of human endeavor. This is accomplished through the responsible stewardship of outside directors engaged in primary career activity in other domains of concern to the company. This may be another economic sector, education, or public or social activity.

The confederation and brokerage forms of organizational relationships also provide an active interface of a board with its neighbors and environment. The interiority of the board thus becomes exposed to forces from the outside world through intimate intraorganizational relationships. Value shifts in governmental regulations and consumerism can be better perceived if a board has interfacial relationships with the outside world.

Common forms of relationships that tend to break down boardroom provincialism include the traditional forms of intracorporate activity. Joint ventures, mergers, partnerships, pooled contracts, volunteer memberships, duty leaves, coalitions, and syndicates are among the architectural variations of company liaison, alliances, and confederations. The legal aspects of these interlocks and activities may appear to be a minefield, but there are legal and useful pathways through the interfacial territories.

The brokerage concept is different. It means the engagement by one organization of another indigenous organization in some other environmental setting to permit the first organization to do the job better. The worldwide agency network of multinational companies is the most common form. Subcontracting for specialized work is another example. Multitiered affiliations and investment interests in associated and subsidiary companies offer opportunities for a corporation to participate in and be sensitive to a diverse range of activity.

The opening of the boundaries between the boardroom and its various worlds mitigates the tendency of directorates to develop an interiority complex to the detriment of their basic functions. More bridges to exteriority will be needed as the world increases interaction and interdependence.

As Ernest Becker has observed, "I have had the growing realization over the past few years that the problem of man's knowledge is not to oppose and to demolish opposing views, but to include them in a larger theoretical structure."[4]

Key Board Functions

This discussion is not meant to imply that the board of directors' function is focused primarily on corporate social responsibility; far from that. An interiority complex in the boardroom can interfere with all four of the board's board functions in a free society: providing for management and board succession, considering decisions and actions with a potential for major economic impact, establishing policies and procedures to ensure law and regulatory compliance, and considering major social impacts of the company's plans and activities.

In June 1977, the Scholars' Symposium was held at the Harvard Business School to appraise the role of boards of directors of large, publicly held enterprises. The Business Roundtable's Committee on Corporate Organization Policy, chaired by J. Paul Austin, reviewed the symposium report and directed a paper to be written on the subject. The statement of the Business Roundtable, "The Role and Composition of the Board of Directors of the Large Publicly Owned Corporation," was thus a recent response of the business community to the rash of public challenges to board conduct and corporate performance.[5] The statement was an attempt by distinguished members of the business community to clarify this murky area of corporate governance. The effort recalls one college professor—a man very much admired as a teacher of medieval history—who confessed that the more he learned about the period, the less he was prepared to say: "The epoch was so complex, so diversified that no general statement could safely be made about it." Corporate governance is like medieval history in this regard—perhaps in other aspects too, with the anachronistic practices still persisting on some boards. The subject is bleary with statements of principles, guidelines, court interpretations, public perceptions, and general misunderstandings.

Given the murk and mist enveloping the function of the board, the Roundtable's statement percipitated four key functional clusters of responsibilities for the stewards of the owners' interests in a corporation. It is vital to note that the directors are also stewards of the owners' legal and ethical obligations to other groups affected by corporate activities or plans. The place of the board of directors in this corporate governance triad of shareowners, directors, and executive operating management calls for more exteriority in the board's behavior and cognition. The first area is in the management and board selection and succession function. It concerns the lack of objectivity and perspective in evaluating the performance of the top management and the board itself. This omission can be life threatening to a corporation. Chapter 10 elaborates on the pathology that may develop with an incestuous board of directors. In the realistic evaluation of boardworthiness of directors and the competence of chief executive officers, it is the "inner-newsreel" of personal human relationships which often obscures impersonal assessment of competence and behavior of our peers. Our private opinions are one of the great tragedies of our interiority; they are often utterly personal and unrevealable. Although we should and want to appraise another member of the board—whether a personal friend or a business acquaintance and colleague—we cannot (and perhaps should not) speak our innermost thoughts, which will intrude upon his inner and separate world. Ernest Becker said this most effectively: "We find ourselves in the ironic situation of having to transact with others with the part of ourselves—our exteriors—that we value least. And we are all placed in the position of having to judge others on this least important aspect."[6]

The criteria for performance, effectiveness, and value of a fellow director are so subjective, dynamic, and unclear that to violate his interiority would often be counterproductive as emotional response and conflicts would take over. Harry Stack Sullivan, a psychiatrist, believes that only during one period in our lives do we normally break down the barriers of separateness. Sullivan refers to "pre-adolescent chumship" as that period when we are striving, perhaps the hardest, to establish the integral domain of our inner identity, and our chum helps us.[7] But as years pass and we move into a career world, the outer or public aspect of our lives takes over, and exteriority is the mode in which we deal with others. Our adult existence, for most individuals, consists only in dealing with the joining of exteriors.

Boards of directors, like persons, also tend to reveal only their exterior feelings when it comes to chief executive or director selection. There are outstanding exceptions. Pillsbury Company's outside directors invite chairman and chief executive William Spoor to meet with them informally before each board meeting so they can evaluate each other's performance on the job. This practice tends to clear any misunderstandings before the official business session. Massachusetts Mutual Life Insurance Company's chairman and chief executive officer, James M. Martin, annually calls for the seven outside director members of the executive committee to enter into executive session to evaluate the performance of the CEO and the top senior officers. The exchange is frank and constructive, and the subsequent transmittal to the management is most effective.

One of the most effective boardroom techniques for introducing perceptive, realistic assessment of director candidates is to separate the nominating process from the overall board process, and certainly away from the management hierarchy. Outside directors, ideally those who can balance the exterior world and interior company perceptions and who can exercise disinterested oversight in the selection and nominating process, are assigned the task of dealing with this key board function, subject to review by the entire board.

One firm that I know had an interesting problem with this succession-selection problem. The situation was complicated by the proprietary interests of one of the directors who had been on the board since the company was founded.

Over a period of time, the management directors took turns in the office of the president, acting in the chief executive role. At all times, there was a plural aspect to the leadership of the company since the founding director remained active in the management. The minority number of outside directors persuaded the management directors that some new and professional top management was needed, not only for succession purposes but to stabilize the leadership of the firm.

An executive recruiter was engaged to seek a new CEO who could lead the company out of its stalemated growth. The problem proved to be the criteria for the new CEO; each of the management directors, including the founder director, had his own bias on the talents most needed. Some consulting help got over this hurdle by forming a CEO selection committee dominated by outside directors, and the problem was resolved to almost everyone's satisfaction. This board, in a somewhat curious and circuitous way, performed its key function despite the boardroom interiority complex.

A second key function of a board in considering decisions and actions that have a potential for major economic impact can also suffer from an interiority complex. I remember from my predirector days in Monsanto an example of provincialism due to interiority on my own part in dealing with the company board. This was back in the mid-1940s when the plastics industry first boomed worldwide. Polystyrene was one of the fastest-growing polymer families supplying the injection molding, plastic film, sheet, and foam business. As general manager of Monsanto's Plastics Division, I was responsible for initiating capital project requests. At that time, one of the outside directors, Charles S. Cheston, a distinguished investment banker with Smith Barney & Company in Philadelphia, was a prime mover on the board because of his perspective of the world about Monsanto. Charlie, as close as one could be to a chum of Edgar Monsanto Queeny, the son of Monsanto's founder and then chairman of the board, shared some of his inner thinking with Edgar, who was also financially astute. There appeared to be few communications barriers between these two business leaders, who generally thought alike. They developed an unusual symbiotic relationship, which lasted until Cheston's death. Their closeness was quite apparent to all of us internal board watchers, who held these great leaders in such reverence and awe with respect to their corporate roles and as dominant director figures.

Given the extent of their primal leadership and the veneration that young, striving managers have for the euhemerism exemplified by these two directors, it was an eventful day when the board decided to hold one of its regular meetings at the Indian Orchard plant at Springfield, Massachusetts. This was then the headquarters of the Plastics Division and the main plant site for Monsanto's plastic raw material manufacture. The purpose of the meeting was not only to conduct its regular business but to expose the outside directors to the key staff of Monsanto's plastics business activity. Edgar Queeny asked me to sit in on the board meeting as an observer. I was also to present and argue for a major capital project to install Monsanto's first commercial polymerization kettle for polystyrene manufacture.

The day came. The written appropriation request had gone forward through the long management hierarchical route and was forwarded to the board on schedule. Our divisional staff, mostly all chemists and engineers, had carefully written the request to answer any question the board might conceivably pose . . . or so we thought. The request was for almost a half-million dollars, at that time a lot of money for this initial scale-up of a relatively simple exothermic process.

The presentation of the project began easily enough with a relaxed atmosphere. As the general manager, I highlighted the virtues of the project, our unique technology, the market acceptance, our plans to control the hazardous aspects of the reaction, and so on. The production cost estimates were down to the third decimal place, the price forecasts were confidently presented, and the return on investment was adequate for this first unit. My exposition focused on our internal capabilities and confidence as to the worth of the project and the ability to pay back the investment in a very few years. My assurance was that we had the skilled operators and the plant management talent necessary to make this big kettle process at the projected rate and that we could sell the output. (In retrospect, I am sure we told the board more than it wanted to know.)

Pleased with my own eloquence and the internal control we had over the project, I finished with a somewhat impassioned request for approval. Charlie Cheston looked at Edgar Queeny, who then asked me: "When could we install four more units in Springfield and place self-contained plants in Mexico, England, Australia, Argentina and Canada?" My interiority complex was slightly jarred as I struggled to give a credible answer to the longer-range, global question, which our division had not thought through. The day was won for the Indian Orchard plant project. And after that we scrambled to open up our inner world to the greater potential, from which we had separated ourselves. Our inner-newsreel approach to a project in our provincial management domain was an inhibiting interiority complex.

A third key function of the board is the establishment of policies and procedures to ensure compliance with laws and regulations. The directors and top management cannot guarantee the lawful conduct of every employee or manager in an enterprise. Legal and regulatory requirements currently imposed on corporations are so numerous, so wide-ranging, so changeable, complex, and unclear in many instances that it is not practical for the directors to see and be assured of compliance in a large, diversified firm. But the responsible and relentless effort to monitor compliance is clearly called for.

Some recent lapses in corporate behavior have emphasized the need for better policies and closer monitoring on corporate law compliance. *Dun's*

Review in 1977, reported on an audit at Pacific Power and Light in 1976 that had some unexpectedly far-reaching consequences when the audit committee discovered that President John Y. Lansing had been making personal use of the company plane in violation of corporate policy.[8] The committee concluded (and it was reported in the 1977 proxy statement) that Lansing "should resign as president and director." Although the board softened the blow by recommending that Lansing be retained as a consultant, the conscientious and obviously influential audit committee summarily ended his presidency.

A March 1977 private compilation of active private shareholder suits against officers and directors arising out of disclosures of improper payments contained the following well-known corporations:

American Airlines (Western District of Kentucky, derivative suit).

AMF Inc. (New York Federal District Court, derivative suit).

Brad Rogan, Inc. (New York Federal District Court, class action suit).

Exxon Corporation (Southern District of New York, derivative suit).

General Telephone and Electronics Corporation (New York Federal District Court shareholder suit).

International Telephone and Telegraph Corporation (Federal District Court, derivative suit).

Occidental Petroleum (Los Angeles Federal District Court, class action suit).

Rorer-Anchem, Inc. (Philadelphia Federal District Court, class action suit).

Sterling Drug, Inc. (Southern District of New York, derivative suit).

Uniroyal, Inc. (Philadelphia Federal District Court, derivative suit).

The list has grown since this compilation along with diligence on the part of directors with respect to their degree of care in ensuring corporate legal compliance. The interiority complex of a board of directors unduly concerned with self-esteem and self-stroking, rather than aggressive monitoring of the duties exterior to the boardroom, has been greatly exposed as insularity from real-world problems attendant to effective corporate governance.

The courts reflect different views as to the exterior reach of a board of directors in fulfilling their duty of diligence. In general there is a tendency to minimize any distinctions among types of institutions from a legal standpoint. Any director must exercise the care that a prudent person would have exercised in a similar position under similar circumstances. The following statement reflects this point of view:

As to the measure of a director's duty in order to avoid liability for allegedly having failed to exercise "due care," some courts have said that he must have exercised that care which a prudent man would have exercised under similar circumstances, while others have said that he must have exercised that care which a prudent man would have exercised in the conduct of his own affairs. And some courts have maintained a distinction between the degree of care required of directors of financial institutions and that required of directors of other corporations, although most courts tend to minimize these differences.[9]

On the other hand, there are decisions—particularly those involving financial institutions and, more specifically, savings banks—that tend to indicate that the directors of a bank owe a higher degree of care than do directors of business corporations. In fact, the Massachusetts courts have suggested that the duty of a bank director approaches that of a trustee. The following excerpt illustrates the point that a director, in carrying out the stewardship function, must extend his or her oversight in the broadest possible sense, a task that is impossible if the board suffers from an interiority complex:

> But these and similar decisions are not applicable to the case of a savings bank under the laws of this Commonwealth. As we said in *Gilson v. Cambridge Savings Bank*, 180 Mass. 444, 446, we have an "elaborate statutory system for the government and regulation of savings banks, which is intended to protect the interests of depositors." As to these depositors, for the encouragement of thrift by the allowance of interest upon small savings, they approximate somewhat to the character of charitable institutions. They are designed to help the poorer members of the community to help themselves by giving them an opportunity to make their small savings productive, and thus to confer upon them a greater and more lasting benefit than in many cases can be derived from mere eleemosynary assistance. Accordingly definite and rigid provisions have been made by our statutes for the administration of savings banks.
>
> Not to go outside the time here in question, see St. 1894, c. 317, SS 13, *et.seq.* It is not without significance that in this statute, as in former and subsequent ones, the governing board of officers is given the name of trustees. Careful provisions are prescribed also for the investment of the deposits that may be received; and it is manifest upon the most cursory reading that the dominant purpose of the legislature has been to provide in this way for the safety of the money entrusted to savings banks and to hold the officers entrusted therewith to a strict accountability.
>
> As was said in *Lewis v. Lynn Institution for Savings*, 148 Mass. 235, 243, "the fundamental idea has never been departed from, that all the funds and investment of a savings bank are held exclusively for the benefit and security of the depositors. This idea was, and still is, the cornerstone of the whole system. . . . To others, to third persons,

the corporation can incur liabilities, in contract or in tort, for which the funds in its hands will be responsible. But to the depositors themselves, the undertaking of the corporation is that it will receive and combine the deposits, and manage and use them to the best practical advantage, according to the judgment of the trustees, and give to the depositors in just proportion among themselves the result of such management." In other words, the savings bank and its managing officers or trustees are held to the same duty as ordinary trustees of a direct trust. See *Newark Savings Institution* case, 1 Stew. 552.

For honest errors of judgment, while acting with ordinary skill and prudence, measured according to the demands of the duties or business which they have taken upon themselves, they are not to be held liable; but the cannot excuse themselves from the consequences of their misconduct or of their ignorance or negligence by averring that they have failed merely to exercise ordinary skill, care and vigilance. And so are the decisions as to the trustees or managing officers of savings banks in New York and New Jersey, in which such banks are not commercial institutions having a capital stock and conducted in whole or in part for the gain of their stockholders, but occupy the same position and are intended to serve the same beneficent purposes as is the case in this Commonwealth. It is held that the relation between the managing officers and the depositors, or the bank as representing them, is that of trustees and *cestuis que trust*."[10]

The fourth function of the board concerns consideration of major social impacts of the company's plans and activities. Although the board's responsibility is to direct the enterprise in the interests of the owners, subject to constraints imposed by law, the interest of shareowners cannot be conceived solely in terms of short-range profit maximization. A balance of short- and long-range profitability better represents owners' interests since the political and social viability of an enterprise over a long period of time, while adjusting to the global environment in which the company operates, is the objective. Shareowners and directors have a common interest in ensuring that institutions with which they are identified behave ethically and as good citizens. The impact of the corporation with society and the interests of groups other than those immediately identified with the corporation are obligations assumed by the board.

The Business Roundtable recently tackled this matter of obligations. It suggests that these obligations can be summed up in this way: to operate profitably; to provide opportunity for private investors to receive a fair return on their investment; to avoid making the corporation a vehicle to solve issues (such as military policy) that should be handled through the political and legislative processes (the private business organization is not an instrument to accomplish ill-defined social objectives, but rather performs specific economic functions); to recognize, but avoid, pursuit of activist-inspired social causes on behalf of minority views rather than prevailing consensus; and to review major environmental impacts, equal employment opportunity, and important relationships with communities or governmental authorities. Therefore boards must address issues such as foreign trade or investment activities affecting U.S. international relations or other such matters of comparable magnitude that are germane to a business operation and therefore are proper for board consideration.

Little more need be said to support the view that a board, obsessed with its own internal state of affairs, cannot fulfill these five functional obligations. Our inner-newsreel propensity cannot be shrugged off as an exaggeration for many boards of directors. The common boardroom agenda includes a constant review of the good aspects of performance and future plans. It is difficult to get equal "newsreel" footage on the bad news and the many external forces at work against the corporation. Such a "merry-go-sorry approach" is suggested in chapter 14. It proposes a cache of eleven issues to which a board with an interiority complex is likely to give minimum attention. These issues gnaw at the door of self-esteem and the inner world of the directorate. Oscar Wilde said it this way: "Egotism itself, which is so necessary to a proper sense of human dignity, is entirely the result of an indoor life!"[11]

Notes

1. Ernest Becker, *The Birth and Death of Meaning: An Interdisciplinary Perspective on the Problem of Man* (New York: Free Press, 1971), pp. 73-74.

2. Gustav Fechner, in *Nanna or the Soul-Life of Plants* (1848), quoted in ibid., p. 48.

3. For a discussion of the board as a structured enclave, see my *New Directions for Directors: Behind the Bylaws* (Lexington: Lexington Books, D.C. Heath, 1977), chap. 3.

4. Ernest Becker, *The Denial of Death* (New York: The Free Press, 1973), p. xi.

5. Business Roundtable, Committee on Corporate Organization Policy, "The Role and Composition of the Board of Directors of the Large Publicly Owned Corporation" Statement of the Business Roundtable, New York Jan. 1978.

6. Ernest Becker, *The Birth and Death of Meaning* (New York; The Free Press, 1962).

7. Harry Stack Sullivan, *Clinical Studies in Psychiatry* (New York: Norton, 1956) pg. 31.

8. "The Innovative Boards" *Dun's Review* 110, No. 4, (October 1977): 93.

9. *Neese* vs. *Brown* 218 Tennessee 686, 405 S.W. 2nd 577 (1964); [925 A.L.R. 3d 941, at 952.]

10. Greenfield Savings Bank v. Abercrombie, 211. Mass. 252, 97 N.E. 897 (1912).

11. Oscar Wilde, quoted in Rudolf Flesch, *The Book of Unusual Quotations* (New York: Harper & Brothers, 1957) pg. 74.

8

Bathtub in the Boardroom

The Sherman and Federal Trade Commission Acts are at least grandly vague. In constrast, the Clayton Act is vague–period; and the Robinson-Patman Act is vague–exclamation mark. Indeed, the Robinson-Patman Act . . . employs more words to say less than any statute in this field. —Jerrold G. Van Cise[1]

Trust-Distrust-Antitrust

Certain business attitudes toward the grandly vague antitrust laws or any other intervention of government in the private sector are largely emotional rather than intellectual or political. Government encroachment is perceived as something to be fought aggressively. But a realistic attitude would be more appropriate toward this inexorable closing in by government in our increasingly complex society. For better understanding, let us look at the historical development and relationships in the field of antitrust laws as they actually affect the boardroom and commercial trade.

The two basic statutes in the field of antitrust law declare our fundamental faith in different ways. This faith is that the nation's economy shall be free of unreasonable restraints of trade and unfair or deceptive acts in commerce. These statutes are the Sherman Act of 1890 and the Federal Trade Commission Act of 1914. They provide that the courts, with certain assistance from the Federal Trade Commission, shall determine case by case which restraints and acts are reasonable and fair and which are not. The Clayton and Robinson-Patman Acts of 1914 and 1936, respectively, provide in greater detail the legislative standards for determining the legality of the practices thus singled out and seek to ensure a free, competitive economy.

Following these basic statutes came a range of statutes and parts of statutes covering miscellaneous regulations as, for example, those administered by the Interstate Commerce Commission and the Department of Agriculture. Many of these antitrust provisions exempted from their rigors specific industries, classes, and transactions. The insurance industry, labor unions, the Webb-Pomerane export associations, the Miller-Tydings and the McGuire acts, and specific agreements approved by the ICC are all illustrative. Patent laws are another group of implied exemptions from the antitrust basic statute. In 1977 the U.S. attorney general, Griffin Bell, announced the Antitrust Division's interest in the many industries in which a small number of companies hold dominant positions ("shared monopolies"). A new period of prosecution seems underway in such concentrated industries.

In administering the antitrust laws from the common-law heritage of this legislation, the courts succeeded in formulating the "rule of reason" by the early 1900s. This segregated good restraints from bad restraints. The Supreme Court in 1911 declared with respect to the Sherman Act: "Unaided by the light of reason it is impossible to understand how the statute may in the future be enforced and the public policy which it establishes be made efficacious."[2]

The rule of reason as applied to the antitrust laws by the courts reflected increasingly what seemed reasonable to business. In Van Cise's words, this was the "golden age of faith in business."[3] Corporate management, to the slight degree that it bothered to consider the antitrust laws at all, found the rules of the competitive game to be confined to selection of customers, quotation of prices, methods of distribution, licensing of patents, agreements with competitors, foreign commerce, and overall size. There was little, if any, invasion into corporate organization or internal conduct.

Because the United States was in a period of dramatic industrial growth, the judicial administrators of the antitrust laws had great faith in business and in businessmen. Executives and directors were high on the public's prestige scale. The theme was that he governs best who governs industry least—the "rule of business."

This golden age was shattered by the Great Depression, and the public looked to the federal government for solutions to the general distress. Unemployment and lost savings caused the role of the businessman, and the director along with him, to plummet on the prestige and faith scales. A new competing faith in Washington was born in the late 1930s and was fueled by the war-emergency psychology, the cold war, and the Korean crisis. Government controls were proliferating, and the courts gradually shifted their deference to business and businessmen. As Van Cise observed, "In turn, however, increasing solicitude to the wishes of government became apparent."[4]

The rule of reason was limited in scope; for example, all price fixing was declared to be unlawful. Patent tying and boycotts, which might have been justifiable in previous years, were condemned as objectionable. The rule of reason became more the reasoning of government. The new faith in government tended to drive from judicial minds their faith in business. Private initiative was pronounced an unlawful method of excluding competitors by "progressively to embrace each new opportunity as it opened, and to face every newcomer with new capacity already geared into a great organization, having the advantage of experience, trade connections and the elite of personnel."[5]

As a result of this dramatic shift in public and judicial attitude from one of trust to one of distrust in business, corporate managements and directors have had to pay much more attention to the implications of the complex, at times vague, provisions and interpretations of various antitrust and related laws.

One of the most pertinent changes in principles of competition regards the concept of overall corporate size. Today's corporation is discouraged from expanding its activities because size is now castigated as an earmark of monopoly power.

The Bathtub Theory

At all times a sincere and zealous minority of the Supreme Court appears to approach business problems with the objective of ensuring that power alone resides with the government. Nowhere has this firmly held objective been more candidly outlined than with the following extract from a recent famous dissenting opinion: "Industrial power should be decentralized. It should be scattered into many hands so that the fortunes of the people will not be dependent on the whim or caprice, the political prejudices, the emotional stability of a few self-appointed men. The fact they are not vicious men but respectable and social minded is irrelevant. That is the philosophy and the command of the Sherman Act. It is founded on a theory of hostility to the concentration in private hands of power so great that only a government of the people should have it." (United States v. Columbia Steel Co., 334 U.S. 495, 536 (1948))[6]

The internal structure of business continues to be enveloped by these interpretations of antitrust philosophy, and this is where the board of directors need take careful note. A theory has evolved to characterize the alleged conspiracy of the internal members of a corporate body to restrain trade: "The component members of each corporate body regularly sit in the corporate bathtub—shut off from customers and competitors—and continuously conspire with each other to restrain trade."[7]

Intrigued by this bathtub theory, I pursued the subject with its creator Jerrold Van Cise. We had several spirited discussions of the subject, which culminated in this letter from Van Cise:

In response to your letter . . . I hasten to report that during certain pre-trial proceedings in a private treble damage action, a corporate executive testified that—when taking a bath—he as president of a parent corporation had agreed with himself as president of a subsidiary as to a certain course of action. Thereafter, in PLI monographs dated 1949 and 1952, I characterized the subsequent Government's theory of intra-corporate conspiracy as a comparable "bathtub" fiction.

Thus, e.g., "Our duly authorized national economic council—namely, the courts and Federal Trade Commission—in critically re-evaluating antitrust law has come to realize that the old cases in this field by and large have ignored the internal structure of business organizations. Now this defect is being enthusiastically remedied. The theory has been evolved that the component members of each corporate body regularly sit in the corporate bathtub—shut off from customers and competitors—and continuously conspire with each other to restrain trade." (*A Practical Guide to the Antitrust Laws* (PLI 1952) p. 41)

Upon reflection, I don't mind if you reveal that I was the perpetrator of this "antitrust prank." Do as you please. . . .[8]

The 1979 version of this antitrust prank might be better called the board-room-bathtub rather than the corporate-bathtub theory. It is divided into three parts: the conspiracy concept ("bathtub"), individual monopolizing ("earmark" of power) and integration ("leverage"). Directors are thus exposed to potential liability for the conduct of a large corporation viewed as a whole (where exercised with the power of "size"), for the agreement of corporate persons (parent and subsidiaries), and for the use of the strength of one part of its integrated structure to give an unfair advantage to another. Van Cise opines, "Perhaps you must say that the 'bathtub' has been enlarged to hold an over-sized ear," the several incorporated "conspirators", and the integrated corporated "spine" to which the others are joined 'til antitrust divestiture doth them part."

Because of the way in which our laws are developing, the board of the corporation must be highly conscious of its strength and assume a more socially responsive stance. The interpretation of this requirement is evidenced by the obligations now imposed by the courts on public-utility industries. Further, the trend overseas has been to deal with the rule-of-government philosophy by nationalizing private industry, by regulating environmental and corporate conduct, and by techniques of social democracy such as requiring the election of employee and public board members.

The clamor for "sunshine in the boardroom" (more disclosure), "police-man in the boardroom" (a public director), and "fishbowl conduct of business" (no competitive secrets and generally open information on almost all activity), are all responses to the old Adam Smith allegation: "People of the same trade seldom meet together, even for merriment and diversion, but the conversation ends in a conspiracy against the public, or in some contrivance to raise prices."[9]

Directors must recognize this relentless swing of the pendulum of judicial and public opinion in the direction of intrusion into the business sector. The challenge for the boardroom is to develop a concept and strategy for aggres-sively and intelligently coping with these external forces. Emotional or purely defensive response is, I fear, a no-win reaction. The compass of the board now embraces its many environmental and societal constituencies.

Guidelines for Directors: A Caesar Thesis

The mental acceptance but emotional rejection of an independent, active role for the board of directors in regard to social responsibility and competitive strategy is a major problem for some chief executives and for many directors. In the recent past, a role of this sort has been the primary response to the antibusiness trends. But some boards of directors are coming alive to the anti-trust and other legal and social yardsticks osmotically penetrating the compass of the boardroom.

One of the most useful responses to the increasing web of laws affecting corporations has been publication of *The Corporate Director's Guidebook* prepared in 1976 by the Subcommittee on Functions and Responsibilities of Directors of the Committee on Corporate Laws of the American Bar Association.[10] Although it does not constitute an official expression by either committee, it was offered, based in part on legal principles, as a contribution to important ongoing and wide-ranging discussions of the role and responsibilities of corporate boards and directors. The Model Business Corporation Act was used as a primary statutory frame of reference.

Some of the concepts, principles, standards, and hypotheses set forth in the *Guidebook* create a modern construct for a progressive board of directors that can serve as a practical derivative of the vague paradigm of pertinent judicial trends and mounting public sentiment. A somewhat misty penumbra overlaps the aura of antitrust legislation and other statutory clusters of principles for corporations. The following sections are selected threads of some consensus. They weave a spiderweb of rules of government in the boardroom and about the entire compass of corporate governance. The norms of conduct recommended primarily for social policy (rather than for legal reasons) lack, in many instances, the underpinnings in precedent or statute; however, they are useful for directors.

The broad areas of concern to directors in the context of seeking an appropriate compass for the board take us in five different directions: standards of conduct, orientation of the new corporate director, responsibilities of the individual corporate director, duties under the federal securities laws, and liabilities and indemnification.

Standards of Conduct

We draw the sword with a clear conscience and with clean hands.
                                        —Emperor William II, speech, August 4, 1914

Duty of loyalty and duty of care, including a duty to be attentive to the corporation's business, are the prime underpinnings of standards of conduct befitting proper directors. Clear conscience and clean hands are, of course, assumed. The basic principle is that directors should not use their corporate position to make a personal profit or to gain other personal advantage. The duty of loyalty is manifest in four concepts regarding conflict of interest, duty of fairness, corporate opportunity, and confidentiality.

The judgment to be used in each of these concepts is that of disinterested peers. On a corporate board, this usually implies nonmanagement, unaffiliated directors. Hence, the current emphasis by the SEC and the business community on an adequate number of nonmanagement, disinterested, unaffiliated directors on every board, if these standards are to be accepted by the corporation's directorate.

Director misbehavior at shareowners' expense for questionable perquisites may be coming under better control after a spate of disclosures during the last two years. Public outrage at the misuse of corporate funds by board members seems surprisingly less vocal than the laughter over these "peccadillos" as revealed on the British scene. A racy series of indiscretions was woven into a hilarious Anthony Marriott hit, *Shut Your Eyes and Think of England*, which played in London in 1977 and 1978. The farce captured a topical theme of an Arab's takeover of the city of London. This was to be accomplished through the purchase of the largest investment house, the Holbrook International Investment Ltd., chaired by the well-known financier, Sir Justin Holbrook. A slapstick run of fiscal chicanery and sex-on-contract compromising the chief accountant was the feature of the main theme. Among other things revealed about board life, the board of directors of the firm and their client investment managers were furnished ladies of pleasure under a contract service. This was depicted as typical of nonmonetary fringe benefits and inducements and the way of life in the City for its boardroom inhabitants. When directors' conduct fails to provide such material for playwrights and packed audiences, I guess our problems of boardroom behavior will be truly lost in a Sargasso Sea of governmental and judicial constraints. We have a long way to go yet, but the trend is clearly toward a clean-up of standards of conduct in most boardrooms.

Duty of Care

Care keeps his watch in every old man's eye.
And where care lodges, sleep will never be.

—Shakespeare

The concepts and words of art, which include *loyalty, good faith, reasonable belief, best interests of the corporation, ordinarily prudent person,* and *in a like position,* are all various expressions of the *duty of care.* The judgment on these expressions is probably best monitored in the boardroom on other than strictly legal terms and by disinterested nonmanagement directors. Also, these directors must be the careful outside kind, who, Shakespeare says, do not sleep at board meetings.

The duty of attention—a form of care—is manifest by such performance as in meeting attendance, required receipt of adequate information, and critical review of documentation. In addition and of significance is the concept of reliance on information, opinions, reports, and statements (financial and otherwise) presented by officers, board committees, employees, counsel, public accountants, or other persons whom the director reasonably believes to be reliable and competent in the matters presented.

The director's exercise of informed judgment calls for critical analysis, relevant inquiry, and discussion of management's proposals. The peer review process in the boardroom is often most credibly served in these regards through a rigorous review by the nonmanagement (outside) directors.

The business judgment rule in decision making is also part of careful duty. Risk evaluation and assumption, acknowledgment of uncertainties, and range of downside and upside range of riskiness depend on the good-faith judgment of the director. Although courts have been less reluctant recently to find directors acting negligently in reviewing business decisions made by a corporation, the concept of the board's acting in the exercise of *free and independent judgment* is reinforced, in appearance if not in fact, if the majority of the voting directors are nonmanagement directors. Management directors, no matter how wise and informed, are subject to the charge of judging their own acts. The name of Pompeia having been mixed up with an accusation against P. Clodius, Caesar divorced her—not because he believed her guilty but because the wife of Caesar must not even be suspected of crime.

Director Orientation

In ancient times, churches were built with their axes pointing to the rising sun on the saint's day. The placing of the east window of a church due east was done so that the rising sun could shine on the altar. This orientation would please corporate activists calling for sunshine in the boardroom. Figuratively, such orientation means the correct placing of one's ideas and mental processes in relation with each other and with current thought. Directors need to get their bearings by sharing concepts, dreams, and hopes with each other and in some relevant perspective to the outside world. Some of this can be done under management's guidance; some of it needs to be done with independent directors alone.

Too often outside directors are elected and left to orient themselves through subsequent exposure to board meetings and by reading materials regularly supplied to the board in the course of its work. Part of the neglect of a more formal orientation of directors stems from the fact that management directors are usually adequately informed on company affairs and nonmanagement directors are often presumed to be similarly informed. In addition, the pressures on directors to be sensitive to their changing legal obligations and the liability exposures have, in the past, been something the directors assumed would be taken care of and adequately monitored by the corporation's legal counsel, its auditing firm, the public relations officer, and the security staff.

Confidence in the top management and in the competence and integrity of fellow directors is a natural frame of mind for a director to assume if this directorship is his first encounter with the boardroom. When a management director becomes involved in a directorship in another firm, tyro directors may become quite nervous about their outsider role and the exposure. Assumed protection by his own corporation for service on his own board tends to seem like a different brand of trusteeship. This comfort can be characterized emotionally as a flight to the familiar. It might be an interesting practice to insist that executives serve on another corporate board before being eligible for membership on their own company's board.

The prohibition of interlocking directorships and the knowledge of certain determining corporate documents and structure are obvious areas in which a new director must be schooled. The articles of incorporation, bylaws, board and committee minutes, disclosure documents, annual reports, proxy statements, prospectuses, resumés of fellow directors, long-range plans, security analyst reports, and other reports filed with the Securities and Exchange Commission or sent to stockholders are all basic disclosure documents that directors must study carefully during their orientation. The sunshine-in-the boardroom concept should illuminate every official document of significance to corporate governance.

Responsibilities of the Individual Corporate Director

Winston Churchill called responsibility "the price of greatness." In the case of publicly owned corporations, this greatness concerns the fundamental responsibility to represent the interests of all of the shareholders as a group of owners of the enterprise and in effectively directing the business and affairs of the corporation. A formal mental step is required of a management director in judging a proposition before the board. He must transcend his advocate, tie-in, or participative role in presenting or considering the management's proposal to the board. He must look at the decision to be made not as an advocate but as a judge of the best interests of all shareowners, large and small. This multiplicity of roles may be too much to ask of a person on critical strategic decisions. A nonmanagement, unaffiliated director, of course, does not have this conflict.

The law does not hold a corporation or its directors directly responsible to anyone other than shareholders. However, the community, customers, employees, suppliers, and any other constituency, such as minority or activist groups, all exert pressures on the boardroom. The invasive rule of government in response to this pressure is manifest by specific constraints imposed by various public laws concerning the environment, occupational safety and health, consumer products, labor unions, securities, and antitrust matters. Trends in law, social norms, and value systems are formidable forces at work on the individual responsibilities of directors.

The duty to manage as expressed in the Model Business Corporation Act sets forth certain relationships of the board and executives of the corporation, which are helpful in examining individual responsibility. (Delegation and retention of powers of the board as a body are further set forth in conventional corporate form in chapter 3 for reference.)

The personal attributes of character, intellect, wisdom, and mature judgment are other obvious requirements for the responsible director. These attributes manifest themselves in the exercise of the duty to object when a director has reservations about a board matter. The areas of special concern to a qualified director embrace those matters of information flow, informed judgment, outside information, orientation opportunities, board organization, meeting schedules and agenda, executive development, management authority, benefit programs, and asset protection. (These critical areas of concern are discussed in detail in the *Corporate Director's Guidebook*.)

Along with specific personal responsibilities, corporate directors have significant rights, such as access to management, inspection privileges of corporate records, ample notice of meetings and adequate minutes of such meetings, and the option to seek outside advice as necessary. These rights should be clearly understood.

All of these responsibilities of directors are primarily geared to the outside or independent-director rather than to the inside management director. By virtue of this conflicting management position, the inside director is usually intimately involved in many of these matters. Too often it does not normally occur to him that these can be separate responsibilities as a director and are not related to his responsibilities as an executive.

Duties under the Federal Securities Laws

The public be damned! I'm working for my stockholders.
                                                          —William H. Vanderbilt, 1883

Vanderbilt was speaking to a newspaper reporter who asked him if the proposed withdrawal of an unprofitable express train was against the public interest. His remark was made in the so-called golden age of business when broader social responsibilities were yet to be awakened by the intervention of government to enforce the plethora of restrictive legislation that followed after the turn of the century. Later, the disclosure requirements of the Securities and Exchange Commission under the act of 1934, insider trading prohibitions, registration requirements under the 1933 act, short-swing profit provisions, and compliance programs all became areas of concern to directors. The basic antitrust and securities act statutes and the *Corporate Director's Guidebook* should be reviewed by directors unaware of their compass in these fields. The sensitivity of management directors' positions in these matters needs no further emphasis. There is an obvious set of duties concerning securities aspects of business that both the management and nonmanagement directors must be very clear about. This concern cannot be delegated.

Liabilities and Indemnification

A punster once defined liability as the ability to tell falsehoods and indemnity as an ill-gotten gain. But in serious boardroom business, these two topics have become very important aspects of being a proper director in this litigious age of business. There is a prevalent view among directors that the potential for personal liability is great. The potential is true in some respects, but standards of conduct formulated recently should show directors how to reduce such liability greatly. I recall, on the other hand, two outside directors who were being sued for several million dollars by disgruntled shareholders for dereliction of duty in allowing a company to go bankrupt. Allegedly they should have perceived this failing trend and done something to arrest the collapse.

The *Corporate Director's Guidebook* is a key handbook in helping directors to minimize liability for activities in connection with their positions. Omitting fraud, the director who acts in good faith and meets the duty of attention can be adequately indemnified by his corporation. A Caesar thesis and advice of counsel is recommended for any time when there is uncertainty about proposed actions and also as a regular checkup on indemnification for safety sake and peace of mind.

Proposed Model Board of Directors

Taking these five broad areas of concern to the director, the *Corporate Director's Guidebook* formulates a proposed model for a board of directors of a publicly owned corporation. Some of the key notions of concern in establishing the compass for a board and for the individual director follow.[11]

Distinction between Management and Nonmanagement Directors

Distinction—the consequences, never the object, of a great mind.
                                                      —Washington Allston, 18xx.

A director is considered a management director if "he devotes substantially full time and attention to the affairs of the corporation, one of its subsidiaries or any other operation controlled by the corporation." Former officers or employees of the corporation are regarded as management directors (or inside directors). All other directors are nonmanagement directors. There is a further distinction of affiliated nonmanagement directors and unaffiliated nonmanagement directors. The first refers to directors engaged in (or proposing to do so in the future) material transactions with the corporation or with close familial ties to a member of key management. Affiliated directors can thus be commercial bankers, investment bankers, attorneys or suppliers of services or goods. The concept here is one of independence from or interaction with the corporation. The inherent involvement of an executive or manager acting as a hired hand to deal with affairs of the corporation puts him in a clearly nonindependent category by this distinction.[12]

Size and Composition of the Board

The model board suggests sufficient nonmanagement directors to staff a minimum of three working board committees (audit, compensation, and nominating). One or more key members of senior management are also indicated, along with a requirement that the board functions effectively in discussions and decision making. Nonmanagement directors normally should be in the majority to ensure both the appearance and reality of independent, objective selection of key management and approval of transactions in which directors have a pecuniary interest (examples are supply contracts, employee contracts, and patent registrations). The integrity of financial reports and control apparatus, the review of ethical conduct, the nomination of director candidates, and appointments to committees are free of suspicion if the majority of directors are nonmanagement. Advocates or beneficiaries of board action should not have a determining voice in such decisions if the directors, like Caesar's wife, are to be above suspicion.

This Caesar thesis that nonmanagement directors should constitute a majority of the board of directors and should have a primary role in management succession and board nominees is a relatively new theory with few legal landmarks.[13] However, it is growing in favor in the society of directors, if not so fast in top management circles. The stage of development, complexity of the business, size of the corporation, nature of the endeavor, tradition, ownership characteristics, maturity of the business, and other factors affect the balance of the equation of inside versus outside directors.

The reliance on outside directors to promote corporate morality has led to some policies, effective June 30, 1978, for the New York Stock Exchange. This requires those listed companies to have one or more outside directors on their audit committees, another reinforcement to the Caesar thesis.

The opponents to this trend toward the primary role of independent directors stress the variety of board situations where unusually strong executive talents, collegial style of management, and plural leadership are often very effective and determining factors in successful corporate governance. To toy with these delicate balances, they fear, will be counterproductive. Instead they believe that more flexibility in the board model is the better answer, although the opposition arguments seem not so convincing from a political or emotional standpoint as the strident call for complete independence and suspicion-free posture of the board.

Role of the Board

A pro-active role of the board in establishing basic corporate objectives in the selection of key management and in monitoring of executive and corporate performance is also a controversial proposal. Many well-managed corporations have boards that cannot be truly called pro-active. They react rather than initiate and confine their role to review and oversight of the quality of management and its handling of corporate affairs in the shareowners' interest. The nature, maturity, complexity, performance, and size of the business can dictate the balance of a board's initiative and evaluative activity.

The staffing of the board's nominating committee is also a controversial subject. Past practice and policy of many boards is to rely on the chief executive or chairman to suggest candidates on the theory that a board and the CEO must have a good working relationship. This matter has more than legal implications; perhaps more importantly, it has political ramifications. Perceptions by the public and the government of any self-perpetuating process of directorships is likely to be attacked by shareowners and corporate activists on appearance alone, if not on the basis of poor or incestuous practice.

Antitrust Pointers

The role of corporate counsel is a vital one in steering a director through the broad compass of corporate governance. Critics of the *Guidebook* imply that the role of counsel should be more strongly emphasized, despite what Arthur Garfield Hays once said: "When there's a rift in the lute, the business of the lawyer is to widen the rift and father the loot!" Lawyers often have to bear such remarks from nonlawyer directors . . . until the director gets in trouble. Then the lawyer's words are usually heeded. The following three sets of check points may be helpful to individuals concerning their legal responsibilities. First are some possible violations that should be avoided:

> Conspiracy of the corporation and/or its subsidiaries to injure others—for example, refusal to deal [*Kefer Stewart Co.* v. *Joseph E. Seagram & Sons, Inc.*, 340 U.S. 211 (1951)].

Contracting between the corporation and an independent person to restrain competition—for example, tying of a franchise to an exclusive dealing arrangement [*Perma Life Mufflers, Inc.* v. *International Parts Corp.*, 392 U.S. 134 (1968)].

Conscious parallelism, tacit collusion, or conspiracy between the corporation and a competitor to restrain competition—for example, price fixing as in the General Electric and Westinghouse electrical equipment cases. [*United States* v. *General Electric Co.*, 272 U.S. 476 (1926)]. Executives convicted of fixing prices received fines and jail sentences.

The corporation alone monopolizing or attempting to monopolize—for example, by excluding others from the market [*United States* v. *Grinnell Corp.*, 384 U.S. 563 (1966)].

Some particularly sensitive areas concerning the liability of directors are these:

Where directors participate in violations of the law.

When directors authorize violations of the law.

When directors who know of violations of the law do not take responsible action.

Finally, here are some suggested practices and procedures for directors:

Have legal counsel present at all board meetings.

Refer all questions to counsel for his or her opinion.

Repudiate any proposed action, and recision of any past action, so referred to and not approved by counsel.

Outside directors may need some guidance quite independently of what the management schedules for formal review. For example, when proxy or registration statements are brought before the board, who should look at these complex documents in the light of the interests of the outside directors? Robert M. Estes, counsel to a New York law firm, calls the outside directors a class having an identity crisis all its own. He has outlined their different interests and responsibilities.[14]

It is unfortunate that antitrust has somewhat lost its way over the years and wandered into a "stream of tendency"—the phrase is Justice Benjamin Cardozo's—about social values. Rededication of antitrust to competitive principles would be salutary to our free American economy.

This chapter is a good topic for a board agenda. The specter of the board-room bathtub is not an easy one to discuss when facing a public that has lost much of its faith and trust in business, businessmen, and directors of publicly held corporations. Unfortunately all directors are not the people of principle that we would have them be.

Will Rogers unwittingly captured the key question about a bathtub conspiracy in the boardroom: "If the father of our country, George Washington, was Tutankhamen tomorrow, and, after being aroused from his tomb, was told the American people today spend two million dollars yearly on bathing material, he would say, 'What got 'em so dirty?'"

Notes

1. Jerrold G. Van Cise, *A Practical Guide to the Antitrust Laws* (New York: Practicing Law Institute, 1952), chap. 6.

2. Standard Oil Company v. United States, 221 U.S. 1, 68 (1911).

3. Van Cise, *A Practical Guide* p.20. See also his *The Federal Antitrust Laws* (Washington, D.C.: American Enterprise Institute for Public Policy Research, 1967). Van Cise's books provide a masterful guide to antitrust law.

4. Van Cise, *Practical Guide*, p. 24

5. United States v. Aluminum Co., 148 F.2d 416, 431 (2d Cir. 1945).

6. Van Cise, *Practical Guide*, p. 41.

7. Ibid.

8. Van Cise to Mueller, January 12, 1978.

9. Adam Smith, *The Wealth of Nations* (1776), bk. 1, chap. 10, pt. 2.

10. *Business Lawyer* 32 (November 1976): 5-52. See the subsequent commentary in ibid. 32 (July 1977): 1841-1854.

11. The material in this section is taken from *The Corporate Director's Guidebook*. Those interested in the entire model should consult the *Business Lawyer*, 32 (November 1976).

12. Personal characteristics and time commitments of directors have been dealt with in my *New Directions for Directors: Behind the Bylaws* (Lexington: Lexington Books, D.C. Heath, 1977), chap. 6.

13. Noyes E. Leech and Robert H. Mundheim, "The Outside Director of the Publicly Held Corporation," *Business Law* 31 (1976): 1799.

14. Robert M. Estes, "The Case for Counsel to Outside Directors," *Harvard Business Review* (July-August 1976).

9

Profiling Conflict in the DMZ

The Turkish Trade-off

This subject really concerns managerial versus director jurisdiction. It involves the broad separation of powers for governance in a classical line and staff and hierarchical type of organization. It concerns the delegation of authority and responsibility, matters of accountability, and decision making that go with division of labor. Above all, it concerns the natural position of organizational entities within a modern corporate organization and the tension that develops at the interface between these separate organs of the institution. The conflicts that inevitably result in conducting the affairs of the corporation cause trade-offs, which must be made by the board and management at various levels in the decision-making hierarchy.

Trade-offs have been made since Adam, Eve, the apple, rib, and the serpent were actors and props in an early decision-making process. In Istanbul during the Ottoman Empire, a lesson in trade-offs occurred that dealt with one of the same issues facing society today. This issue is the struggle with the trade-offs of safety and health against the benefits and risks of chemicals, pollutants, and transport hazards: the silent spring conflict of the plant shutdown and unemployment versus zero base pollution. Mandatory seatbelts and airbags versus automobile fatalities require trade-offs to be made on the safety front. The Turkish solution is not recommended, but it makes an interesting story.

Mahomet II, the mad sultan, used to sit on his pavilion and practice archery—on his subjects. It was not long before people began to stay away. The annoyed sultan countered by having his bodyguards act as beaters to round up the people and drive them past the pavilion where he waited. However, after a while, even the Turks began to complain, if carefully, about the number of citizens who were maimed and killed. As a strategy, they persuaded the head of the church to approach the mad sultan fearlessly. Sheik-ul-Islam tried to reason with Mahomet II, but the sultan wanted his sport. A satisfactory compromise—a Turkish type of trade-off—was reached: the sultan would continue to have his game but he was restricted to killing no more than eight people a day. While this solution did not help the unlucky eight, the rest of the population were given considerable relief. A mitigating factor in this Turkish trade-off was the fact that "most of the eight were recruited from prisoners of war anyway."[1]

The Decision-making Zone

The concept of profiling conflict or potential conflict in the decision-making zones of corporate governance helps develop a better understanding of the areas of actual or potential stress and tension. It identifies where trade-offs must be made in the corporate decision process and by what level of management authority. Approached as a technique—a tool for top management to analyze these situations—profiling reveals the official power structure and helps to develop a realistic appreciation of the actual power structure and influences used in the decision-making process.

A profile of a board is a representation of the organization in an outline form. It is a distinctive representation of its nature and composition, and indicates the way it looks to outsiders. Psychologists call such a profile analysis a method for appraising individual uniqueness and traits of the organization. This would include a search for characteristic patterns in the trait profiles of individuals on the board. A trait is an enduring or persisting characteristic of a director by means of which he or she can be distinguished from another director. A board profile is a display of the individual director's unique characteristics, which, composited, determine the nature of the board. As always, management information flow (intelligence) is a major source of power. The decision-making process is inextricably involved and interdependent with the management information systems—who gets what information, what type of reporting is required, and the formal policy and procedures that prescribe the corporate activities.

The normal executive managerial functions of setting objectives, planning, organizing, operating, measuring, controlling, feedback and corrections are carried out in various formal and informal ways by different elements of an organization. Corporate staff group, line groups, board of directors, the chief executive office, counsellors on tax, legal, accounting, and other functions each have inputs to the total managerial system for governance of the institution. The problem of managerial jurisdiction and the changes that are required as growth, development, and problems are encountered indicates that any profiling of tension, conflicts, and trade-offs involved in the decision-making zone is a transitory and mobile phenomenon.

The opportunity presented for profiling at any time shows how the organization is functioning. In fact, much profiling is usually called for when troubles, such as significant differences of opinion and conflicts between jurisdictional heads, arise. Profiling can permit an unbiased analysis of the problem and provide insight into solving the problem. The least it accomplishes is setting aside the issues clearly so that intelligent tolerance can be attained for all parties until a final solution is achieved.

The concept of using a diagnostic tool of profiling the conflicts in the decision-making zone, including the boardroom, is dependent somewhat on an open-ended, organic style of management structure and policy. It relies on an organizational climate that will tolerate some deviance, some conflicts, and some tensions in the interest of finding a best solution for the long term. Success in the profiling exercise is dependent upon the sophistication, maturity, and experience of the directors, the executive group, and, particularly, the CEO and the heads of the functional and line departments. It involves examining the political process and confronts such issues as management hierarchical succession.

The normal drive of individuals to accumulate power in order to exercise influence with respect to their organizational position is often exposed in the analytical exercise. Profiling recognizes a competition for resources in the separate units within a corporate system. It also recognizes that there may be different value systems at work and that different standards of measurement of performance are necessary for professional groups, service groups, and operating groups. All such measures of performance are not necessarily bottom-line items; many are subjective. Hence, profiling of organizational conflict is a working tool and is not meant to be a solution that is final for all times and all situations. But there can be an enduring boardroom profile.

Organizations often have to reestablish equilibrium within the institutional milieu from time to time. This requirement depends on changes that are imposed on the organization from the outside plus stresses and strains from organizational conflicts and growth internally. Careful analysis can sometimes help to identify these force fields and the politics involved.

Definition of Political Elements

In order to conduct a useful conflict profile, it is necessary to agree upon certain definitions of key elements in the concept of the exercise. There are two primary elements normally present in a tension-conflict-trade-off construct. The first is the DMZ, the decision-making zone. It refers to any collection of corporate activities, internal and external, where conflict, stress, and tension are building up. This may occur in the marketplace, in the laboratory, between internal staff departments, in the boardroom, or in the financial community. These zones may be concerned with conflicts with any of the managerial functions, such as objectives setting, strategic planning, organizational development, measurement and control, operating activities, and advisory activities. A careful analysis of these conflict, stress, and tension areas usually reveals the significant issues as problem areas and indicates which are secondary ones. These are then ranked by some subjective priority—for example, by their impact on the corporation or whether they concern primarily certain different hierarchical levels. For example, are they issues to be managed or for the directors to decide? Where is the proper zone for decision making: the executive level or the operating level of management?

The second element is the accountability system. This involves a way of describing the relative degrees of authority and responsibility that by policy or by law are delegated or withheld in connection with a certain role in the organization. Relative degrees of delegation or withholding of authority and responsibility establish a system of accountability for each organization. Assignment of degrees of authority and responsibility is a constantly changing activity within a broad framework of corporate policy and procedure. It is changeable because conditions and incumbents change, as well as the experience and maturity of those holding different positions. Degrees also change with time and organizational evolution. Differentiating between degrees of authority and responsibility in five levels, as in the following accountability scale, is useful in profiling conflict in the boardroom, executive suite, or operating theater.

Degree of Authority and Responsibility	Description
1. Independent authority and responsibility	Incumbent takes action subject only to limitations of broad corporate policy.
2. Independent authority and responsibility after counsel	Incumbent takes action only after advising or obtaining counsel from the appropriate corporate officer. Such counsel may not be determining in the course of action; therefore, responsibility remains with the one taking action.
3. Shared authority and responsibility	Incumbent seeks approval of appropriate officer before taking action.
4. Prior consultation and no authority	The executive manager is advised or consulted prior to action taken by corporate manager or officer. The person has no authority for action but may be responsible and accountable for carrying out the action as it applies to his area of jurisdiction.
5. No responsibility and no authority	The executive or manager has no authority for action and resulting specific responsibility or accountability. The manager refers these matters to the appropriate officer or decision-making authority as required.

Sorting out the accountability in this way helps determine who has the initiative and who has the supportive role. This sorting leads to the role criteria element of the concept.

Role Criteria

A formally organized corporation (defined as one with positive descriptions, an organizational structure, and management processes) has a description of the role, scope, function, and duties of each executive or staff position. This reveals interfaces or overlaps that can cause conflict, stress, and tension in the decision-making process or zones. Interface between the directorate, the executive office, and operations are fertile areas for such conflict and tension.

At least six different modes of activity are normally considered in assigning a position description:

1. Initiative role. The incumbent is the primary power—the catalyst and developer.
2. Supporter or service role. The incumbent responds when asked.
3. Monitoring role. This is the control role. For example, a corporate comptroller monitors performance on behalf of the corporation but is not subservient to line-operating executives on this particular score. He monitors for the chief executive officer, who monitors for the board.
4. Evaluative role. In this role, an analysis is performed for the benefit of the incumbent in a position. This, of course, is a prime supervisory function.
5. Resource role. The incumbent is available for counsel, planning, help, or guidance to get perspective, but he does not function as such unless asked.
6. Operating role. This is the traditional "getting things done" function.

Most corporate governance positions have a mix of these different roles. It is useful to check them off when examining a position description in relation to any conflicts. A good organizational set-up will indicate who has to make initial moves by the position description and the accountability system imposed upon them.

Process of Diagnosis, Assessment, and Evaluation

When two or more organizational units are in the state of tension or conflict, the first step is to determine the position descriptions involved and the accountability delegated to each position. This process sorts out the sectors of activity where there is a conflict as to, say, managerial jurisdiction. These conflicts should be ranked in order of priority, impact on the corporation, and various hierarchical levels. An example concerns the nomination of prospective board of director candidates for a second-tier international subsidiary. This is a good situation to clarify who takes the initiative and who has the responsibility and authority needed to complete the action. Quality control is another example that involves the issue of central versus decentralized control. Investment in new enterprises versus expansion of existing business is another area to determine who has the initiative and who has the supportive role so that strategic growth and development can progress with minimum stress, tension, and conflict.

After identifying the sectors of tension and conflict, the next step involves examining the official (and unofficial) delegation of authority and responsibility by the five degrees of accountability for each one of the conflict issues. This must be done in relationship to the role criteria for the unit positions of the incumbents involved. These should be outlined by position descriptions, organizational departmental charters, or otherwise. If such are not explicit, there will be areas of uncertainty that should be identified in order to clarify the causes of conflict.

Step three takes the accountability degrees as determined for each conflicting party (assuming there are two at minimum) together with the role criteria as identified. These are plotted on a diagram to show where there are potential conflicts, areas of uncertainty, or tension. (See figure 9-1.) This plot will identify issue areas where there are differences of opinion concerning the role of the parties, managerial jurisdiction, and what degree of authority and responsibility is appropriate for resolving these issues, and it will usually elicit suggestions if the differences can be resolved.

Because of the realistic nature of things, certain issues can be resolved on a short-term basis, some on a long-term basis, and some, unfortunately, are never resolved. Identification of each issue on a time frame is therefore important. After this is done and a policy decision is made where it is possible to resolve the issues, some areas may still be left open. This is where creative tolerance can recognize the malintegrative accountability factor. One organizational approach to handling this tolerance is the concept of plural governance.

Response to the increasing pressures of the executive suite, and particularly the demands on the CEO, has caused companies to try to pluralize the executive office into a multiperson office. This is an organizational device toward a group solution to increasing accessibility by permitting decisions to be made by more than one person. The arrangement is a controversial device that diffuses accountability and can work only if the actors involved have great empathy and understanding for each other.

An office of the president is often a somewhat vague approach to the plural leadership box on the organization chart where more than one person participates in decision in a sort of collegial form. Accountability is with the group. Responsibility and authority are often shifted between the parties like a basketball rally. In order to become operative in a going organization, certain areas may require this creative tolerance and malintegrative accountability. A policy statement can be made that such matters are to be resolved by the group, a plural office, or a committee. One interesting organization I know not only has a plural chief executive office of three persons but a rotating tour of duty as CEO. That is, a CEO of the month concept.

This plural approach is often the way in which matters are resolved at the board level. The board (as a group of individuals) comes to a position by trading off the advantages and disadvantages of one option versus another and functioning as a plural entity. A decision is made in the interests of those most concerned. Such a decision is, of course, best made by persons who have no beneficial interest and have an external perspective. The outside director, or a corporate officer whose scope is corporation-wide rather than a single functional assignment, is in the best position to wrestle with an issue of conflict. Political considerations are important in this issue-resolution process. Depending in its importance, the decision can be handled either at the chief executive level or, if necessary, escalated to the board of directors' level and dealt with by outside directors who are disinterested, unaffiliated stewards of the shareowners' interests.

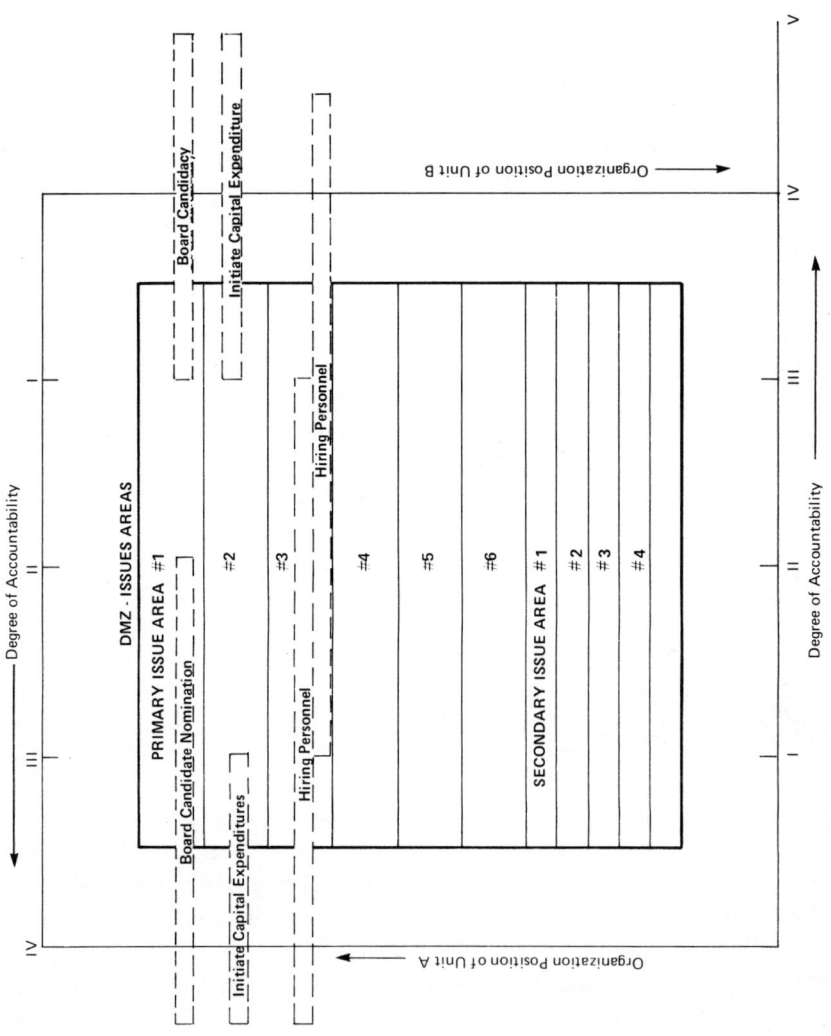

Figure 9-1. Profiling Conflict in the DMZ

When areas of potential or actual conflict reach a counterproductive stage, policy changes and sometimes belief, attitude, or guidance changes must be made. It is important to recognize points at which decision making must go to the next, that is, meta-level, for decision or corporate tolerance. Often certain issues cannot be easily resolved. Assumption of the risk involved in nonresolution at a lower level in the organization without the knowledge of the top management (or, in some cases, the board) can be hazardous mothering of a conflict situation. Mature management judgment is required as to when to reveal and when to tolerate these conflict situations, at what level in the organization for either making a decision one way or the other, or for receiving knowledge and permitting tolerance of the liabilities and risks that may be inherent in inaction or action. (The legal implications of these problems were discussed in chapter 8.)

Philosophy and style of management have a lot to do with how much conflict is allowed to exist and how much tension is permitted in an organization due to lack of firm policy guidelines on certain areas needing decisions. One school insists that conflict is strengthening; total harmony does not create the best and most vital organizational climate for achieving corporate success. This position is credible as long as the conflict and tension are not counterproductive and the incumbents in the system are able to tolerate and deal naturally with the conflict and the uncertainty involved.

Trade-offs

American adolescents regularly deal in "trade-lasts," compliments in exchange for another. They will tell you something flattering about yourself after you tell them a flattering remark you have heard about them. This practice has the elements of a trade-off used in a corporate sense. Every party gets something out of the deal, even though it is a kind of compromise rather than a zero sum game—you win, I lose. Often the result is like warming yourself at an artificial fireplace. The trick is to make the trade-off a reasonable and intelligent one. This is often the job of the board of directors, which can take a more Olympian view than can the executive management who are the advocates of a course of action by virtue of their role in corporate governance.

World disarray in social, political, economic, military, and environmental sectors indicates a period of continuing trade-offs for the immediate future. The business community, with a few outstanding exceptions, does not fully understand the concept of trade-offs except in a simplistic sense of giving up one thing to get another. Boardroom education is needed on examining these trade-offs of economic and social issues particularly.

A conflict-trade-off frame of reference is useful. In this regard, the term *trade-off* refers to an enhancement of the characteristics or values of any one factor at the expense of another. It may also refer to the selection of conditions for more than one factor that improves the whole result, even if it does not provide the optimum conditions for any one factor.

If the substantive result of a trade-off is negligible, the economic criteria may come into full play. Social, human, or environmental considerations fade into the background. Trade-off analysis is a well-known technique for indicating consequences of alternate decisions, the relationship among such corporate factors as development time, total resource requirement, and technical performance of a corporate system.

There are at least four sets of key equations that usually reflect these conflict-trade-off systems concepts. Most corporate governance issues can be placed in one of these equations.

1. *Security versus opportunity.* This has both an inside and outside dimension in terms of external and internal security within a system, a society, or institution and the opportunities both internal within those entities or external to them. For example, high security in a government position trades off in favor of less opportunity in such a structured system. Changes in an organization like many corporations have, with degrees of freedom allowed the executive managers and staff, are trade-offs in favor of security or tenure with the company.

2. *Equality versus reward.* This equation reflects a difference in risk potential versus reward potential. It introduces the egalitarian concept that all people are born equal and should be treated alike.

3. *Efficiency versus dependency.* This trade-off focuses on the concept of efficiency as distinct from effectiveness. The equation always operates in accord with the second law of thermodynamics to interact with other factors and the environment. Interdependency and interaction exist in any but a static system of governance.

4. *Resource versus consumption.* The limits-to-growth concept introduces the need for controlled consumption on the global level. The resource allocation process in a corporate boardroom deals with the trade-offs of authorizing one project versus another when resources are less than the project demand (or consumption) coming from the management to the boardroom for decision.

One final approach to resolutions is to take your pick from a semiserious list compiled by Leslie E. This. This collected the following kinds of reactions managers have identified as having been useful in dealing with protests and conflicts in corporate governance matters.

Kick the problem upstairs; it's their baby.

Go on leave—sick or annual, 'till it blows over.

Call the police; it's a community or social issue or problem.

It will pass. Wait it out.

Ignore it.

Take over and give leadership to this protest.

Lay down the law. Let them know who's boss.

Make an example of key persons the first time the method is tried.

Make concessions as you are forced to. Give way only when defeated.

Maybe the thing called organization development/organizational renewal is the answer.

Get young people, minority groups, pressure groups, etc., on your boards, committees, policy-making groups, etc.

Join the protest (conflict).

Find another less hectic job.

Pray a lot.[2]

There is an old German saying about reactions in these conflict resolution matters: "He who considers too much will perform little."

Rather than consider conflicts in the decision-making process further, it is helpful to end with a more philosophical note with some words from James Russell Lowell:

Once to every man and nation comes the moment to decide,
In the strife of Truth with Falsehood, for the good or evil side;
Some great cause, God's new bloom or blight,
Parts the goats upon the left hand, and the sheep upon the right;
And the choice goes by forever 'twixt that darkness and that light.

Notes

1. Paul Tabori, *The Art of Folly* (New York: Chilton, 1961), p. 47.
2. Leslie E. This, "Coping with Organizational Influence Methods," *Consultants' Communique* 3 No. 3, (July-September 1975): 3.

10 Concinnity, Groupthink, and Independence

A Galactic View

Any board trek into the future will encounter a forbidding universe of systems. Included are external force fields in rapidly changing environments. Stresses are produced by interface conflicts, by inconsistencies, by discontinuities, and by knowledge advances and knowledge gaps. In addition, there are systems interactions because of changes in value systems and beliefs. These unknown territories of corporate governance are not unlike the inhospitable, hostile, and complex physical universe in which we exist with the millions of solar systems similar to our own.

This galactic view of the future environment for the board of directors presents a constellation of problems and opportunities. The very nature of the board becomes altered as it assumes its discrete part of the corporate governance system. Such a role views the board of directors as an increasingly vital element in a complex system of corporate metadevelopment. The simple abstraction of life cycle—birth, growth, maturity, and death of a corporate governance system—is inadequate to deal with the complex system requirements in the future context in which corporations will find themselves. The nature and relations of being—the ontological drive—are precursors of levels of abstraction for the orderly development of the board. There is need for a higher metalevel of conceptual thinking about the absorbing phenomenon of board functioning in the future.

The continuum of creation, discovery, concept shaping, innovation, survival, defense and security, growth and change identity, value exchange, sociocultural, and environmental concerns are topped by the teleological doctrines of purpose and legitimacy of the board of directors as a subsystem in corporate governance. It is a very dynamic and complicated subject.[1]

Beyond these abstractions are the meta-aspects—over and beyond—of the future role of the board of directors. Some of the constellations of problems can be identified at the board interface with society. Certain external driving forces that may become imperatives include changing demographic factors, increasing emphasis on full social-cost accounting, technology and work ethic changes, shifting ideologies, and more concern for natural resources. The intervention by government to meet group needs, the use of government to achieve greater social control, and the social consequences of advancing technology, which make the world increasingly interactive and interdependent, are among the other forces at work. The growing scale for application of technology and the scarcity of resources are advancing the lead times required for a business enterprise. All of these problems require more attention to the system of governing corporations in order that they become more effective. This attention should be paid in the boardroom.

Most forecasters, futurologists, and board watchers center their attention on external factors that impact the corporation. These, of course, have to be dealt with by the board of directors. A relatively neglected area of thought at the board level concerns the internal workings of the board and the behavioral aspects of a board of directors that is attempting to function to the best of its ability. While the board of directors can be designed to facilitate institutional flexibility, the very design has become a serious constraint on institutional change.

Board of directors' practice, the organizational system employed within the board itself, and particularly its relationship with the organization that it serves often tend to support what some have called timidity, mediocrity, and encapsulated decision making. Everyone is familiar with the enormous difficulty experienced in persuading a board of directors (or any other organization, for that matter) that is established as a going concern to change its way of administering its own activities. Very few boards are structurally geared for accepting continuous innovation or are capable of facilitating changes in the corporate governance system. The challenge before the board of the future is whether it can respond to the imperatives for institutional change through organizational innovation or whether it must experience this through the ordeal of revolution forced upon it by the reform activists.

Imperatives for Change

Three of the formidable imperatives for change encountered by boards of directors are internal phenomena: the concinnity bias, the groupthink tendency, and dispassionate pursuit of independence.

The Concinnity Bias

Many boards tend to develop a clubbable, if ellusive, characteristic of organizations which place internal harmony and fitness before such attributes as objectivity and independent judgment. This is called concinnity. Thus boardroom decision making tends to beget graceful and regularized behavior, neither of which is necessarily an attribute of responsible stewardship. Harmony and often elegance—of either design or a board protocol or continuity of its activity—is the trade-off achieved. Harmony is sought rather than facing up to conflict, tension, and possible disruption through the significant differences of opinion aired in the boardroom.

The importance of thinking, speaking, and acting independently with confidence and courage cannot be overestimated in directorship. A freestanding posture where independence of decision is important is required. It must be free of real or apparent conflicts of interest. This requirement makes the role of an inside director very difficult because of the built-in conflict that he or she has in serving both as a member of management and as a board member charged with looking after the interests of all shareowners. Tendencies of boards to be self-perpetuating protectorates that are unresponsive to change are not abnormal phenomena in the board world.

An objective role is required of individual directors who should take a thoughtful position considering all of the trade-offs involved and their consequences. The willingness of a director to risk rapport and collateral with the chairman, with fellow board members, or with the chief executive is involved. Taking independent action is very difficult for a person who is placed in a hierarchical management structure as an executive, in addition to attempting to function as an independent board thinker. This conflict does not indicate that management directors are necessarily captive to the CEO or chairman, but it points to the fact that the peer system of governance in the boardroom mitigates against independent, objective views if the tendency is not properly managed. Conflicts with individuals' management and career interests within the corporate hierarchy are distinct from those with shareowner interests. Rather, there tends to be some lack of reality in expecting a judgment to be made without the concinnity bias either consciously or subconsciously entering into the equation. The board should carefully assess this illusive factor in relation to the appropriate balance of inside and outside directors to serve a corporation in the best way at all times.

Groupthink

The concept of groupthink in a board of directors introduces a risk bias and pinpoints a different source of potential trouble. This problem resides neither in the individual director nor in the organization setting. Beyond all of the familiar sources of human error is the powerful source of defective judgment that can arise in cohesive groups according to observers of organizational behavior. This problem refers to decision quality and the concurrence-seeking tendency that can foster overoptimism, an illusion of invulnerability, a lack of vigilance, stereotypical views, the practice of self-censorship, and sometimes sloganistic thinking about the weakness and immorality of so-called out-groups.[2] In the corporate context, out-groups can mean those persons not involved in the management: the outside directors. If the outside directors are prone to groupthink, the out-group can dominate the management directors.

Studies show that groupthink occurs most often in a company when the decision-making body is insulated from the advice of qualified experts or when a strong leader actively promotes a solution to a problem or takes a policy position. Of course, not all cohesive groups are prone to groupthink, but many tend in that direction when these attributes are present. One hazard of continual domination of a board by a majority of either outsiders or insiders is the risk of drifting into a groupthink mode and not recognizing it.

Virtually the same group of individuals of the U.S. government were involved in the decision processes that led to the Bay of Pigs invasion and to the blockade at the time of the Cuban missile crisis. The effects of groupthink in the first situation are well known: a disastrous course of action. The second action is often considered a model of rational crisis decision making.

Students of groupthink point out eight major symptoms of it. These can be identified for a board if it tends to develop these manifestations:

1. The illusion of invulnerability promotes excessive optimism and encourages decision making in very high-risk areas.

2. The board ignores negative feedback and warnings that might force a reassessment of a board decision. Instead it attempts to rationalize the status quo.

3. Board members display an inviolate belief in their morality and the integrity of the system. Often they may ignore the ethical and moral consequences of boardroom decisions entirely when this symptom is in high gear.

4. Stereotypical views of the competition are often developed by boards of directors or individual members facing an adversary business situation. The competition or adversaries are regarded as unreachable as far as genuine negotiations are needed to resolve conflicts or that they are uninformed or too weak to take any effective counteractions. In our Arthur D. Little consulting practice, probably the most frequent failure found in corporate planning activities is for the corporation to underestimate the position and potential of competition.

5. When a director expresses doubts about a course of action or questions arguments and supporting policies that are favored by the majority of the advocating management, the board tends to apply pressure to the fellow board member. This situation can result in lack of discussion of the potentially negative ramifications of a different course of action. The concurrence-seeking norm is reinforced. This pressure can be overt, covert, real, or psychological.

6. Self-censorship is often practiced by individual board members when the symptom of groupthink has taken hold. The director tends to avoid deviating from group consensus and remains silent about his own doubts and misgivings. A highly politically motivated director, whose ambitions may cause him not to rock the boat, is often a management director who strives to retain his relationships with his bosses and fails to be an independent director. This situation occurs not because of a lack of faith of an individual director's own ideas or judgment but through fear of losing the approval of fellow board members (both inside and outside directors) and of facing the consequences outside

the boardroom context that may come of this lack of approval. The assumption that silence means consent reinforces the practice of self-censorship.

7. Board members can develop a tendency to share an illusion that unanimity in their decision means truth. In the case of decisions on a particular course of action, the course is therefore wise.

8. Boards of directors can develop what are called mindguards; for example, self-appointed members of the board or staff to the management of the board try to shield the board members from information that may go against shared beliefs.

A board of directors that displays any of these symptoms tends to produce poor-quality decisions. Also these dynamics of groupthink may reinforce other dysfunctional individual behavior patterns. One study found that decision makers in some instances may increase their commitment to poor decisions even at the risk of further negative consequences in order to avoid cognitive dissonance.[3]

Understandably, management directors can become committed to group decisions by a sense of shared responsibility, trust, and mutual support. As a result, their own personal attitudes and models of reality may tend to reflect those of the group in an attempt to maintain some inner consistency. This is merely another way of expressing the conflict problem of the director who is both a member of management and of the board of directors. Another problem with this potential pathology of groupthink is the apparent credibility to the external world of a director's making an independent decision when he is also part of management. The fidelity in assessing trade-offs of the aspect of the insider-outsider balance for the board of directors deserves careful consideration when designing the membership mix that best serves the board role.

An interesting study of key decisions and crises that were made by a small, tightly knit group of individuals has shown that decision quality is inversely related to the rates of the four types of decision errors: rejecting a correct course of action, accepting a wrong solution to a problem, solving the wrong problem, and solving the right problem but too late.[4] The author of this study points out further that decision quality depends upon three factors: the quality of the information inputs into the decision process (in this context, the boardroom deliberations); the fidelity objective or articulation of trade-off evaluation (the completeness of proposals and discussion before the board with alternative options); and the cognitive ability of the decision group (the background, expertise, and understanding of the individual directors on the board). The major impacts of decision quality are identified by the phenomenon of groupthink, which introduces a risk bias, and the general cognitive abilities (or scope and perspective) of the board. This means the ability of board members to interpret information, to consider options creatively, to understand and evaluate calculated choices between alternative courses of action. Changes in such cognitive ability, particularly during a crisis, are attributed mainly to the groupthink phenomenon and to the stress existent (in this case) in the boardroom.[5]

One technique for preventing errors in judgment that result from board-room groupthink is to experiment with role playing and scenario building. Solutions to problems such as the propensity to take increased risks and illusions of their vulnerability may be exposed through these techniques. Techniques such as building scenarios of the worst possible outcome can aid a board in evaluating the seriousness of proposed programs or investments realistically and reduce the propensity toward high-risk alternatives.

Boards dominated by groupthink try to rationalize away early warnings and other disturbing data that may require a reevaluation of a policy or ensure further evaluation of alternatives. A technique of the devil's advocate is useful to cope with this problem. It is based on the premise that conflict is the best way of exposing hidden assumptions. Both good and bad aspects of a proposal are carefully examined. In some companies there is a danger, however, that devil's advocates may become tokens or become domesticated. The institu-tionalized devil's advocate can, paradoxically, lead to a false sense of security on the part of the advocate because of comforting feeling that he has considered all sides of the issue. The policy may be challenged by one or two members of the decision-making circle after the devil's advocate has spoken. One way to avoid tokenism in this regard is to rotate the responsibility for being the devil's advocate from among the different staff members or board members or to use outside expertise.

The board decision-making process can be only as effective as the analytical phase of decision making permits. Too often little attention or time is devoted to managing this analytical process. Boards are often made up of generalists rather than specialists. They must rely on the expertise of others and hope that the analytical intricacies hidden within any management-submitted pro-posal are thoroughly treated in an objective, realistic, and correct manner.

Critical strategic analysis of plans often flushes out these tendencies. There are well-established methodologies practiced by most of the prominent con-sulting firms. Arthur D. Little's version of this is especially effective because of its organic nature, the elimination of a stereotype of patterned methodology, and the integration of methodology with knowledge of industry and business dynamics. The strategy center concept can be broadly characterized as follows. The keystone of a contemporary business organization is a market-investment system based upon multiple strategies—a separate one for each identifiable strategic business segment or unit. Each is geared to the stage of develop-ment and rate of growth of that unit. In specific terms, the way in which this system of strategies is built is by classifying companies or sections of com-panies in terms of maturity and competitive position using the standard curve for the life cycle of a new product or service. Businesses may fall into either embryonic, growth, mature, or aging stages. The corporation's recognition of its variety and its flexibility in managing the variety is what makes the corporation contemporary.

Although some organizations may be moving or groping in the direction of diversity, they may not yet have integrated all of this into a coherent management whole. The concept of strategy centers, which are explicitly managed in the context of real-industry situations, can be a way to cope with some of the problems that groupthink poses in a complex organization.

But back to the institutionalized role of devil's advocate. Formalizing of this dissent role is as old as history itself. Within the Roman Catholic church, the devil's advocate, formally termed "promoter of the faith," has been a continuing functional office since the early 1500s. The prescribed function is to investigate proposals thoroughly for canonization and beatification. In the church context, the devil's advocate must bring to light any information that might cast doubt on the qualifications of a candidate for sainthood. The bestowing of sainthood is not taken lightly by the church since it represents extensions of doctrinal fabric and affects the lives of congregation members. The negative side of evaluation of a candidate for sainthood has to be thoroughly and rigorously investigated. The organizational separation of the functions of the promoter and dissenter thus ensures that both sides of the question are thoroughly analyzed and presented. It is unfortunate that the director-nominating process does not have at least some of the rigor involved in the sainthood candidate process.

In the church context, the roles of the promoter and dissenter are not subject to intrapersonal conflict by residing in the same person. In this respect, it differs often from the problem that a management director has in proposing and advocating a course of action or candidate nomination to fellow board members and then joining in the voting on a decision to be made in regard to the proposal.

In the Catholic church, the very existence of a formal adversary may pressure the promoter of a candidate for sainthood to be much more rigorous than if only the positive side of the nomination were presented. Unfortunately, political and other considerations often prevail.[6]

In our Anglo-Saxon legal system, the dissenting function is formalized. The jury and the judge examine the merits of the prosecution's case and the counterproposal by the defense's presentation of all available evidence to show the defendant's innocence. The process is carefully structured so that prosecution and defense attempt to show the fallacy and omissions in the other's presentation to the impartial jury. This system allows a complete airing of positive and negative sides of questions.

The role of the loyal opposition in the British parliamentary system is another evidence of the effectiveness of the devil's advocate phenomenon. This system balances the unilateral programs of the party in power by questioning almost routinely the government's proposals. In the United States, a similar dissenting role is built in for those opposed to a bill placed before the legislature with the practice of hearings and debate of the floor of the legislative house clearing the air in this regard. If an economic institution, such as a business corporation, had to carry out this political-judicial process to the same extent, very little progress would ensue.

Consumer advocate groups in the United States also present negative information to the consuming public in an attempt to balance what they consider one-sided advertising claims. The self-appointed dissenting role thereby provides more complete information to the decision makers who have neither the time nor the expertise to gather and analyze data for their ultimate consumers.

Learned societies and academic organizations incorporate a more formalized dissent procedure to insure rigorous treatment of the substance of research and theoretical papers. This practice calls for a discussant, often an aspiring assistant professor who is assigned to study a paper presented before a society. So far business corporations have been unable to match this technique very effectively and still get on with their primary tasks.

In the corporate world, internal auditors provide a check on investment decisions and other proposals by questioning the basic issues and integrity of the system. When outside CPA firms give a "comfort letter" to the board, the management, and the shareholders regarding compliance with regulation and conventional standards of accounting, they are performing a task not unlike the check and balance in the devil's advocate mode. Manufacturing and business firms that operate on the leading edge of technological applications quite often employ outside consulting firms to appraise internally developed products, or process developments from a devil's advocate viewpoint.

Applying the devil's advocate concept to the corporation is tricky. Volunteering criticism of a fellow manager's proposals can be taken as a personal attack, and, as a result, constructive criticism may be withheld. This occurs quite often, and very naturally, when management directors are fellow members on the board. They in effect may take turns applying for allocation for corporate resources to support the business unit for which they are responsible in their executive role. One large national service company I know fell into this practice of "your turn to get approval" to a point where the corporate growth was stalemated because of the political maneuvering.

To expect a director to contribute insights and criticisms is difficult under certain circumstances and corporate climates even though the opportunity to contribute such does, in fact, exist. Directors may choose to withhold involvement for personal or group-related reasons. One way to get around this problem is to institutionalize the dissent function and thus help to depersonalize the conflict generated by a critical analysis. This may be done inside the organization or outside by providing specialists, who are technically competent and have no beneficial interest in the outcome, to analyze proposals and to operate as staff to the management or to the board. This critical review process can be most appropriately applied to the major strategic or single-time propositions (rather than to routine administrative or recurring matters).

With many boards of directors facing turbulent, externally created conditions and interaction with other institutions, use of the institutionalized dissent function is a sophisticated way of dealing with this problem. The delegation and retention of powers and policy for the decision-making process within an organization are the factors involved. The troublesome problem often relates to the interface between the executive management and the board of directors.

The corporate dissent function may be pursued in the form of an organizational unit at corporate staff level. Alternatively it may be a separate group, such as an outside advisory council composed of external and otherwise unaffiliated persons, or it may be an outside individual, who is expert in the area, to consult in this type of analysis. No single model fits the nature of all problems, proposals, or corporate circumstances.

Corporations often use a task-force approach in this regard. The devil's advocate role is a temporary one and functions on an ad hoc assignment. Some companies use this type of position as a management development device, rotating it among the brighter junior experts who have upper-management potential. It is important that such a devil's advocate role not be exposed to status or rank differentials in any assignment. Good practice dictates that the analyst whose proposal is critiqued should always be at the same hierarchical level as the devil's advocate to avoid status pressure or other repercussions. Quite often this analytical function reports directly to the chief executive of the firm to avoid undue political pressures.

Merely establishing an organizational function is not sufficient since the concept must be understood and accepted in order to be workable in a corporate context. The board in particular must understand this technique. The Justice Goldberg approach proposed some years ago to the TWA board was an extreme version. The outside directors were to be equipped with a separate staff to analyze and question all matters before the board. Although this idea had certain interesting features, it has not been accepted in any serious corporate sense. Divisiveness and adversary positions that are destructive have little attraction to the contemporary boardroom.

The purpose of a version of the corporate devil's advocate role is suggested to ensure valid decision making. The persons or unit charged with the responsibility of dissenting and providing recommendations by pointing out flaws in logic or other fallacies or inaccuracies in what otherwise might be onesided proposals is an interesting, if touchy, approach to increasing the overall validity of the complete decision making process. I know of one multinational corporation in the billion-dollar class that employs this technique very effectively. An official dissenter can heighten the probability that decisions will be thoroughly researched and that proposed solutions will be soundly based on reality. Such a role can also do a great deal to make sure that marginal or unwise decisions are not made at all.

There is one obvious risk in an organizational sense. Some corporations rely greatly on outside experts, consultants, and advisers, and they may develop a tendency not to rely on the judgment of those in the firm who know the business best. A careful balance between expert input and the input of those who will be held accountable for actions and proposals needs to be considered carefully. Morale, retention of key people, and development of a belief in equitable and fair management decision making and accountability are at stake.

Independence

One of the primary criteria for selecting an individual for board membership is his ability to bring to the boardroom a dispassionate, objective point of view. A management director whose working experience has been entirely within the one company on which board he is serving may be a very objective person. However, it is only reasonable to expect that because of his long experience in the corporate culture, where personal commitment and success are strongly controlled and influenced by the environment, he will tend to foster a strong personal bias. This bias is in favor of the culture of—in the extreme—the group-think state-of-mind of the management. The need for a dispassionate, objective perspective is the reason for the trend toward increasing the number of non-management directors on boards.

The matter of whether a board member can be characterized as independent, outside, or nonmanagement is a subject of considerable debate. The *Corporate Director's Guidebook*, prepared by a subcommittee of the American Bar Association, takes the position that former officers or managers should not, regardless of circumstances, be considered to be independent of management for any purpose, including audit committee membership.[7]

An expert in the field of corporate governance at the board level, Brian F. Smith, general director of Texas Instruments Incorporated, testified before the Senate's Subcommittee on Citizen and Shareholder Rights and Interests of the Committee of the Judiciary on June 27, 1977. Smith stated that "the audit committee policy of the New York Stock Exchange provides that a former officer of the company may qualify for membership if, in the opinion of the board, such a person will exercise independent judgment and will materially assist in the functioning of the committee. In other words, the Exchange is determined that former officers may be considered to be independent of management. As originally proposed, the policy employed the term 'outside' director and excluded former officers from the category; the policy became much more meaningful when the worn out term 'outside' director was dropped, together with the shadow it cast on the potential independence of former officers."

The Exchange does require that a majority of the audit committee consist of directors who are not former officers. In February 1977, Korn/Ferry published its fourth annual study regarding boards. In this report, it indicated that over 38 percent of the surveyed companies believed the Exchange's treatment of former officers is restrictive.[8]

The American Society of Corporate Secretaries has also questioned the *Corporate Director's Guidebook's* automatic assignment of a retired officer to insider status. This view highlights the other argument regarding the independence of former officers. A September 1977 report from the Conference Board showed that of 167 major U.S. manufacturing companies surveyed, 83 percent had boards on which outside directors—defined to include former employees—were in the majority. However, if former employees were counted as insiders, only 60 percent of the manufacturing companies would be considered to have boards on which outside directors are in the majority.[9]

In an effort to reduce the confusion surrounding the use of the terms *outside* and *inside* director, Texas Instruments, Inc., prepared a paper concerning criteria for determining the independence of directors (see the appendix to this chapter). This study of criteria was developed in the context of the changing state of legislation, administrative regulation, stock exchange listing requirements, statements by the accounting profession, and a series of academic studies. From the study, it is apparent that there is essentially a consensus on present management directors who are deemed to lack independence with respect to their employer and former officers who are not presumptively deemed to lack independence with respect to their former employer. This supports the T.I. rationale for its innovative concept of general directors of the board.

Notes

1. For more on this, see my *Metadevelopment: Beyond the Bottom Line* (Lexington: Lexington Books, D.C. Heath, 1977).

2. Irving L. Janis, *Victims of Groupthink* (Boston: Houghton Mifflin, 1972), chap. 13.

3. Barry M. Staw, "Knee-deep in the Big Muddy: A Study of Escalating Commitment to a Chosen Course of Action," *Organization Behavior and Human Performance* 16 (1976): 27-44.

4. Howard Raiffa, *Decision Analysis* (Reading, Mass.: Addison-Wesley, 1968).

5. For more on this subject, see Carolyne Smart and Ilan Vertinsky, "Design for Crisis Situation Units," *Administrative Science Quarterly* 22 (December 1977): 640-657.

6. Theodore T. Herbert and Ralph W. Estes, "Improving Executive Decisions by Formalizing Dissent: The Corporate Devil's Advocate," *Academy of Management Review* (October 1977: 662-667, reveals no evidence on the effectiveness of these techniques as used by the Catholic church.

7. American Bar Association, Section of Corporation Banking in Business Law, Committee on Corporate Laws, Sub-committee on Functions and Responsibilities of Directors, *Corporate Director's Guidebook Business Lawyer*, 32 (November 1976).

8. Korn/Ferry International, Board of Director's Fourth annual Survey, No. 10 (February 1977).

9. J. Bacon and J. Brown, *The Board of Directors: Perspective and Practices in Nine Countries*, New York Conference Board, 1977, pp. 84-85.

Appendix 10A
Criteria for Determining
"Independence" of
Directors

Two recent major studies have emphasized the desirability of boards of directors and audit committees dominated by "independent" directors.[1] An "independent" director is, primarily, a director who is not subservient to management.[2]

The purpose of this memorandum is to explore the criteria which may be applied in determining the independence of directors and, specifically, to consider if former officers of a company should, as directors, bear a presumptive lack of independence.

I. Summary.

Criteria for determining the "independence" of directors (and others in analogous circumstances) have been developed in the context of legislation, administrative regulation, stock exchange listing requirements, pronouncements of the accounting profession, agreements and academic studies.

Although the criteria represent a wide variety of approaches, from simple to complex, from subjective to objective, there is a near consensus in at least two respects: (1) present officers are presumptively deemed to lack independence with respect to their employer, and (2) former officers are *not* presumptively deemed to lack independence with respect to their former employer.

II. Terminology—Use of "Outside" Director.

At the outset, it should be noted that the term "outside" director is frequently used to describe a director possessing independence.[3] The multiple connotations ascribed to the term "outside" director, however, impair the utility of its use.

For example, in a statistical study[4] supporting the thesis that insider boards out-perform outsider boards, former officers were deemed to be insiders, an approach which has been questioned.[5] On the other hand, the New York Stock Exchange, in bolstering the statement that almost all listed companies have at least two outside directors, cited statistics which include former officers as outsiders.[6] These examples suggest the content of the term "outside" director is uncertain, confusing and can be colored by the immediate bias of its user.

In an effort to avoid what one author has called a "linguistic quicksand,"[7] this memorandum avoids the use of the terms "inside" and "outside" director and attempts, when possible, to clarify the intended meaning when such terms are used by others. In particular, an attempt will be made to determine if a particular use of the term "outside" director is intended to exclude former officers.

Brian F. Smith, general director of Texas Instruments, Inc., in testimony to the Securities and Exchange Commission, Chicago, Illinois, November 1, 1977.

III. Criteria for Determining "Independence."

A. Legislation.

1. *Canadian Prototypes.* Since 1970, the Ontario Business Corporations Act has required publicly-held corporations to have at least two directors who are not officers or employees and, in addition, to maintain an audit committee composed of a majority of such directors. The statutory provisions are set forth in Exhibit A to this memorandum. The recently enacted Canada Business Corporations Act contains similar requirements.

2. *Proposed International Contributions, Payments, and Gifts Disclosure Act.* On May 5, 1976, Senator Church introduced a bill (now apparently defunct) which would have required that at least one-third of the board of each company (presumably limited to companies reporting under the Securities Exchange Act of 1934) be composed of "independent outside directors" and that such directors constitute an audit committee. "Independent outside directors" were identified as "individuals having no direct or indirect financial ties with the company."[8]

3. *New York Insurance Law.* Section 56(3) of the Insurance Law of New York provides that the number of officers and salaried employees serving as members of the board of a mutual insurance company must at all times be less than a quorum of the board.

4. *Investment Company Act of 1940.* The Investment Company Act requires that a certain portion of the board of a mutual fund be persons not associated with the advisor to the fund. In defining persons who are appropriately independent of the advisor, the Act suggests, by analogy, that the existence within the past two years of a material business or professional relationship with the company or its principal management officers should result in a director not being considered an independent director.[9] Consequently, if this model were followed, a former officer could be considered independent so long as he was not an officer within the preceding two years.

5. *Japanese Commercial Code.* Under Article 276 of the Commercial Code of Japan, those serving as a company's *kansayaku* (person elected by stockholders to supervise activities of directors in effort to assure their proper and lawful performance of statutory duties) may not, at the same time, be a director, manager or other employee of the company (or certain related companies).

B. Administrative Regulation.

1. *SEC Actions to Enhance Board Independence.* The Chairman of the Securities and Exchange Commission, Roderick M. Hills, has requested the New York Stock Exchange to consider amending its listing requirements to require audit committees of "independent" directors and, in the case of larger companies, boards composed of a majority of "outside" directors.[10]

It appears that Mr. Hills is not using the terms "independent" or "outside" in a manner which would exclude former officers. In his testimony before the Senate Commerce Committee (in which he reviewed the SEC's recommendations to the Exchange) he clearly used the term "outside" director to include a former officer in his discussion of Connecticut General Life Insurance Company.[11]

Mr. Hills cited both Connecticut General and Texas Instruments Incorporated ("TI") as examples of "numerous corporations who already are experimenting with their boards to create a management team that is more responsive and accountable." His remarks regarding TI indicate a clear understanding of TI's use of former officers as directors.[12] It is unlikely that Mr. Hills would have cited TI as an example unless he felt TI's use of former officers as directors was compatible with, and contributed to, the type of board independence which he and the SEC are encouraging.

2. *SEC Rules Governing Independence of Accountants.* Rule 2-01 of Regulation S-X provides the formal requirements as to independence of accountants for purposes of qualifying to certify financial statements filed with the SEC. The rule provides specifically that so long as a former officer does not participate in auditing financial statements of his former employer for periods of his former employment, an accounting firm "will *not* be deemed *not* independent in regard to" the former employer if the former officer "is employed by the firm and such individual has completely dissociated himself from" his former employer.

The relevant portions of Rule 2-01 are set forth in Exhibit B. Additional material regarding independence of accountants is discussed below in connection with pronouncements of the accounting profession.

C. *Stock Exchange Listing Requirements.*

The New York Stock Exchange requires two "outside" directors for newly-listed companies and recommends a minimum of three.[13] Although the Exchange has not published a formal definition of the term "outside" director, as it is used in this context, it is understood that the informal definition used by the Exchange excludes former officers.

In the context of the Exchange requirements, the exclusion of former officers from the definition of "outside" directors is understandable. The requirements would typically result in a token representation of the "outside" directors. Under such circumstances, the criteria for determining independence should be more stringent than if, for example, the "outside" directors constitute the majority of the board. Exclusion of former officers would not appear appropriate in the context of a board with a majority of "outside" directors. The position of being in the majority is thought to strengthen the independence of the included members, thus permitting a correspondent easing of the criteria for independence. As one of the recent studies concluded: "[A] clear-majority rule would put much less strain on the statutory definition of independence in the case of persons whose independence is debatable, such as commercial bankers and retired executives.[14]

D. *Pronouncements of the Accounting Profession.*

1. *AICPA Statement on Audit Committees.* In the AICPA Executive Committee Statement on Audit Committees, July 20, 1967, it is recommended that audit committees be composed of "outside" directors. Such directors are identified as "those who are not officers or employees."

2. *Independence of Accountants.* Rule 101 of the AICPA Code of Professional Ethics requires that public accountants, who express an opinion on financial statements of an enterprise, be independent of that enterprise. Examples are given of instances in which independence will be considered to be impaired. The text of Rule 101 is set forth in Exhibit C.

There is no provision requiring that former officers of an enterprise be presumptively deemed to lack independence with respect to the enterprise. To the contrary, Ethics Ruling 40 indicates that a controller who severs all connections with, and disposes of all financial interest in, his former employer may join the accounting firm serving the former employer and, presumably, have responsibilities for future audits of his former employer's financial statements.[15]

The irony would be obvious if any member of a board's audit committee were held to a stricter standard of independence than the company's outside auditor.

E. Agreements—Settlements of Suits Against Northrop and Phillips.

In settling suits based on illegal political contributions, Northrop Corporation and Phillips Petroleum Company agreed, among other things, that a clear majority (ultimately 60%) of each board, and the entirety of each audit committee, must consist of "independent outside directors." (The plaintiffs in each suit were represented by the Center for Law in the Public Interest.) Each settlement contains an elaborate definition of "independent outside director." (The definition used in the Phillips settlement is set forth in its entirety in Exhibit D to this memorandum.)

With respect to *existing* directors, the definition in the Phillips settlement includes any director who was not an officer or employee of Phillips at the time of his most recent election (and at the time of subsequent elections).

The Phillips settlement contains a provision otherwise excluding persons from the definition who had individually received payments from the company in excess of $25,000 (other than as fees as a director) for services provided during any one of the four preceding calendar years. The Northrop settlement contained a similar provision. Consequently, it appears that an existing officer or employee of these companies who is newly elected as a director in the future would, unless his annual compensation were less than $25,000, have a waiting period of four years before being considered an "independent outside director."

F. Academic Studies.

The study by Professors Noyes Leech and Robert Mundheim of the University of Pennsylvania[16] makes persistent use of the term "outside" director without providing a definition. That the term is not intended to exclude former officers seems clear, however, from the discussion regarding Texas Instruments Incorporated in which its "General Directors" and "Directors" are identified as "outside" directors (despite such positions being filled to a substantial extent by former officers).[17]

The study by Professor Melvin Aron Eisenberg of the University of California, Berkeley,[18] as noted earlier, indicates former officers may be considered independent, particularly if independent directors constitute a majority of the board.

With respect to criteria of independence, the Eisenberg study indicates that any person who is an executive of the corporation, or who has a professional relationship or material business dealings with the corporation, and any close relatives of such persons, must be treated as not independent.[19]

The Leech-Mundheim study adds some miscellaneous criteria. For example, the study indicates independence is impaired if CEO's serve on the board of each other's company.[20]

IV. Effect of Litigation Threat.

In part because of efforts by the SEC, the threat of litigation against directors for inadequate performance is widely felt.[21] The positive aspects of litigation (or the threat thereof), as it affects independence, should not be overlooked.[22]

The AICPA, in establishing criteria for independence, has indicated that in deciding what types of relationships should be prohibited it is necessary to weigh the magnitude of the threat posed by a relationship against the force of countervailing pressures (such as the possibility of legal liability and loss of reputation).[23] Consequently, relationships of directors which were considered to impair independence ten years ago (the *BarChris* case in 1968 is generally thought to have begun the movement toward increased director liability) would not necessarily be so considered today.

V. Consideration of Potential Contributions.

In determining what relationships should be presumed to impair independence, it may also be appropriate to weigh the potential threat to independence arising from an individual's history and experience against the potential contribution available from the individual because of his history and experience.[24] In other words, what is the cost of excluding such persons and is it worth the supposed benefit?

It should be noted that the inadequate performance of nonmanagement directors is typically caused not by personal bias but by a lack of knowledge, insight and understanding regarding the company.[25] Therefore, in preparing persons for audit committee membership, for example, neither of the available alternatives is totally satisfactory: (1) recruit a stranger whose objectivity may be unassailable and attempt to bolster his knowledge of a complex company, or (2) recruit a former officer whose knowledge of the company may be unequaled and attempt, to the extent necessary, to bolster his objectivity.

In this context, the approach of Texas Instruments Incorporated, cited by Roderick Hills, . . . is illustrative. To assist a former officer serving as a director to develop and maintain a dispassionate perspective toward the company, TI expects that he will enter into activities outside of the company which will supplement his experience in the company in a meaningful way. Such activities are intended to expose him to environments in which a diversity of viewpoints is expressed, where the performance of individuals in quite different endeavors from the company's may require evaluation, and possibly where some of the approaches developed in the company might be tried and further evaluated. Typical of such activities are: (1) service as trustee or director in an educational institution, a charitable foundation, or a hospital; and (2) membership on boards of other business corporations, including banks, where there are no conflicts of interest.

In addition, the company provides former top officers with a measure of financial independence through their assured retirement allowance, payable whether or not the former officer serves as a director. Such allowance includes, in the case of early retirement, a supplementary retirement allowance sufficient to bring a former top officer's total retirement allowance up to an amount approaching the allowance he would have been entitled to at normal retirement age. Under the company's retirement policy, its chairman, president, and executive vice presidents, after serving a specified minimum number of years in those posts, may choose early retirement after their 55th birthday. Retirement for the chairman, president, and executive vice presidents will be compulsory shortly after they attain age 62. Executive vice presidents ordinarily will retire shortly after reaching 55, but may be asked to serve to a later age when the company's needs so require or in order to attain the required minimum length of service in that post. In addition to providing an orderly succession of top officers and opening promotion opportunities, the company's policies are expected to make available independent candidates as future members of the board.

With respect to preparing persons for audit committee membership, it is apparent that both knowledge and objectivity are necessary to do the job, to ask the right questions, to probe the soft spots. It is not apparent, however, that any overriding basis exists for preferring or excluding either strangers or former officers (although it would seem foolhardy to expect an audit committee—absent an extraordinary expension of time and money—to function effectively without the insight provided by some members drawn from management). Rather than agonize over achieving the ideal mix of knowledge and objectivity in a particular individual's make-up, it would seem better to establish an audit committee with a membership including, and perhaps roughly balanced between, individuals whose principal experience has been outside the company and former officers intimately familiar with the company.

VI. Conclusion.

Perhaps the most appealing approach for determining independence of directors is the definition of "independent outside director" in the Phillips settlement. (See Exhibit D hereto.) While the definition appears complex, that complexity is primarily the result of its effort to provide objective standards which avoid debate over whether a particular interest is "material."

Admittedly, the objective standards are somewhat arbitrary. For example, paragraphs ii through v, which cover payments for property or services (presumably including services as an officer) and engagement of legal counsel, extend four years into the past. This seems an inordinately long period. As noted earlier, the Investment Company Act, in dealing with independence, is only concerned with business relations occurring within the preceding two years. Many other models, of course, have no period of presumptive non-independence at all.

On balance, it does not appear that a waiting period is a necessary element in determining independence. Nevertheless, a waiting period may appeal to some because, as a token, it recognizes that independence is not gained overnight. Consequently, if a waiting period is deemed to be desirable at all, it is recommended that the period be limited to one year. An example of a one-year period to shed a previous interest is provided in Rule 16b-3 under the Securities Exchange Act of 1934. A person serving on a committee administering, for example, a stock option plan, is deemed by the Rule to be a "disinterested person" with respect to the plan if he has not been eligible for the grant of options under the plan for a period of one year prior to serving on the committee.

VII. Epilogue—Proposed Definitions.

A. No Waiting Period.

The following proposed definition of "independent director" is modeled after the Phillips example but omits any waiting period:

"The Term 'independent director' means any person who, on the date of his election,

(i)   is not an officer or employee of the company or its subsidiaries (the 'Company');
(ii) is not an officer or employee of, or does not own directly or indirectly in excess of 1% of the shares of, a corporation which is proposed to receive during the following year payments from the Company for property or services in excess of 1% of its gross receipts as determined by its financial statement for the immediately preceding year;
(iii) is not a member, officer or employee of any business or professional organization (other than a corporation) which is proposed to receive payments from the Company for property or services in excess of $250,000 during the following year;
(iv) is not a person who individually (as a share partner or otherwise) is proposed to receive payments from the Company, directly or indirectly, in excess of $25,000 (other than fees as a director, retirement allowances or payments required under non-competition agreements) for property or services sold or provided by him during the following year; *and*
(v)   is not a member of or associate in a law firm which is proposed to be engaged by the Company."

B. One-Year Waiting Period.

The following definition of "independent director" is modeled after the Phillips example but reduces each waiting period to one year:

"The term 'independent director' means any person who, on the date of his election,

(i) is not, and has not in the calendar year immediately preceding such date been, an officer or employee of the company or its subsidiaries (the 'Company');
(ii) is not an officer or employee of, or does not own directly or indirectly in excess of 1% of the shares of, a corporation

(A) which has received payments from the Company for property or services in excess of 1% of its gross receipts during the calendar year immediately preceding such date, as determined by its financial statement for such year, or

(B) which is proposed to receive during the following year such payments in excess of 1% of its gross receipts as determined by its financial statement for the immediately preceding year;

(iii) is not a member, officer or employee of any business or professional organization (other than a corporation) which

(A) has received payments from the Company for property or services in excess of $250,000 during the calendar year immediately preceding such date, or

(b) is proposed to receive such payments in excess of $250,000 in the following year;

(iv) is not a person who individually (as a share partner or otherwise) has received payments from the Company, directly or indirectly, in excess of $25,000 (other than fees as a director, retirement allowances or payments required under non-competition agreements) for property or services sold or provided by him during the calendar year immediately preceding such date, and is not proposed to receive such payments in excess of $25,000 in the following year; *and*

(v) is not a member of or associate in a law firm which is proposed to be or in the preceding calendar year has been engaged by the Company."

Notes

1. M. Eisenberg, "Legal Models of Management Structure in the Modern Corporation: Officers, Directors and Accountants," 63 Calif. L. Rev. 375 (1975) (hereinafter cited as Eisenberg); and N. Leech & R. Mundheim, "The Outside Director of the Publicly Held Corporation," 31 Bus. Lawyer 1799 (1976) (hereinafter cited as Leech & Mundheim). Also see Testimony of Roderick M. Hills, Chairman of the Securities and Exchange Commission, before the Senate Commerce Committee on "Corporate Rights and Responsibilities," June 21, 1976 (hereinafter cited as Hills).

2. "The term 'independent' is not used to suggest indifference to the corporation's concerns, but the capacity to advise or monitor (whatever the board role) without subservience to management, in particular the chief executive officer. As previously indicated, independence is consistent with an effective working relationship between management and the board. It does not require the outside board member to carry a bias against management or to believe that management is not dealing with the board in good faith. Independence does not mean that the director must characteristically vote against management or otherwise dissent from its proposals." Leech & Mundheim, *supra* note 1, at 1830.

3. "In the experience of the authors, what most people have in mind in using these words ["insider" and "outsider"] is to distinguish degrees of objectivity. They use the word 'ousider' in the sense of having objectivity, breadth, freedom to speak without restraint. They use the term 'insider' in the sense of a lack of these things. But we see from the analysis of [a hypothetical] board that the words 'insider' and 'outsider' are not only vague; they can be downright misleading as to objectivity and outspokenness.

"The authors would like to see industry throw overboard the tired terms "inside director' and 'outside director.' The need is to choose or coin new words which carry the connotation of objectivity and of freedom to put it on the line." J. Juran & K. Louden, The Corporate Director 170 (1966) (hereinafter cited as Juran & Louden). Also see Hills. *supra* note 1, in which the terms "independent" and "outside" are used interchangeably.

4. S. Vance, Boards of Directors: Structure and Performance (1964).

5. See Juran & Louden, *supra* note 3, at 177.

6. NYSE, Recommendations and Comments on Financial Reporting to Shareholders and Related Matters—A White Paper 5-6 (1973) (hereinafter cited as NYSE White Paper); J. Bacon, Corporate Directorship Practices: Membership and Committees of the Board 2 n.1 (1973).

7. Juran & Louden, *supra* note 3, at 172.

8. S. 3379, 94th Cong., 2d Sess. §8 (1976).

9. 15 U.SC §80a-2 (19) (1970); see Leech & Mundheim, *supra* note 1, at 1804 and 1831.

10. See Hills, *supra* note 1; also Address of Chairman Hills to New York Law Journal Seminar, June 30, 1976.

11. "Connecticut General Life Insurance Company has a Board consisting *only* of the *Chief Executive Officer* and *outside directors*. The *Chairman* will no longer be a management officer, although *he may previously have been a member of management* and he will devote only about one-half of his time to the company."

Hills, *supra* note 1 (emphasis added). Mr. Hills also refers to Connecticut General in a May 11 letter to the newly-elected Chairman of the Exchange with the same use of the term "outside" director.

12. "Texas Instruments Corporation [*sic*] has divided its board into three categories:

"'General Directors' who are expected to devote approximately thirty days per year (or up to eighty in more unusual circumstances) to the work of the Board, 'Directors' who are expected to devote only fifteen days, and 'Officers of the Board.' Neither General Directors nor Directors are employees of the Company. Officers of the Board are employees who will retire from operations within a few years and who are then expected to become General Directors."

Hills, *supra* note 1.

13. NYSE White Paper, *supra* note 6, at 5-6.

14. Eisenberg, *supra* note 1, at 407.

15. Ethics Ruling 40 on Independence, Integrity and Objectivity, Controller Entering Public Practice:

"*Question*—A controller of a client of a member's firm wishes to enter public practice. Arrangements have been made for him to join the firm's staff, with a view toward ultimate partnership. Prior to employment with the firm, he will have severed all connections with the client and will have disposed of all financial interests. He would have no responsibilities for the current audit of his former employer's financial statements. Would the independence of the member's firm be considered to be impaired under these circumstances?

"*Answer*—Independence of the member's firm would not be considered to be impaired under these circumstances because precautions are being taken to maintain the firm's independence for the period covered by the financial statements. The other precautions taken by the firm appear to assure compliance with both the letter and the spirit of Rule 101."

The Ethics Rulings are made by the AICPA's professional ethics division's executive committee after exposure to state societies and state boards.

16. Leech & Mundheim, *supra* note 1.

17. "Some companies have adopted systems designed to permit at least some members of the board to devote their principal time to board matters. Texas Instruments, for example, has included on its board at least one full-time employee who has few or no other management functions. *Aside from the chairman and the president* (and occasionally an executive vice president), *This Officer of the Board is the only insider* on the board. The officer of the board concept underscores an increasing time committed to the work of the board, at least for the person occupying that position.

"The concern for increasing the time that directors will spend on board matters underlies several other developments at Texas Instruments, supplementing its institution of the Officer of the Board. *The company makes provision for two categories of outside director*: 'General Directors', who are expected to devote at least thirty days per year to the company and a smaller number of 'Directors' who are expected to devote only fifteen days of service per year.

"Under the Texas Instruments plan, a person who has served as Officer of the Board will retire at age 55 and is expected to be designated as General Director. The company states that a primary consideration in the selection of a Director, General Director and Officer of the Board is his ability to bring to the board a 'dispassionate point of view.' To insure that persons occupying those positions after a working experience largely within the company will develop such a perspective, it is company policy to expect that appointees will enter into activities, such as directorships, outside the company. The process whereby the Officer of the Board remains on the board following his retirement from full-time employment insures a cadre of board members who have intimate historical knowledge of the company. *The Texas Instruments system seems particularly suited to companies that want their outside directors to play a substantial role in actively participating in the company's management* rather than to confine their efforts principally to a monitoring role."

Leech & Mundheim, *supra* note 1, at 1809-10 (emphasis added).

18. Eisenberg, *supra* note 1.

19. Eisenberg, *supra* note 1, at 407.

20. Leech & Mundheim, *supra* note 1, at 1830-31.

21. See generally, 31 Bus. Lawyer (Special Issue; March 1976) relating proceedings of the ABA National Institute, "Current Problems of Corporate Directors Discharging Developing Responsibilities."

22. "[T]he several judicial decisions over these past few years that have emphasized the responsibilities of directors were appropriate government interventions to improve the functioning of corporations in the private enterprise sector."

P. Haggerty, The Productive Society 143 (1973). (At the time of his statement, Mr. Haggerty was the chairman of Texas Instruments.)

23. "While it may be difficult for a CPA always to appear completely independent even in normal relationships with clients, pressures upon his integrity or objectivity are offset by powerful countervailing forces and restraints. These include the possibility of legal liability, professional discipline ranging up to revocation of the right to practice as a CPA, loss of reputation and, by no means least, the inculcated resistance of a disciplined professional to any infringement upon his basic integrity and objectivity. Accordingly, in deciding which types of relationships should be specifically prohibited, both the magnitude of the threat posed by a relationship and the force of countervailing pressures have to be weighed." AICPA Code of Professional Ethics, Section 52.08.

24. For example, in an ideal world it may be desirable to require that the Secretary of Defense and other high government officials not be former

officers of companies holding government contracts, or to require that members of regulatory agencies not be former officers of regulated companies. In the real world, however, such former officers are often regarded as possessing knowledge, insight and understanding which uniquely qualify them for the government position. It is considered sufficient if they sever their relationships with the contracting or regulated companies. See W. Meigs, J. Larsen & R. Meigs, Principles of Auditing 45 (1973).

25. See, e.g., Report of Investigation in the Matter of Sterling Homex Corporation Relating to Activities of the Board of Directors of Sterling Homex Corporation, SEC Release No. 34-11516, July 2, 1975; J. Daughen & P. Binzen, The Wreck of the Penn Central (1971).

Exhibit A: Ontario Business Corporations Act

Sec. 122(2).—The board of directors shall consist of a fixed number of directors,

(a) in the case of a corporation that is not offering its securities to the public, of at least one; and
(b) in the case of a corporation that is offering its securities to the public, of not fewer than three, of whom at least two shall not be officers or employees of the corporation or of any affiliate* of the corporation.

Sec. 182.—(1) The directors of a corporation that is offering its securities to the public shall elect annually from among their number a committee to be known as the audit committee to be composed of not fewer than three directors, of whom a majority shall not be officers or employees of the corporation or an affiliate of the corporation, to hold office until the next annual meeting of the shareholders.

(2) The members of the audit committee shall elect a chairman from among their number.

(3) The corporation shall submit the financial statement to the audit committee for its review and the financial statement shall thereafter be submitted to the board of directors.

(4) The auditor has the right to appear before and be heard at any meeting of the audit committee and shall appear before the audit committee when required to do so by the committee.

(5) Upon the request of the auditor, the chairman of the audit committee shall convene a meeting of the committee to consider any matters the auditor believes should be brought to the attention of the directors or shareholders.

Exhibit B: Regulation S-X of the Securities and Exchange Commission Rule 2-01. Qualifications of Accountants

(b) The Commission will not recognize any certified public accountant or public accountant as independent who is not in fact independent. For example, an

*Sec. 1(4) defines "affiliate": "For the purposes of this Act, one body corporate shall be deemed to be affiliated with another body corporate if, but only if, one of them is the subsidiary of the other or both are subsidiaries of the same body corporate or each of them is controlled by the same person."

"Subsidiary" and "control" are defined in Sections 1(2) and 1(5), respectively.

accountant will be considered not independent with respect to any person or any of its parents, its subsidiaries, or other affiliates (1) in which, during the period of his professional engagement to examine the financial statements being reported on or at the date of his report, he or his firm or a member thereof had, or was committed to acquire, any direct financial interest or any material indirect financial interest; or (2) with which, during the period of his professional engagement to examine the financial statements being reported on, at the date of his report or during the period covered by the financial statements, he or his firm or a member thereof was connected as a promoter, underwriter, voting trustee, director, officer, or employee, except that a firm will not be deemed not independent in regard to a particular person if a former officer or employee or such person is employed by the firm and such individual has completely dissociated himself from the person and its affiliates and does not participate in auditing financial statements of the person or its affiliates covering any period of his employment by the person. For the purposes of Rule 2-01 the term "member" means all partners in the firm and all professional employees participating in the audit or located in an office of the firm participating in a significant portion of the audit.

(c) In determining whether an accountant may in fact be not independent with respect to a particular person, the Commission will give appropriate consideration to all relevant circumstances, including evidence bearing on all relationships between the accountant and that person or any affiliate thereof, and will not confine itself to the relationships existing in connection with the filing of reports with the Commission.

Exhibit C: AICPA Code of Professional Ethics, Rule 101

Rule 101—Independence. A member or a firm of which he is a partner or shareholder shall not express an opinion on financial statements of an enterprise unless he and his firm are independent with respect to such enterprise. Independence will be considered to be impaired if, for example:

A. During the period of his professional engagement, or at the time of expressing his opinion, he or his firm

1. Had or was committed to acquire any direct or material indirect financial interest in the enterprise; or
2. Had any joint closely held business investment with the enterprise or any officer, director or principal stockholder thereof which was material in relation to his or his firm's net worth; or
3. Had any loan to or from the enterprise or any officer, director or principal stockholder thereof. This latter proscription does not apply to the following loans from a financial institution when made under normal lending procedures, terms and requirements:

    (a) Loans obtained by a member or his firm which are not material in relation to the net worth of such borrower.
    (b) Home mortgages.
    (c) Other secured loans, except loans guaranteed by a member's firm which are otherwise unsecured.

B. During the period covered by the financial statements, during the period of the professional engagement or at the time of expressing an opinion, he or his firm

1. Was connected with the enterprise as a promoter, underwriter or voting trustee, a director or officer or in any capacity equivalent to that of a member of management or of an employee; or
2. Was a trustee of any trust or executor or administrator of any estate if such trust or estate had a direct or material indirect financial interest in the enterprise; or was a trustee for any pension or profit-sharing trust of the enterprise.

The above examples are not intended to be all-inclusive.

Exhibit D: Definition of "Independent Outside Director" in Phillips Petroleum Company Settlement*

The term "independent outside director" means any person who, on the date of his election, (i) is not an officer or employee of Phillips; (ii) is not an officer or employee of, or does not own directly or indirectly in excess of 1% of the shares of, a corporation (A) which has received payments from Phillips for property or services in excess of 1% of its gross receipts during any one of the four calendar years immediately preceding such date, as determined by its financial statement for the year in question, or (B) which is proposed to receive during the following year such payments in excess of 1% of its gross receipts as determined by its financial statement for the immediately preceding year; (iii) is not a member, officer or employee of any business or professional organization (other than a corporation) which (A) has received payments from Phillips for property or services in excess of $250,000 during any one of the four calendar years immediately preceding such date, or (B) is proposed to receive such payments in excess of $250,000 in the following year; (iv) is not a person who individually (as a share partner or otherwise) has received payments from Phillips, directly or indirectly, in excess of $25,000 (other than fees as a director) for property or services sold or provided by him during any one of the four calendar years immediately preceding such date, and is not proposed to receive such payments in excess of $25,000 in the following year; and (v) is not a member of or associate in a law firm which is proposed to be or in the preceding four calendar years has been engaged by Phillips. Any person elected a director at Phillips' 1975 annual meeting of stockholders, who was not an officer or employee of Phillips when so elected and is not such an officer or employee on the date on which his status is determined. shall be considered within the definition of "independent outside director."

*Wall Street Journal, February 23, 1976, at 13.

11 Bank Holding Company Boards

In March 1942, the abortive Cripps mission, in which the British proposed that India would have an assembly with powers to draft a constitution after the war, took place. Mohandis Karamchad Gandhi retorted that this was "a post-dated cheque on a crashing bank." Today candidates for a "noncrashing" bank holding company board of directors find themselves in a similar Cripps mission mode if they do not circumspectly explore the characteristics of the banking system's multiplicity of chartering, supervising, and examining agencies.

Prospective directors should understand the guidelines that the dual banking system presents to both federally and state-chartered banks. These constraints rest on the separation of federal and state powers in our legal code, as well as the diffusion of powers among different federal agencies. National banks receive their charter from the office of the comptroller of the currency, and each state can also grant a charter to a bank that does not wish to be organized under federal law. Although the U.S. banking system is predominantly one of unit banking, branch banking has developed in a context of uneven restrictions imposed by various federal and state laws. Because of these restrictions, chain banking and group banking have evolved. Chain banking refers to the use of interlocking directorates to link banks together; and in group banking, a holding company is formed to control the common stock of a number of banks.

A statutory web of regulations surrounds such banks. By comparison, these regulations make Jonathan Swift's figment of Gulliver's fetters a gossamer-like check on any action. Prospective holding company directors must fully appreciate the stewardship implications of a holding company board. These special fetters and features are especially interesting to any student of directorships. Before tackling the special aspects of directorship on a bank holding company board, it is helpful to examine bank directorships in general.

Duties and Responsibilities of Bank Directors

William H. Bowen, a bank president, recently pointed out seven differences between service on a bank board and service on a regular corporate business board.

1. Bank directors take the oath of office; business corporation directors do not (12 USC '73). 2. Bank directors have residence and citizenship

requirement; their peers in business may, but often do not. *3.* Investment bankers may not serve as bank directors (12 USC '78); no such barrier exists in business corporations. *4.* A bank director may have a financial commitment in stock ownership (12 USC '72); business corporate law typically exacts no such requirements of its directors. *5.* Statutory machinery exists for summary prohibition of unsound practices which bank directors permit or even are about to permit. In addition, the bank director may be removed from office with these practices with recited statutory liability for damages that may result from willful violation of the law—12 USC 1818 (b)(1) and (e)(2). Vague or less summary procedures if any at all appear in a typical business corporation codes. *6.* With exceptions, the national bank directors may not serve on more than one national bank board (15 USC 19); there is no such general prohibition in non-banking corporations. *7.* Criminal laws abound which expressly prohibit certain acts by bankers—embezzlement (18 USC 656), making false entries (18 USC 1005), taking fees for loans (18 USC 215), falsely certifying checks (18 USC 1004), making or granting a loan or gratuity to a bank examiner (18 USC 212), and borrowing funds entrusted to a bank under its trust powers. No such direct targeting of criminal laws confronts the business corporate director. Clearly the bank director is set apart for different attention, and it may be argued that a higher duty of performance and behavior is expected of him than of his business corporation peer.[1]

According to the American Bankers Association (ABA), the U.S. banking system is unique among the financial structures in the world and has spawned a unique institution: the American bank board of directors. Our commercial banking system now comprises over 14,000 banks with approximately 240,000 bank directors. The ABA calls this system "a typical American experiment. Imagine one state (Texas) with 1400 independent banks! It is a widely held opinion that this diverse, multi-unit system breeds innovation, more competition, closer relationship between management and customer and contributes to a vital and expanding American economy."[2]

The community bank is still a very significant part of American banking. More than 90 percent of the nation's 14,300 banks have assets of $100 million or less. In contrast to the community bank, a bank holding company is a corporation that owns or controls one or more such banks. The organization of a holding company is not easily portrayed because there are differing policies and opinions (as well as state laws) involved in showing the functional lines of authority and responsibility. Banks in both unit-banking and branch-banking states can be owned by a holding company. Typically, these banks have their individual boards of directors, which may retain substantial autonomy in establishing local bank policy.

Most holding companies have been formed by the banks themselves in order to broaden their operation potential. A holding company can often serve a wider geographic area than an independent bank can. They can be in the form of one bank or multibank holding companies. The holding company may also engage in certain nonbanking activities, such as operating mortgage and finance companies; providing investment counseling, data-processing, and bookkeeping services, and leasing real estate and other property. These activities require the approval of the Federal Reserve Board and are considered by the FRB as long as the activities are closely related to banking.

There are special characteristics of directorships in chain banking and group banking as compared with those attendant to the usual business corporation directorships. Fundamental, but often so obvious that it is overlooked, is the fact that the bank's basic stock in trade consists of funds that are borrowed from others: its depositors. The federal government and each state has formulated statutes and regulations to impose special rules on the conduct of the banking business because of this special characteristic.

Commercial banking always has been (and probably always will be) a highly regulated industry. Reasonable regulation in the public interest does establish a climate for operations that may be foreign or uncomfortable to directors who are more oriented toward governance of private business or the professions. Bank directors learn to recognize not only the legal restrictions but also other implications that such regulation has on their function and the bank's performance. The philosophy and approach to bank problems are so fraught with consciousness of regulation that serving the variety of masters makes the bank director's job difficult. The bank holding company, one tier removed from the depositors, makes this role even more complicated.

In addition to the usual director responsibilities, bank directors have a responsibility to the depositors and to the public to see that the bank is operated in a fashion that safeguards deposited funds and does not imperil public confidence in the entire banking system. As Theodore Brown, president of the First National Bank of Denver, put it, "The responsibilities of bank directors are awesome; in most instances the remuneration is not compensatory for those responsibilities; but the opportunity to be of real service to the bank, the banking system and the community is impressive. Commercial banking, as we have known it in our nation's history, could not have played the role it has played in national development without the participation and contribution of able, dedicated bank directors."[3] The holding company, as owner of one or more banks having their own directorates, poses the problem to its directors of reifying these awesome responsibilities to the banks, the banking system, the public, and the depositors.

The Bank Holding Company Movement

The nation's banking system is undergoing basic structural changes, the most prominent of which may be referred to as the bank holding company movement.

A bank holding company as regulated by the Federal Reserve Board under existing law is permitted to engage in only banking and closely related activities. The impetus behind the bank holding company movement is the desire of more than one bank to create a business network where branch banking is limited or prohibited. There are other motivations: ability of dividends to flow on a tax-free basis from a bank to the parent, the ability of the parent to service member banks more efficiently and to furnish capital downstream in the form of equity into its banks, and many other reasons.

Some history here may be helpful to candidate directors of a bank holding company. The first regulation of bank holding companies was in the Banking Act of 1933. By that act, the Federal Reserve Board was empowered to withhold or to issue a voting certificate for corporations owning a majority of the stock of a bank that was a member of the Federal Reserve system. A corporation had to agree to open up the books of the bank for examination by the Federal Reserve in order to obtain a permit from the board to vote the stock of a bank. In addition, agreement had to be made to refrain from participation in the securities industry.

The Bank Holding Company Act of 1956 basically confined bank holding companies to the business of banking and closely related services. Further, the U.S. Congress empowered the Federal Reserve Board to regulate bank holding companies. The act was amended in 1966 and in 1970 to provide uniform standards for bank agencies and the courts in evaluating the legality of bank holding company acquisitions. The amendments also established that acquisitions that had taken place prior to 1966 were immune from antitrust legislation unless litigation was already in process. Holding companies must be registered under the Securities and Exchange Commission.

The 1970 amendments also eliminated the exemption contained in the 1956 act of the one-bank-holding company. By 1970, 33 percent of all bank deposits in the United States were in banks owned by a one-bank-holding company. The exemption of 1956 had no more validity and one-bank-holding companies became a significant factor in the banking community.[4]

Bank Holding Company Survey

Among the advantages and disadvantages of the bank holding company concept, one disadvantage seems particularly pertinent to this discussion. Because of the two-tier corporate architecture involved between the parent company and the subsidiary bank(s), there is an understandable perception that a bank holding company can become and remain impersonal in its approach to a community; it can be unaware and unresponsive to the same degree that a local board of directors or the local president can provide with this often nonresident and remotely located parent. Of course, this same concept pertains to other corporate institutions that have two, three, and four levels of corporate architecture in their subsidiaries and subsidiaries of subsidiaries. Because banks are held so much in public view and are concerned more apparently with public trust, the holding company operates under a perceptive disadvantage because of the very nature of its structural setup. This second degree of abstraction can be dealt with by policy by having the holding company board be especially responsive to the local boards of directors' role and interests and by providing enough flexibility to decide which service and control functions can be centralized and which functions should be decentralized. The purpose of a 1977 survey of bankholding company executives was to determine the perception of the chairman and chief executive officers of medium-sized bank holding companies (those in the billion-dollar class) on the issue of the role of the board and particularly to the relationship between the parent board and the subsidiary bank board. Although the literature is replete with articles about bank holding companies, little is apparent in dealing with this policy and attitudinal question. Hence the survey strives to take a reading on the actual state of mind of those in responsible charge of bank holding companies with regard to their director function.

A private survey was conducted in the fall of 1977 of senior executives of twenty-three-bank holding companies. It was designed to elicit a broad but detailed response to issues in a fast-growing area of corporate interest: the board of directors. William M. Crozier, chairman and CEO of BayBanks, Incorporated, a Massachusetts bank holding company, assisted by soliciting the respondents. Kenneth K. Talmadge and my associates at Arthur D. Little performed the major analysis of the survey results.

The primary topic areas were board concept and nature; board structure, organization, and process; board context; liability and indemnification; and future outlook. Respondents were promised that their responses would be aggregated to avoid identification of the individual or his institution. Copies of all material prepared from the questionnaires were sent to the individual respondents so that they could position themselves with respect to the rest of the sample.

Companies were chosen at random from the Bank Holding Company Association membership list. The assets of these companies comprise more than two-thirds of total banking assets in the United States. Companies excluded from the inquiry were the very largest bank holding companies with international activities as a principal corporate component and small bank holding companies, particularly where a larger company existed in the same state. Thus, the bank holding companies selected for the survey could best be described as leading regional banks.

Twenty-three detailed responses were received. Twenty-one could be identified; two were anonymous.[5]

All identifiable respondents had nonbanking financial subsidiaries. Five were single-bank holding companies with numerous offices. Sixteen were multiple-bank holding companies.

The range of scope	two to seventy-five banks in the holding company system.
Average	twenty-three banks in the holding company system
Medium	fourteen banks in the holding company system

Of the individuals who responded to the questionnaire, eleven were titled chairman of the board, eight were titled president, two were titled chairman of the board and president, and nine were titled chief executive officers. In seven of the companies, no chief executive officer was designated as such, and in five cases the CEO was someone else.

The responses to the questionnaire were composited into the summary shown in table 11-1. It seems apparent from this survey that the stage of board reform underway in these holding companies lags behind a similar state of reform consciousness underway with many unregulated industrial boards. In many manufacturing corporations, change in the role and conduct of the directorate has been under more aggressive scrutiny by directors, shareowners, activists, and management.

Board Concept and Nature

1. *To what degree does your board (versus the management) take initiative action with respect to holding company objectives, plans, strategy? What initiative action does the board take with regard to financial performance, CEO performance appraisal?*

Bank holding company boards take very little initiative action in either strategic planning or financial performance, although this latter area receives primary focus. Directors are more active in CEO performance appraisal, usually on an informal and indirect basis. Roughly a third of the bank boards interviewed formally appraise the chief executive officer's performance. Initiative (versus participative) action is primarily in setting the CEO's compensation and in management succession. The board's functions are to keep well informed; review performance; discuss financial statements; question, probe, monitor, and ultimately give approval; but not initiate.

2. *To what degree does your board take participative action with management in respect to company activities through active committee or consultative assignments?*

The primary thrust of a director's participation on a bank board is through committee membership. The larger the bank holding company, the greater the number of committees. Some smaller bank holding companies had no

Table 11-1
Responses to the Questionnaire

	Response Category				
	Largest Size	Medium Size	Smallest Size		
100 largest U.S. bank holding companies by rank	1-15	16-50	51-100	N/A	N/A
Number of responses	0	5	8	4	4
Responses as % of category	0	15	16	N/A	N/A
Range of assets of individual bank holding companies ($ Billion)	74.0-10.2	9.4-3.0	3.0-1.5	1.5-1.0	Below 1.0
Total assets of all members of category, 12/31/76 ($ Billion)	415.5	161.4	100.4		
Total assets of respondents 12/31/76 ($ Billion)	N/A	26.8	16.5	4.9	2.6
Responses as % of category	0	17	16		
Geographic concentration	New York, 8; California, 5; Illinois, 2	varied	varied	varied	varied

committees because the reduced size of the board permitted regular meetings for consideration of all matters. This, however, is the exception. Occasionally selected directors are informally asked by management to work on special projects or problems. A board member was not used on a consultative assignment in any instance.

3. *What was the total cost to the company in 1976 of the holding company board (fees, expenses, retainers, perks, travel)? What was the total of the CEO's 1976 compensation as the latter is reflected in the proxy statement?*

The range of answers was from $6,000 to $177,000, with the average at $67,000 and the median at $55,000. The CEO's 1976 compensation ranged from $63,000 to $242,000, averaging $137,000, with the median at $129,000.

Board Structure, Organization, and Process

4. *How large is the board? How often does it meet and for how long at a regular meeting?*

The range was from six to twenty-six directors; the average was eighteen and the median nineteen.

Regarding meeting frequency, two respondents had twenty-four meetings per year, ten had twelve meetings, three had eight meetings, two had six meetings, one had five meetings, and five had four meetings.

The meetings generally lasted between an hour and a half and two and a half hours each.

5. *What are the standing committees? How often do they meet—for how long? How are committee members selected—how long do they serve? Briefly describe their activities versus those of the board.*

The traditional standing committees include executive, audit, and compensation, which usually meet more frequently than other committees. Almost all institutions also have a trust committee. The larger bank holding companies have up to eight to ten committees in some cases, but the majority of the holding companies have three to five. Other committees include pension, acquisition, capital and dividend, stock plan, salary, public policy, investment, examining, management and corporate development, and marketing. Only two of the companies surveyed had a public policy committee.

In large institutions where the executive committee functions as a small board of directors, the committee may meet monthly, on call, or three to five times a year. The audit and compensation committees usually meet three to six times a year, and other committees usually meet two to four times a year or on call. Some of the holding companies (three or four) have very active trust committees, which meet approximately once a month.

The appointment of directors to committees is usually made by the chairman, CEO, and management. In about half of the cases, it is made with board approval, although this often appears to be token. Committee members usually serve for one year; few terms are longer. An exception is a company that appoints committee members for three years.

6. *Are criteria for director candidates nominations clearly set forth? Are there criteria for subsequent director performance after election?*

In an overwhelming number of cases, there are no formal criteria either for candidate nominations or for director performance. Subsequent director performance is usually associated with attendance at meetings which reflects an interest level.

7. *In the director candidate selection and nomination process, how do outside directors participate?*

In approximately 50 percent of the cases, the initiative for the selection of new directors comes from management. In 20 percent of the cases, the initiative comes from outside directors, and in the remaining 30 percent, the initiative is mixed between management and outside directors. The process is informal in more than half of the cases. When outside directors have the initiative, selection is handled through the executive committee or a nominating committee. The board often gives routine final approval to a nomination.

8. *Do you have any formal provision for automatic disqualification as a director, or for involuntary separation of a director from the board? What is your director retirement policy?*

In almost every case, there are no formal provisions for automatic disqualification or involuntary separation. It is understood that a director cannot serve as an officer or as a director of a directly competing institution. Retirement age, in most cases, is at seventy. In far fewer cases, it is at sixty-five or seventy-two. The other major stipulation is that a director retire from the bank at the time that he retires from his outside business or his bank position. Some institutions use a director emeritus position to ease people off the board.

9. *Where does the responsibility for the selection process for CEO succession lie within your board organization and board process? Is there a regular directors' review of potential candidates?*

The responsibility for succession falls in an equal number of cases to the CEO, the full board, executive committee, personnel committee, a committee, a committee specially composed for this purpose, or there may be no established procedure. Most institutions have chosen a new CEO only once or twice in recent history, so responsibility may not be well institutionalized. About 75 percent of the banks do not have a regular review process. Rather they have a periodic informal review of in-house candidates by the chairman and/or CEO with directors.

10. *What do you think of having a separate role for the chairman, distinct from that of the CEO?*

This question drew the strongest response in the entire survey. Answers ranged from "absurd" and "absolutely opposed" to "desirable" and to "very good—we do this in all of our banks." Some institutions have never considered this idea. Conclusions are that if this were done, roles and responsibilities must be clearly delineated; that by dividing authority, the leadership focus is not undercut or detracted from; and that the idea may be very helpful in management succession.

11. *Are directors provided with information in advance of board meetings, and how extensive is it?*

In a third of the cases, directors are not provided with information in advance. The two-thirds that are given information receive financial data, information on issues and votes to be recommended by management, charts, tables, and analyses, an agenda, minutes of the last meeting, and a summary. In some cases the information is limited to a financial analysis and a brief summary. It is usually sent out a week prior to the meeting. Sensitive data are not included.

12. *What steps are taken to familiarize a new director with the company? What measures are taken to aid in the continuing education of directors in the affairs of the company?*

The process of familiarizing a new director with the company is informal and may include a tour of the facilities, meeting and presentations by senior management, a reading list, and considerable time with the CEO. To continue director education, reports and readings are mailed. Many institutions regularly have an in-depth presentation by a division of the bank holding company at board meetings.

13. *Does the presence of certain unique individual personalities, behavioral patterns, style or traditions of importance affect the manner in which your board functions?*

The answer is evenly split: half said "yes" and half said "no."

Board Context

14. *What relationships of importance or interactions are there as a part of corporate policy or practice between holding company directors and subsidiary bank boards?*

Answers to this question depended on the number of banks under the bank holding company umbrella. If there is a single institution, the boards of directors are usually identical. There is an overlap of directors between the individual bank boards and the holding company board when there are several institutions. When there is a large number of subsidiary banks, generally none of the subsidiary boards' members serve on the holding company board, but communication is effected with an annual meeting of all boards.

15. *Do you have any restrictive policy applicable to your board members (other than that required by law or regulation) regarding linkages with or separation from outside organizations and activities?*

The only restriction is association with a competitor, a fact that would emerge during nomination of a new director. One institution has a stricter policy.

Liability and Indemnification

16. *To what extent does Director's & Officer's insurance cover your directors? Is insurance limited to the holding company board, or are subsidiary boards covered as well?*

Of the twenty-three respondents, five do not have D&O insurance for their directors, but three of these are now considering it. Eighteen have this insurance. In one case, it does not include subsidiary boards as well. The amount of this insurance is predominantly $5 million to $10 million. In one case, it was $1 million and in another $15 million.

17. *What indemnification is provided for the board?*

The bylaws of bank holding companies generally indemnify their boards of directors to the fullest extent permitted by law. The articles of the corporation follow state statutes. The area not covered is that of negligence and misconduct. One respondent indicated a willingness to defend its directors in legal suits, but another provides no indemnification.

18. *What explicit provisions do you have for protection of board members against ransom, extortion, kidnapping?*

Five holding companies have made no explicit provisions for protection. Provisions cover only officers in four cases. Two banks have made provisions primarily for officers but also cover directors. Seven bank holding companies said they had insurance to cover directors; and two others have funds designated for such an eventuality. Two companies said that they had made provisions but did not comment further. This is understandably a topic of great sensitivity to bank holding companies and should be treated cautiously. One company said: "We have provided some rudimentary instructions to alert directors to the possibility of extortion."

19. *Regardless of the current level of your directors' fees, do you feel that these should rise substantially, stay about where they are, or be lower?*

None of the respondents felt there should be any decrease in the amount paid. Eight respondents felt that the fees would stay roughly at the same level; nine felt there would be an increase in fees; and five thought there would be a substantial increase in fees. Fees paid by industrial companies have traditionally been larger than the honorariums paid by banks. Directors' fees may well be expected to rise from the current level paid by holding companies to reflect increased director responsibilities and more closely approximate fees paid by industrial companies.

20. *Could you cite the three most troublesome issues of any kind to be faced by your board during the next five years?*

Government interference and increased regulatory requirements were seen as the primary issue to be faced by boards in the future. A number of respondents expressed product- and market-related concerns: coping with the advent of electronic funds transfer, NOW accounts, unbundling and pricing of unbundled services, and keeping ahead of the competition. Financial challenges were addressed in two ways: in terms of profitability and sources of capital for expansion. Tied to this latter point were questions of geographic and nonbank expansion policy. Chairmen were still concerned about the normal responsibilities of the board, including management succession, personnel, and the relationship of the board to its company. Personal liability by directors, interestingly, did not emerge as a primary concern but received some mention, as did issues relating to the directors' privileged position, like conflicts of interest, inside transactions, and personal financial disclosure.

The implications of the survey are interesting. The following commentary attempts to interpret some of these findings.

Issues Confronting Bank Holding Company Directors

There is a universal problem in the difference of expectation among the parties at interest. The first of these parties are the member banks in the holding company, which is the permanent core of the economic enterprise. The separate management and operations of these member banks are vital in relation to the identity and purpose of the holding company. Member bank boards or directors at the second-tier level are interested parties, as are customers, legislators, public officials, neighbors, and the press. The management and the directors of the holding company each have their own definition of good stewardship and will press claims in fulfilling their roles. The management at the two levels of the organizations will have expectations of the various director levels and vice-versa. Each party will feel some conflict and controversy, and each must lean on each other as they function in their interdependent ways.

The concept of a governing board type of directorate for the holding company with directors representing the public interest is a topical idea that can lead to special kind of misunderstanding. If individual board members represent special groups such as minorities or women, the board itself cannot fulfill its responsibility to the whole public and shareowners. In order to do this, the holding company would be forced to establish formal representation for any group that could muster strength to support its claims for special treatment.

There are conflicting notions, however, about the essential nature of a bank holding company as an institution. Among the various concepts, each has its supporters and each has some degree of validity. These notions are not totally in conflict, although when carried to extremes, each becomes unacceptable.

> The holding company as a community of banks for whose benefit each bank is organized. The holding company should therefore respond to individual bank interests.

> The holding company as a public agency to be operated for the public good, responsive to the society of which it is a part.

The first duty of a director is to understand the purpose of the holding company, to determine its direction, and to assist in holding it to a steady course. The purpose may change with changing times, but these changes are matters for serious deliberation and sober judgment. Given an understanding of the purpose of the holding company, its specific role and the tasks attendant to being a director warrant careful consideration. Some of the following comments may be helpful in this regard.

The Role of a Governing Board

A holding company board has several roles to play in order to deal with the following functions:

> To hold the assets of the member banks and interpret the management of assets for the benefits of shareowners.

To act as a buffer.

To arbitrate internal disputes between banks.

To stimulate change.

To be a resource for member banks in terms of management and money.

To provide for a governance guiding system, with adequate control and adequate freedom to encourage banks to develop on their own.

To fulfill fiduciary and statutory requirements.

To evaluate the performance of each member bank and the holding company and to evaluate the performance of the chief executive officers of the member banks and the holding company.

To participate in assisting and auditing member banks activities—for example, by holding company director committees on auditing, organization, and compensation.

Some of these ideas are controversial. The concept of the board as a stimulator of change, a change agent, or a catalyst often runs counter to the objectives of management and certainly is often in conflict with second-tier bank management and director groups.

Director Tasks

Here is an obvious list (that bears repeating) of the obligations confronting directors of holding companies:

To study their own membership continuously. This means developing an effective board that is fully independent but has devoted members who are sensitive to, but not committed to, the views of the major constituencies that relate to the institution.

To protect the independence of the bank holding company from external control.

To review periodically the purposes of strategic direction of the bank holding company and its members.

To provide for appropriate strategic growth in assets and in management capability, including management succession.

To manage the assets entrusted to it by the shareowners in an effective manner.

To have a long-range plan for the business and management development.

To be alert to forces at work in the external environment for changes in attitude, motivations, interests, and life-styles of the customers and the employees. To remain in touch with other domains of activity on which the bank holding company and its member banks are interdependent.

To ensure a voice for directors at the state and federal levels when matters of common concern are under discussion. This would include tax policies, regulation, insurance, and other matters affecting the operation of the bank holding company.

The delicate balance of a director's being active—yet not hyperactive—is a matter to be dealt with through experience. To attempt to know everything about an institution would be foolish, but to know too little is to be helpless. Directors are responsible by law to be properly informed. This means that directors must take time to understand the purposes of the holding company, to develop a vision of its future potentialities, and to relate effectively to the other members of the board and to the management—not to say the other elements of the total community in which the banking system operates. A spirit of controversy with basic commitment to a healthy company is important at the board level. Problems arise when there is a failure to understand the nature of the board and its role, failure to understand the distinctive nature of the holding company as distinct from an industrial establishment or a single bank, and—perhaps most troublesome of all—failure to distinguish between broad strategic policy direction and the administrative or management function.

Directors are responsible for the process, as well as for the property, in a bank holding company and are responsible for the activities of the company, as well as for its assets. The problem is how to live up to this heavy obligation. The three functions that a board must focus on in order to carry it out are planning, authorization, and review.

Planning is not a subject for the board itself but rather a source of demand for adequate strategic planning for all aspects of the holding company and member banks. The function of planning is never static, never finished. It must remain in a state of continuous revision as experiences dictate. Individual members of the board can act as resources to planning, but the responsibility for the board is to see that the CEO of the holding company provides an intelligent planning function.

Given competent planning, the board performs its function of authorization. It authorizes capital expenditure, salary approvals, executive appointments, management succession, and so on.

The third stage of review means adequate attention to follow through after planning and authorization to close the loop in a learning process as well as a control function.

One of the most widely quoted concepts of the law regarding banking in America was rendered by the New York State Court of Appeals in 1880. It captures the essence of a director's stewardship, whether it be at a bank director or holding company director level:

> When one deposits money in a saving bank or takes stock in a corporation thus divesting himself of the immediate control of his property, he expects, and has the right to expect, that trustees or directors who are chosen to take his place in the management or control of his property, will exercise ordinary care and prudence in the trust committed to them—the same degree of care and prudence that men prompted by self-interest generally exercise over their own affairs.

Notes

1. Richard B. Johnson, ed., *New Perspectives for Bank Directors* (Dallas: SMU Press, 1977), pp. 3-4.

2. *Focus on the Bank Director: The Job* (Washington, D.C.: American Bankers Association, 1977), p. 1.

3. Richard B. Johnson, ed., *The Bank Director* (Dallas: SMU Press, 1974), pp. 10-11.

4. Charles E. Banks, "Holding Companies: One- and Multi-Bank," in Johnson, ed., *New Perspectives*, pp. 216-225.

5. The following material was developed from *Moody's Bank and Financial Manual, 1977*, vol. 1, to characterize the twenty-one identifiable respondents.

12 Advisory Boards

It's always a silly thing to give advice, but to give good advice is absolutely fatal.
—Oscar Wilde

Remember when President Carter, amid great fanfare, announced in August 1977 that the number of federal advisory committees would be reduced by 40 percent that year? Criteria for the hit list of advisory groups were three: the lack of compelling need for their continuation, a lack of balance in their membership, and lack of openness in the way they conduct their business.

From a political standpoint, the sacred criterion—lack of balance in membership—spawned a yearly index to advisory committee membership, which is published by the Senate Subcommittee on Reports, Accounting and Management. The 1,340-page index for 1976 revealed the following:

> Representatives of 28 large companies held more than a thousand seats on the advisory committees. American Telephone and Telegraph led the list with 120 employees on advisory committees, RCA had 94 members on 24 panels advising eight federal agencies, and General Electric was third with 74 seats.
>
> Fourteen universities held more than 1,800 seats on committees. University of California led with 394 seats, University of Texas had 160 representatives, and Harvard University was third with 140 seats.
>
> Four labor unions held nearly 200 seats.
>
> One hundred seventy-three individuals, most of them from corporations, held between 4 and 12 seats each.

The president's objective was worthy but early results from just one of the federal agencies, the National Science Foundation (NSF), reflected what a formidable and illusive task this zero-based review of adviser panels proved to be. *Science* magazine reported that although thirty-six NSF advisory committees were consolidated into fourteen, the overall membership would actually rise from 378 to 540.[1]

Originally the overall government total of advisory committees was 1,189. First efforts pared off 304 committees (25 percent) from a number of agencies. Efforts to reduce further will undoubtedly continue for a long time, for, as

Josh Billings observed long ago, "Advice is a drug on the market; the supply always exceeds the demand."

Advice being more blessed to give than receive, it is understandable why persons are reluctant to lose their status as advisers. This problem has arisen, in my experience, with some advisers selected by corporations to serve to keep management informed on various industrial, disciplinary, or geographical areas where an enterprise has interests. Unless a carefully planned scheme is developed to make service on such an advisory board meaningful, the advisers tend to become disenchanted, and their attitude may do more harm than good from a public relations standpoint. If the value of the advice proves to be limited, the management becomes disenchanted, and a delicate problem may arise in disbanding a group of distinguished outside advisory directors.

There are some great benefits from selectively engaging advisory boards. An examination of the basic elements will help in deciding whether an advisory board is appropriate for an enterprise at a particular time.

Role of an Advisory Board

The advisory responsibilities of the statutory board of a company have been discussed thoroughly elsewhere.[2] To recap these, the key statutory board roles are concerned with the following board functions:

Statutory and fiduciary responsibilities.

Evaluation of the corporation and the CEO's performance.

Participative action on board committees.

Resource bank of experience, wisdom, and expertise, available to advise management and the board.

Catalytic or change agent role to initiate constructive suggestions or evaluations for the board and management to consider. Action in crisis is included in such a role.[3]

In another context the advisory board has no statutory or fiduciary role but offers evaluative advice or active participation as requested. It is primarily a resource committee with a mandate to initiate suggestions, warnings, or criticism to improve the effectiveness or potential of the enterprise.

An advisory board functions as an open organizational device to broaden horizons; develop new business or new thinking; improve the contacts, trade, and professional relations of the corporation; and do so especially in world areas or in disciplinary domains where local or specific knowhow is needed. There are few, if any, legal requirements regarding functions of an advisory board or duties of an advisory director.

The circumstances indicating the need for an advisory board are somewhat parallel to those calling for utilization by the board of any outside experts.[4] In adapting and expanding this checklist to the rationale for a corporation, at least a dozen reasons for an advisory board can be indicated. The advisory board may be organized to do the following:

1. To pass on the reasonableness and propriety of a proposed corporate decision without necessarily endorsing it as the only, the best, or the wisest decision that could be made.
2. To identify and evaluate alternative courses of action not foreseen by the management or the main board.
3. To confirm or verify important factual data underlying a particular proposition, project, or policy request.
4. To relieve some of the pressure on inside management and the decision-making process in times of explosive growth or business pressure. Advice by an advisory board on key decision elements can facilitate management decisions if the advisers are expert and trustworthy.
5. To provide independent assistance in the formulation of long-term objectives, goals, and strategy and advice on how to operate in an uncertain or foreign environment.
6. To provide objective and disinterested evaluation of corporate or management performance and competitive or government activity.
7. To supplement management with needed expertise and experience not available internally.
8. To assist the company in resolving or reconciling serious internal differences of opinion by an objective outside judgment.
9. To provide a level of confidence to top management when there is some lack of confidence but no desire or ability to bring in new better-qualified management at the time (a short-term solution at best).
10. To advise the company where there is a high risk of material litigation or other potentially serious adverse consequences to the community, environment, or corporate reputation.
11. To watch for conflict-of-interest (real or apparent) overtones of a proposed transaction. This could involve an acquisition, merger, joint venture, spin-off, stock issue, or entry into a new business.
12. To provide introductions to potential customers, suppliers, or clients; help develop business and enhance trade relations; recruit assistance for key personnel; assist in obtaining industrial property rights, permits, and licenses; and offer knowledge to keep abreast of social, legal, and technical developments in industry, government, or universities.

One suggestion worthy of consideration has been made by John E. Martin, an independent consultant. This concept is that certain specialized functions requiring board attention can be handled by a single director with the support of advisory councillors. The concept is referred to as a committee or council of peers. The peer director thus defined provides services for the others on the board, either as an individual and liaison between the advisory councillor and the board or as a chairman of a board committee.

In order not to compromise his independence, the peer director should not also be an officer of the company. The concept proposes "instituting a board structure that would provide specialized communications and counsel to the directors. A diverse group of independent advisors and corporate monitors, or examiners, would constitute a council selected to service the numerous needs of the directors.... The services they would provide would be in the nature of advice and counsel, analysis and special studies, auditing and monitoring sensitive operations, answering inquiries and advocating the views of special constitutencies."[5]

Although this approach has obvious problems of potential conflict with management, information overload, and duplication of staff, it is an idea to be aware of even though use of the full blown concept is yet to be seen extensively. The concept has many of the ingredients of the less complicated and traditional advisory board that have proven of value to many corporations.

Activity and Societal Scan

Effective management action or reaction is contingent upon adequate advance or current information. Normally a corporation has its own network of plants, laboratories, offices, agents, and representatives who furnish a continuing flow of information necessary to plan and operate the business. But when it comes to sensing developments in remote locations or in broad economic, cultural, or social trends, it is important to tap outside experts to avoid the groupthink pathologies that tend to develop internally. The illusion of invulnerability held by many internal decision groups (and hence high-risk propensity), the rationalization of warnings that may force reassessment of current policies, the belief in the inherent morality of the decision group, the pressures on members of management to conform to accepted company or group policies, the suppression of personal doubts, and the cognitive biases or faulty conceptualization are all symptoms of company groupthink pathologies.[6] An advisory group consisting of independent, well-situated, experienced, and expert persons can avoid these characteristics of groupthink, which may breed in some corporate organizations. (This concept has been explored for the statutory board in chapter 7.)

The advisory board can be viewed as an adjunct to the corporation's intelligence-gathering system. In this context, two useful conceptual approaches have been employed in describing the setup of information systems for social reporting.[7]

The first approach may be characterized as an activity scan. (See figures 12-1 and 12-2.) The activity scan can be positioned in at least two different sectors. The most obvious is when the advisory board is made up of industrial, specialized disciplinary, or nation-oriented experts. This is represented in figure 12-1 as an industry-focused advisory board. Justification for situating an advisory board in an industry domain may be dictated in a new venture or at the start-up or crisis stage. Or it may be targeted at a selective industrial market where the determining factors for viability of the enterprise are in the hands of competition, a set of particular customers, a restricted source for raw materials, or in a regulated or service-regulated industry. The statutory board may need input from a special group of advisers who are unaffiliated, disinterested, and independent and who are credible and outstanding in the industry involved. The broader social concerns may be shielded from the enterprise at that particular stage of its development. Knowledge of long-term trends may be of secondary or tertiary consequence at a particular stage of development.

The model in figure 12-2, with the business (versus industry) focus, calls for an advisory board made up of persons with broad business and business-related backgrounds, but not necessarily from the particular industry or business in which the corporation has its primary interests. Financial, economic, political, scientific, or technological advisers are obvious advisory director candidates where such a broader cognitive sweep of the business community and its trends are germane and determining to the company's operations and future plans. Examples of companies utilizing the business-focus-activity-scan type of advisory boards are conglomerates, multinational companies, multiproduct and service firms, holding companies, and investment management or financial services organizations. Large, fairly complex organizations in services and manufacture can often utilize an advisory board so composed that its perspective is that of the broad international community.

Figure 12-3 is a model of the advisory board concept at a higher-level of information sensing and cognitive scope. The societal focus of such a board dictates an entirely different board mix, locale, and composition. Its purpose is more long-range, futuristic, global, and social-change oriented. The issues studied are more sweeping and concerned with the purposeful and normative nature of the enterprise. (Chapter 13 illustrates this metalevel of corporate concern in a scarabaeus structure with four levels in the relevance tree of corporate governance zones.) The overview metascan type of advisory board serves the corporation at the highest level of this relevance tree. Such advisory boards are being employed by many large multinational companies, such as financial institutions and international manufacturing corporations.

The strengths of each of these three separate approaches—the industrial, business, or societal focus—give rise to their respective limitations. An advisory board formed for either of the first two activity-scan situations offers the advantages and familiarity with the company's current activities, problems,

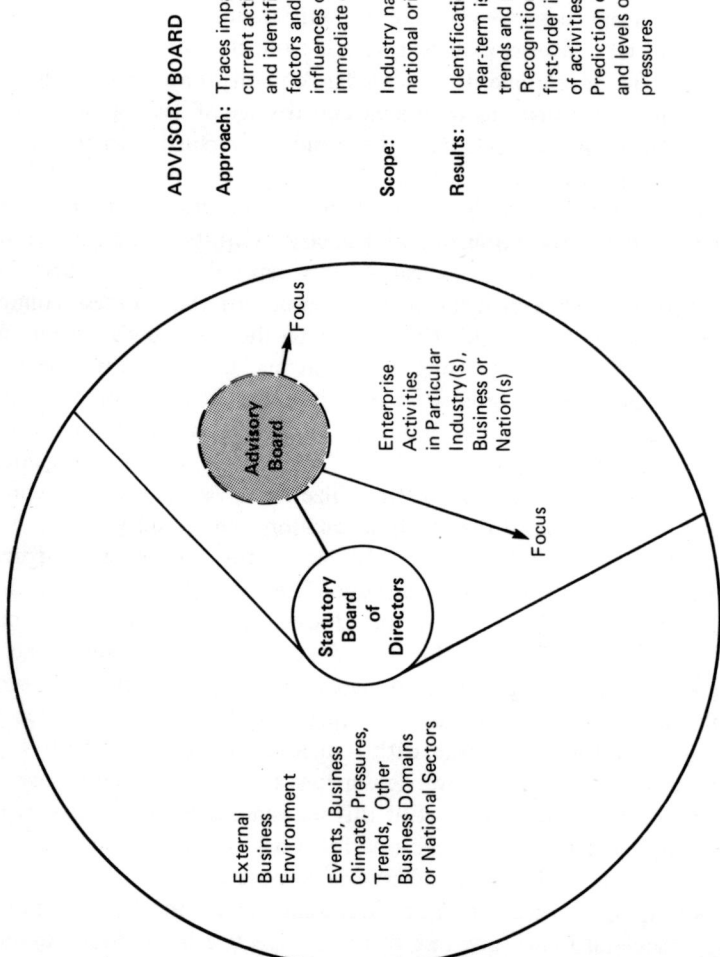

INDUSTRY FOCUS

ADVISORY BOARD

Approach: Traces impact of current activities and identifies factors and influences of immediate concern

Scope: Industry narrow or national orientation

Results: Identification of near-term issues, trends and influences. Recognition of direct first-order impact of activities. Prediction of sources and levels of near-term pressures

Focus

Advisory Board

Enterprise Activities in Particular Industry(s), Business or Nation(s)

Focus

Statutory Board of Directors

External Business Environment

Events, Business Climate, Pressures, Trends, Other Business Domains or National Sectors

Figure 12-1. Activity Scan of an Advisory Board: Industry Focus

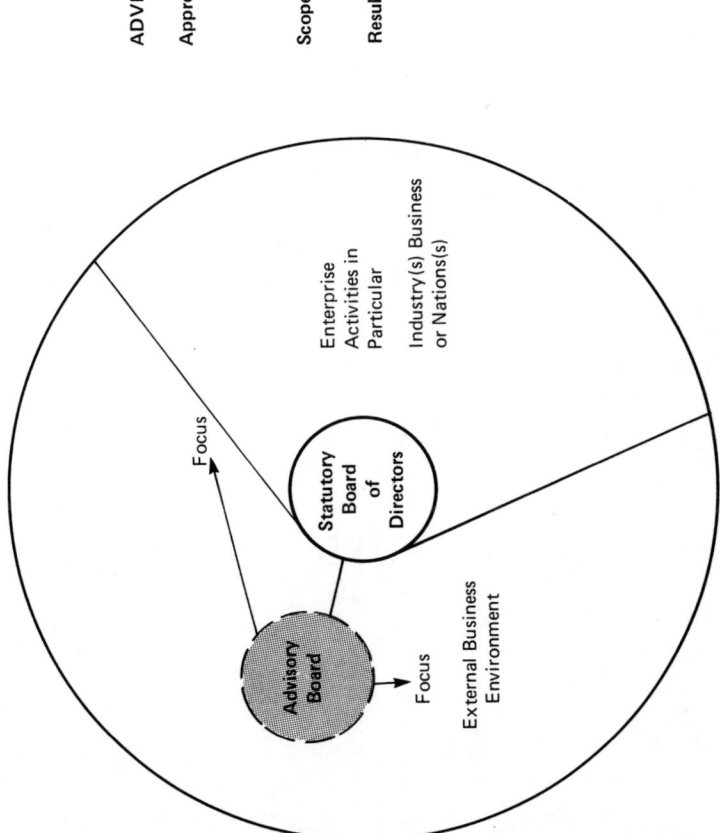

ADVISORY BOARD

Approach: Same as Figure 12-1 against broader business range of activity

Scope: Business community oriented

Results: Figure 12-1 plus interrelationship with world-wide business interests. Identifies some second-order impacts and cross-impacts with industry and business more broadly

BUSINESS FOCUS

Focus

Enterprise Activities in Particular

Industry(s) Business or Nations(s)

Statutory Board of Directors

Advisory Board

Focus

External Business Environment

Figure 12-2. Activity Scan of an Advisory Board: Business Focus

ADVISORY BOARD

Approach: Identifies broad social trends, movements, issues, conflicts, interactions, potential surprises, discontinuities, force fields, patterns of change, value shifts, traditions, beliefs, ideologies

Scope: Global and meta-system view of economic, military, social, cultural, political, ethical, moral, legal, religious, scientific, technological and environmental factors and change. Understanding society and human affairs as a whole.

Results:
- Forecasts of alternative futures, trends and impact of forces at work
- Projection of long-term continuity and discontinuity between activities and trends
- Visualizes end state of society of the future, including new roles, issues, dilemmas and opportunities for the corporation

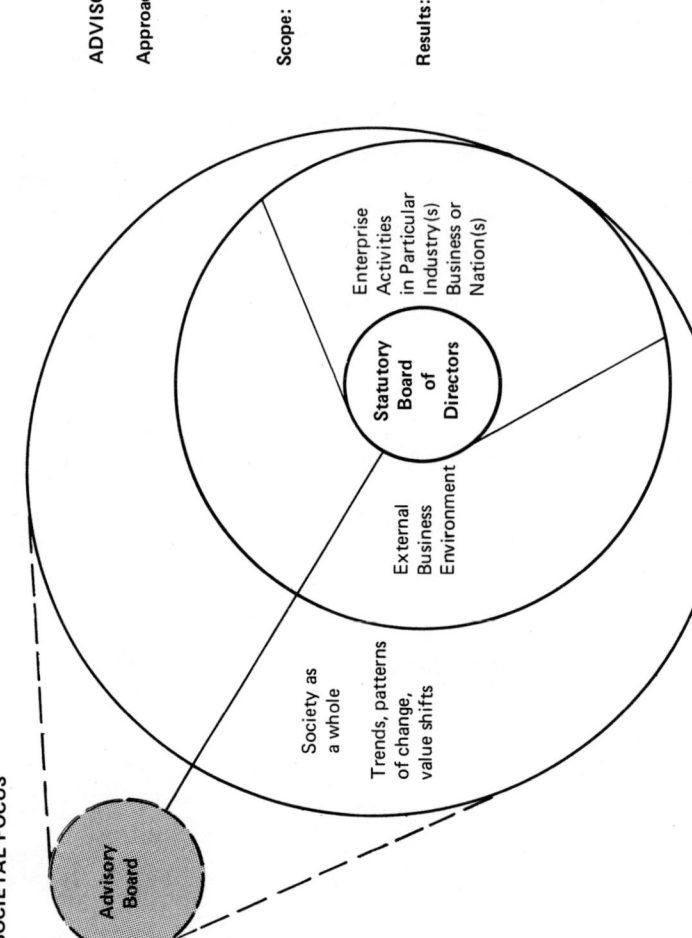

SOCIETAL FOCUS

Advisory Board

Society as a whole

Trends, patterns of change, value shifts

External Business Environment

Statutory Board of Directors

Enterprise Activities in Particular Industry(s) Business or Nation(s)

Figure 12-3. Metascan of an Advisory Board

and opportunities. It also provides knowledge of previous crisis, conflicts, disputes, pressure points, and vulnerabilities of the firm. The shortcomings stem from these same sources. Familiarity with the activities lends itself to some of the pathological conditions referred to previously. Other related shortcomings may be a priori notions, predispositions, or prejudice regarding sources of pressure and conflict or the merit of certain claims. In addition there may be a tendency to overcommit to certain goals.

The overview or metascan approach, shown in figure 12-3, balances the weaknesses of the more provincial scans by analyzing broad societal trends that are often relatively detached from the firm's current activities. By refraining from assumptions about the significance of these invasive and illusive trends or forces and by offering alternative futures, the advisory board can force a continual redefinition of the parent organization's activities. Such reexamination is becoming more necessary as the world increases in interaction and interdependency.

This broad societal approach has some obvious shortcomings, including its unlimited scope of inquiry, its often abstract level with inconclusive indicators, and the difficulty in relating results of the advisory group's perceptions and suggestions to the real activities of the company that it is supposed to serve. It can also be expensive and inconclusive. Only certain firms can afford to explore this approach. It is being used with increasing effectiveness by large, multinational corporations.

The complementarity of these three approaches suggests the development of an advisory board that combines the focuses in an integrated approach. This can be done by careful design of the composition of the advisory board to achieve a proper balance of advisers who can contribute the different perspectives. A planned turnover through specified terms of service can keep such an advisory board tuned into and intelligently related to the current activities and the future course of an enterprise.

International Advisory Boards

Lyndon B. Johnson once hankered: "I wish there were some giant-economy size aspirin tablet that would work on international headaches. But there isn't. The only cure is patience with reason mixed in." If a corporation has the time and the patience, an advisory board can provide some of this necessary reasoning.

With the growth in influence and the challenges facing multinational companies in recent years, the utilization of international advisory boards has come into vogue with a welter of U.S. and foreign-headquartered firms. A few well-known American firms that have established such boards are General Motors, Westinghouse, IBM, Exxon, Chase Manhattan, R.J. Reynolds Industries, Inc., Sperry Rand Corporation, Corning Glass Works, W.R. Grace, AMF, CPC

International, and Merck. Europe, Latin America, the Far East, the Middle East, and Africa are the broad regions into which these various companies have extended their advisory networks. Firms with headquarters outside the United States also use the advisory board device to tap world area knowhow. Swiss Banking Corporation, Volvo, and Thyssen come to mind in this category.

The viewpoint of the foreign nationals—usually distinguished citizens in their own noncompeting company and country—can offer a guest company some obvious insight and knowhow of the international scene in a foreign region. The value to a guest company of having expert advice from prominent residents of the host country is the obvious advantage. No legal or statutory entanglements are involved, and the meeting schedule requirement is usually limited to three or four times a year for formal meetings. In addition, contacts with advisory board members in overseas locations are frequently made on an individual basis to help with spot assignments, effective introductions, or an exchange of views with visiting executives or by trips for the advisory director arranged to the home office.

Advisory board member compensation is reported to be at least $10,000 per year for U.S. companies. The average board numbers six to ten, and sometimes more. Chase Manhattan has twenty members on a worldwide advisory board.[8]

One general observation may prove valid over the next few years. Frank X. White, vice-president of Business International Corporation and an experienced internationalist of long standing in the business world, points out that "in the industrialized countries, the trend seems to be among U.S. companies to move away from the traditional 'dummy' inside boards to boards with numerous local, outside directors. This would seem to militate against advisory boards at the national level, but they seem to be multiplying at the regional and world level."

Board-Mentor Service

Consultants abound worldwide to offer their advice for a fee to companies needing outside expert orientation, counsel, problem solving, introductions, industrial-business-societal scans, or just plain handholding. Not a small part of these professional solo or team advisory services are at the board level, subsidary and main board. Recruiting services are offered to boards of directors and management to help find members for their advisory committees and international advisory boards. This type service is par for the course and has existed since the first company went abroad.

In a more innovative direction, an interesting development is underway in the educational field that is related to advice for boards. It is worth including here as a possible new approach to improving board effectiveness. The

Board-Mentor service was conceived in 1974 by the Association of Governing Boards (AGB) to provide assistance to colleges and universities troubled with their trustee effectiveness and to provide member boards with on-campus workshops to assess their organization and performance. This concept could well have application in the business world as an addition to the environmental scan function of advisory boards.

In September 1976 the first group of experienced and knowledgeable trustees and administrators, representing a broad range of higher education institutions across the United States, were invited to serve as Board-Mentors. They were then given an intensive orientation session conducted by the AGB with the assistance of the Institute for Educational Management of Harvard University and the Cheswick Center of Boston.

Field tests with these thirty-two Board-Mentors began in January 1977, and a second orientation session was launched for a new batch of volunteers. The cost of employing a Board-Mentor is nominal to the educational institution, and the service is available only to AGB member boards. The thrust of the advice is on trusteeship in the evolving societal context. In addition to offering filmstrips on topics ranging from the board's role in institutional strategic planning to fund raising, the basic role of the Board-Mentor is to serve as a catalyst to engage boards in discussions of matters of special concern. In this regard the technique and contribution of the Board-Mentor is to the proper role of the trustees, the most useful concepts, and the methodology of the stewardship process. Through this process, there is an awakening of the trustees to the realities of functioning in the future world of education.

In this respect the Board-Mentor concept features more functional advice than environmental scan-type advice. Both types of advice are needed when a company seeks to operate in a new business environment, or geographical locale. What is going on there that is different from other operations, and how best to function are equally valuable advisory inputs. Perhaps some business corporations could use a Board-Mentor for their subsidiary boards—even for their main boards perhaps. To mention the use of consultants for this advisory or counseling purpose is an obvious and valid suggestion.

Early Warning Systems

The Center for the Study of Social Policy at SRI, Inc., Menlo Park, California, recently set out to try to identify the problems that may become critical in the years ahead. Eight different problem search strategies or techniques were developed for bagging their elusive quarry. The work was conducted under a grant from the U.S. National Science Foundation and was specifically aimed at providing guidance for the president's science adviser. The results are relevant to our discussion of advisory boards, which are usually created for the parallel purpose of forecasting trends in the future as well as advising on current activities.

Of the eight different techniques used, some will be of interest to management long-range planners and advisory directors:

Problem lists: review of existing known problems.

Problem level analysis: compare alternative interpretations of problems at different societal levels.

Opinion surveys: a conventional technique.

Trend discontinuities: looking for trend breaks or gaps.

Missed opportunities: latent or stymied technological or social innovations for exploitation.

Cross-paradigm analysis: modeling and comparing societal conceptualization.

Alternative futures: an obvious task for advisers.

Science fiction: a controversial source of subjective anticipation, far-out and risky but playful.

The study identified more than a thousand problems found in the literature. After consideration, only twenty of these ended up on the final list of forty-one potential crises or future long-term problem areas that were judged to be representative of the more critical problems that society may face in the years ahead. Surprisingly, many of these national- and international-scale problems are not widely recognized as such at the present time.[9]

This search method for early warnings can be contrasted with other interesting forecasting techniques. The management science literature is replete with different approaches to the appropriate tools and conceptual framework for a useful business-related forcasting program.[10]

The generic categories hypothesized indicate the complexity of the subject. Psychologists would refer to this as the misery of choice surrounding selection of an appropriate method to use in devising forecasting or early warning function. Forecasting techniques were placed in the following esoteric if generic categories: single-variable extrapolation, theoretical limit envelope, dynamic models, mapping, multivariate interaction analysis, unstructured expert opinion, structured expert opinion, structured inexpert opinion, and unstructured inexpert speculation.

One of the most controversial approaches to forecasting theory is intriguing because of the great scientific debate underway about this mathematical concept intended to explain and predict events as disparate as chemical reactions, stock market crashes, dog bites, and the outbreak of war. The catastrophe theory is a concept that says that sudden events will occur and can be accurately forecast by plotting developments mathematically. Critics of the theory contend that it is mathematically unsound, that it has little or nothing to do with the real world, and that the predictions drawn from it are so vague and general as to be worthless. Eminent mathematicians have taken sides on the argument, with the tide turning in favor of the critics.[11]

One of the members of the scientific establishment identified with catastrophe theory is Russian-born Immanuel Velikovsky, a psychiatrist who first became well known with the publication in 1950 of *World in Collision*. In his eighties now, Velikovsky has endured furious storms of attack by the scientific community in attempts to discredit his theories, which have produced some answers to questions that established science could not come up with and some of whose predictions have come true even though scientists scoffed at them.

The theories contend that in the unpredictable world of nature, disorder and catastrophe are as much a part of the universe as are order and clockwork progression. These physical events, of course, have profound impact on human affairs and are of concern in dealing with the long-range future of civilization and its institutions.

One of the reasons Velikovsky draws so much fire—and ire—from other scientists is his method, which is quite different from the ordinary methods of empirical research. Starting with myth and literature and developing hypotheses from these areas, Velikousky applied the interpretation to natural phenomena. His approach is to speculate rather than experiment. As Lionel Rubinov, professor of philosophy at Trent University in Canada, observes: "The incredible thing is that when experimental data is finally produced, it tends to confirm his hypotheses."[12] Velikovsky's theories bridge such widely diverse disciplines as archaeology, astronomy, chemistry, genetics, geology, history, mythology, paleontology, and psychology.

Science writer Fred Warshofsky describes the approach: "From the memories stored in myth and legend, from the testimony of broken pillars and archaic calendars, from the records of bones and stones, Velikovsky concluded that the vision of a safe, orderly, unchanging universe, with planets and satellites moving with clockwork precision since the beginning of time, was wrong. And if the earth's path about the sun had been changed or interrupted, it was logical for Velikovsky to speculate on both the causes for the change and the effects they would have on the planets and on the creatures that lived upon them."[13]

The record of Velikovsky's predictions points up an unyielding, unremitting refusal of the scientific establishment to accord him even the slightest hint of legitimacy. Whether his theories have validity is not to be discussed here except to indicate that Velikovsky has a large part of the world's thinkers reexamining the techniques of forecasting. Advice to our international and national institutions can undoubtedly benefit by the furor and intellectual ferment. In a humble way, an advisory board can stimulate a corporation's long-range fixations or lack of reality by discussing long-term events, both physical and social. The best thing for the long-range future of corporations is to devote some energy and resources to sensing the world about them and the changes that may take place.

Like a good advisory director, Velikovsky is sticking to his opinions and judgments. His parting shot at his critics in the world's largest scientific organization, the American Association for Advancement of Science, at a recent meeting was: "None of my critics can erase the magnetosphere, nobody can stop the noises of Jupiter, nobody can cool off Venus, and nobody can change a single sentence in my books."

Notes

1. R. Jeffrey Smith, "Carter Reducing Plan Adds Pounds," *Science* 198 (December 2, 1977): 900.

2. J.M. Juran and J. Keith Louden, *The Corporate Director* (New York: American Management Associations), chap. 8. See also appendix F.

3. Robert Kirk Mueller, *New Directions for Directors: Behind the Bylaws* (Lexington: Lexington Books, D.C. Heath, 1977), pp. 42-45.

4. Bruce Alan Mann, *Preventing Directors' Liability under the Securities Laws* (New York: Practicing Law Institute, 1974).

5. John E. Martin, *"The Board Advisory Council and Peer Directors," Directors and Boards* 1 (Fall 1976): pg. 46.

6. Carolyne Smart and Ilan Vertinsky, "Designs for Crisis Decision Units," *Administrative Science Quarterly* 22 (December 1977): 640-647.

7. James E. Post and Marc J. Epstein, "Information System for Social Reporting," *Academy of Management Review* 2 (January 1977): 81-87.

8. Roger M. Kenny, "Helpful Guidance from International Advisory Boards," *Harvard Business Review* (March-April 1976): 14-19, 156.

9. Peter Schwartz, Peter J. Teige, and Willis W. Harman, "In Search of Tomorrow's Crisis," *Futurist* 11 (October 1977): 264-278.

10. Don Lobell and J. Krasner, "Selecting Environmental Forecasting Techniques from Business Planning Requirements," *Academy of Management Review* (July 1977): 374-383. This review suggests ways of applying these management science concepts to a business organization.

11. See *New York Times*, November 19, 1977.

12. Fred Warashofsky, *Doomsday: The Science of Catastrophe* (New York: Reader's Digest Press, 1977).

13. Ibid., p. 41.

13 Corporate Governance

The surest way of governing, both in a private family and a kingdom, is, for the husband and the prince sometimes to drop their prerogatives.
—Thomas Hughes (English author)

Corporate anomy by a few unprincipled businessmen has brought down upon the corporate world a cloud of suspicion about many aspects of company and executive conduct. Corporate prerogatives are being challenged. Privilege does not include the running of a business in such a way that sanctions of the society that is served are taken for granted or that they are something abstract that will be taken care of by someone else.

Linkages

The chief executive officer and the board of directors cannot function in a privileged or private social vacuum. Governing a corporation in a competitive, complex environment requires linkage to other sectors of society and a respect for the impact that company affairs have on the world around it. This goes far beyond the economic interests of the owners and employees. It embraces consumers, suppliers, competitors, and communities at all levels and faces an increasing number of constraints in the form of laws, regulations, customs, traditions, beliefs, rules of conduct, taxes, public opinion, changing value systems, and activities of special interest groups. Phrasemakers like to refer to some of these constraints as the "rule of law:" respect for important social and political obligations that are crystallized in the statute books.

A recent proposal provides a formal, structured response to social demands and the interest of individual shareowners by creation of a corporate governance officer. This CGO position separates the governance role from management by placing it instead at the highest point in the corporate board.[1]

Linkages of a corporation, a board of directors, and/or the key principals involved may take various forms. The most commonly recognized ones are legal, technical, commercial and political. There are also more subtle and less recognized linkages, which can be classed as psychological, cultural, social, familial, religious, and ethnic.

One organizational dynamics term for some of these linkages is *permissive coalition*. This means an optional union form of organizing relationships between domains—for example, the corporation and the educational institutions. The

161

purpose of such permissive coalition can be a loose alliance for achieving joint action. In the example of a corporation teaming up with a university, it may be to solve an urban problem or to develop a city plan. In 1977, Massachusetts Mutual Life Insurance Company developed a loose alliance with the University of Michigan Graduate School of Business Administration to create a one-week course on business management to help train the company's general agents to cope with the increasing size and complexity of running an insurance agency.

The structure of a permissive coalition type of linkage is usually fragile, mobile, and frequently temporary. It is remindful of a common-law marriage, without civil or organizational ceremony or sanction.

Certain processes are used in making organizational linkages. At least five are in common use in the business world today.

Osmotic Linkage

This is the type of subtle linkage with members of one organization permeating the boundaries of another organization by virtue of some special attributes. The very nature of an active outside director on a board, who is gainfully occupied in his profession or business, provides a link penetrating the parameters of the two organizations involved. The analogy is from physics or physical chemistry in which diffusion takes place through a semipermeable membrane typically separating a solvent and a solution that tends to equalize their concentrations.

The osmotic action in the organizational world is illustrated by the corporate employee who is a professional lawyer serving on a police board of a city or town by virtue of his legal training, maturity, interest, and experience in society and human affairs. Conflicts of interest must be managed carefully. The obligation of Swiss citizens to serve in the military on a regular basis forms a strong bond between business organizations who employ citizens and support their leaves of military absence in the interests of national defense. Penetration by civilians through the military establishment boundaries is required by law. This forms the osmotic pressure to force a vital military-industrial linkage.

Implant Linkage

This form of linkage is the basis for many successful marketing programs by companies providing technical services on site in a customer's plant where the vendors' products, equipment, or machinery are used on a purchase or leased basis. Successful plywood adhesive manufacturers provide the customer plants using their adhesives with constant resident technical advisers in the plywood manufacturing plants. Computer and office equipment manufacturers rely on competitive advantages by providing constant field service help. The implant of a technical service engineer in a large customer plant affords a mutually beneficial commercial linkage. The whole concept of diplomatic representation with consulates and embassies in a foreign country is a political linkage of inestimable value in global political relationships between nations.

The controversial practice of having investment bankers on a board of a company has been examined critically as to its propriety as an implant with insider aspects and conflicts of interest.

Genetic Linkage

The analogy of biochemical "heredity condons" that determine the specific sequences or antecedents between forms of life is best illustrated in an organizational context by the following examples.

Some professional service firms make it a policy, or do not discourage the practice, of performing a training-school function for professionals who leave the service firm to work in client organizations. Patent and law firms, accounting firms, public relations firms, management consulting firms, and trade associations are prime examples. A member of such an organization may be weaned away to work for a client or customer, who becomes impressed with an individual professional's potential, and proselytes him, with or without due notice to the professional firm. The alumni relationship forms something akin to a genetic linkage. While an arms-length one, it is still often in the best interest of the supplying source to have a friend in the customer's tent. While this practice can backfire, it still is a common genetic-type of linkage.

The old-boy school network, which pervades industry, government, military, politics, education, and many other domains, is another obvious genetic linkage. The Ecole Polytechnique network in government and industry, the Oxford-Cambridge heritage in the United Kingdom, and the Stanford and Harvard business schools' alumni networks can also be considered genetic linkages between organization.

The nepot on the board is a subject of many novels, plays, and journalistic articles as to the influence of the genetic influence of a family director on a public company board.

Lightning Rod Linkage

These linkages are often short-circuit mechanisms vertically placed in an organization. Creation of the ombudsman role in government, the consumer relations vice-president in a company, and the direct complaint letter "to the president" device in hotel and transportation company practice are examples of attempts to provide a linkage between levels of activity in an organization—specifically top administration and the person served. Special sales persons assigned to large accounts perform this lightning rod function in large business organizations. President Carter's experiment with an open White House switchboard to handle calls from individual citizens was a highly publicized use of this technique in an attempt to siphon off questions from the public at the citizen level right to the highest office in the land. In this case the White House lightning rod was designed for political effect.

The controversial practice of providing constituency directors on boards to represent minorities, special interest groups, or labor representatives are other examples of such lightning rod linkages.

Sub-rosa or Moonlighting Linkage

This type of permissive coalition or linkage is becoming more common. Necessarily there is nothing illegal about a sub-rosa arrangement. In ancient times a rose hanging over a council table indicated that all present were sworn to secrecy. The origin of this practice is wrapped in obscurity, but the story is that Cupid gave Harpocrates (the god of silence) a rose to bribe him not to betray the amours of Venus. Hence, the flower became the emblem of silence and was sculptured on the ceilings of banquet rooms to remind the guests that what was spoken *sub vino* was not to be uttered *sub divo.*

Organizational sub-rosa linkages of this type can usually be imagined by reading the roster of the Links Club or Chemists Club in New York, the Eccentric Club in London, and the Club l'Ommegang at the Gran Place in Brussels. Membership in these social type of clubs affords an easy linkage between persons in different organizations under club auspices. Country clubs at Augusta, Sunningdale, Forest Hills, and the like are obvious centers of sub-rosa linkages, other than golf or cuff links. These interstitial type of organizations provide a cement between other organizations in business, government, and education that are of great value in developing an understanding and rapport.

Moonlighting linkages occur in many ways. Professional persons, managers, and homemakers who moonlight as teachers, professors, consultants, counsellors, and volunteers of all sorts provide an important bridging linkage between organizations, corporations, associations, homes, and other centers of activity.

Linkages thus provide mechanisms for organizations coping with the world around them. Changes in the environment in which an organization functions are more easily detected if the organizational linkages are in place and are recognized. When an organization gets into a hostile environment and cannot cope with it, it dies. Private enterprise examples abound with the failure rate of companies that cannot compete successfully and go bankrupt. There must be some form of exchange between an organization and its environment to accommodate the adaptation necessary for an organization to survive.

Organizations do adapt and cope when their linkages signal the necessity for this. Eskimos build igloos to survive; political organizations often co-opt another organization and the alliance survives. The organization can influence its environment. Boston, for example, identified its adult entertainment district to sequester certain entertainment, services, and products from the rest of the city.

The environment created in such zoned areas influences the type of enterprises that will flourish there, no matter how controversial their activites may be.[2]

Levels of Concern

Corporate governance has a generally accepted hierarchy, which goes like this in relation to the levels of concern in corporate governance matters:

1. Philosophy and ideology.
2. Concepts and principles.
3. Nature and character.
4. Functions and duties.

These four levels form a relevance tree in the interdisciplinary system that is utilized to govern a modern corporation. This relevance tree can be more specifically described in the corporation context as follows.

Purposeful Level. This level of concern is philosophical and ideological. It deals with teleological aspects or the study of evidence of design, meaning, purpose, and destiny of the corporate organization with its doctrines. The very nature and relations of existence or being of a corporate organization relate to its ontology and all of such existential and metaphysical questions that surround the nature and kinds of existence. At this lofty level, values and value systems, behavioral norms, aspirations, and goals come into play. Too often boards of directors neglect thinking about the purposeful level of concern about the institutions they serve. This is a difficult and abstract overlay on the relevance tree of corporate concerns, which are intrinsic with enlightened corporate governance. There are outstanding examples of board of directors that are tackling these philosophical questions in the form of ethics, corporate conduct, environmental concern, political and social responsibilities, committees, and reports. Citicorp's effort in 1977 to institutionalize ethical conduct into its mode of operations has been eloquently expressed by Walter Wriston, its chairman and CEO, in several public forums.

Normative level. Concepts and principles constitute the normative level on the relevance tree, which concerns the framework of morality, canons, or principles that constitute what should be done from a conceptual target basis. It includes standards, norms, traditions, beliefs, organized systems, strategies, and plans. It deals with the concepts and directions of a corporation once the purpose and raison d'être are clear in the minds of the directors. It represents the executive level of the relevance tree.

Pragmatic level. This level of the relevance tree gets down to the practical interconnections, character, and control of the corporation, its organizational elements, divisions, hierarchies, and the very nature and character of operations.

In another context, it concerns tactical implementation rather than philosophical or strategic pondering about corporate governance. This level exhibits style of practice and relates to matters of fact, often to the exclusions of intellectual or moral matters. It concerns the problem-solving mentality and consists of the product of science and the effort of production, distribution, or service as distinct from dealing with social morality, environmental responsibility, egalitarianism, or other concerns that are higher on the relevance tree.

Empirical level. This is the functional level and deals with specific duties in the matter of corporate governance. As the lowest level on the relevance tree, the subject matter deals with matters that are experienced or are based on observation alone. Little regard is given to the system or the loftier levels of concern involved in corporate governance. Duties and functions are spelled out. Bureaucratic procedures prescribe all activity, and little thought is required to perform. Certainly little thought regarding the nature and requirements of organizational relations, corporate governance, or institutional purpose is involved—even acknowledged—at the empirical level.

The linkages between levels on the relevance tree are based on philosophy and principles adopted by the board of directors. These are manifest in the bylaws, statements of policy, and codes of behavior. The organizational and business concepts employed, as well as the character, identification, and style of governance, are all linked together in a scalar relationship of the four levels of concern on the relevance tree of corporate governance. These levels overlap and get misplaced hierarchically in the real world. For analysis, it is helpful to envision them in an orderly progression as shown in figure 13-1.

Zones of Corporate Governance

These zones are jurisdictional echelons within a corporate structure. The conventional corporate organization consists of three separate zones: the trustee-steward-director, the executive management, and the operating management zone. Not all organizations are content with this three-tiered conventional structure because it limits the number of positions and titles that can be assigned. Like the trend in the military and government, some license is often taken with organizational structure to serve personal or political purposes.

In the late seventeenth century, Prince Frederick William succeeded to the head of the Mecklenburg duchy, The principality of Hohenzollern-Sigmaringen, a six-square mile, 20,000-inhabitant, sovereign territory, one of about three hundred independent entities in that crazy quilt that formed Germany's map after the Thirty Years' War. The prince decided after much thought to define everyone's place in the hierarchy of his subjects. Their status would be fixed, and only the ducal power could move them up or down from this position. He declared a long list of precedences with no fewer than twenty-four degrees of rank. They started with the president of the Privy Council, who was followed

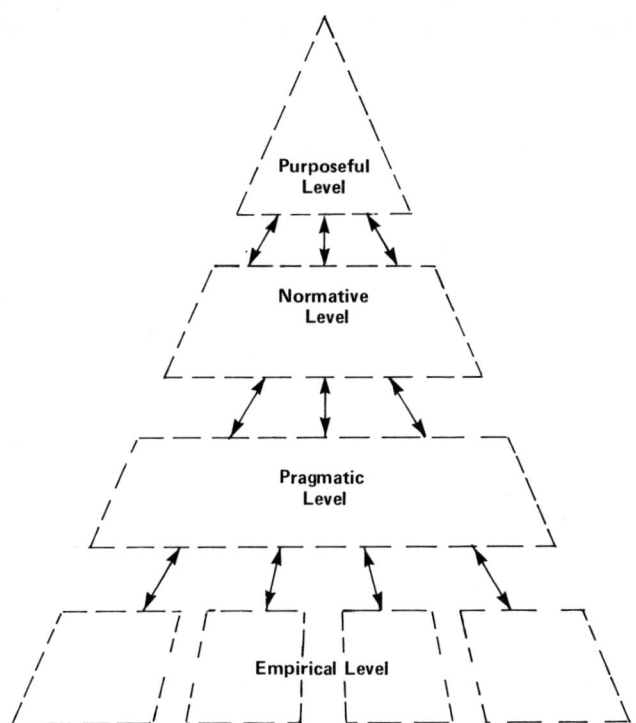

Figure 13-1. Corporate Governance Relevance Tree

by the field marshall, the Privy counselors, and district (or provincial) counselors. The latter were ranked by seniority, and the long list ended up with the coachmen and wood carriers. (Interestingly, in this seventeenth-century hierarchy, university professors ranked with the head butler, the bailiffs, and the aldermen of the city of Rostok.)[3]

Our twentieth-century simplistic three-tiered zones of governance are these:

Trustee-steward-director zone. This is the directorate level where the principals act as trustees and fiduciaries on behalf of the owners of the enterprise. Legally constituted, the board of directors is concerned with the overview and standards of conduct applicable to individual directors. The duty of loyalty, duty of care, duty to manage, duty to object, areas of special concern, rights, liabilities and indemnification, and fundamental responsibilities at this level are legally defined in many instances. The body of law, regulation, public expectation, and sentiment about the activity at this zone of corporate governance are growing.

Executive management zone. This zone is the active management level of the CEO and his top staff who carry out the activities of the corporation under the general oversight of the directors. Organizational schemes for best carrying out the affairs of a corporation vary considerably, but it is clear that this executive zone should be recognized as a separate force field in corporate governance, if accountability is not diffused or confused. Responsible charge of strategic activity is the maxim that goes with this zone.

Operating management zone. This is the tactical area of carrying out affairs after the strategic objectives and directions have been set by the previous two zones of governance. The separation between the operations and executive zones is normally clear and violated only in crisis management situations or when the executive management fails to delegate appropriately.

These three zones form an iconic-type pictorial representation of the interdisciplinary, multitiered system of corporate governance in its simplistic conventional image. (See figure 13-2.)

The linkage between zones is based on law, bylaws, charter, policy, and procedures. The classical management processes of organizing, planning, measuring, controlling, and feedback interconnect as well as separate the respective zones.

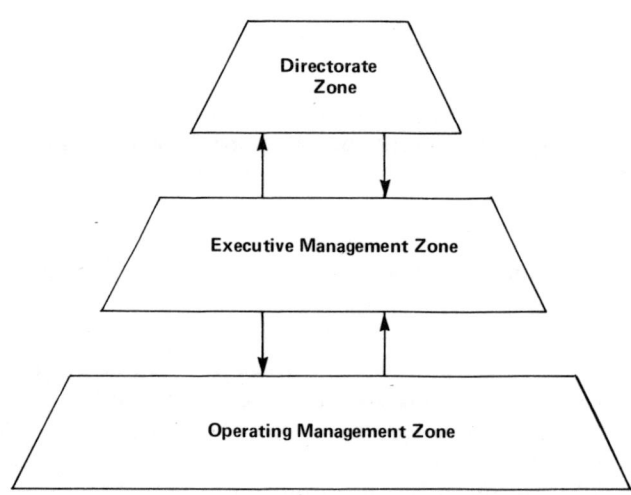

Figure 13-2. Corporate Zones of Governance

Corporate Governance as a System

> The classical theory of organization, dealing almost exclusively with the anatomy of formal organization, revolves around four pivotal concepts: The division of labor, scalar and functional processes, formal structure, and control span. Useful as these concepts are, they are of limited value for they ignore the interplay of personalities, informal groupings, interorganizational conflict, and the ever present decision-making processes.[4]

Modern organizational theory has been termed system theory. Systemic components are the interdependency of parts, linkage processes, organizational goals, environmental ambiance, formal and informal organization, role theory, equilibrium and steady state cybernetics, decision-making processes, and diverse objectives. One way to view the situation is to consider that any corporate organization is an instrument for attaining known goals. The aspect that we are concerned with on behalf of the board and management is their corporate governance system in such a context.

The three architectural zones of this type of construct are the director-trustee-steward zone (the board), the executive zone, and the operations zone.

Another dimension of the conceptual framework is the nature of the institution's business: the business sector in which the board of directors chooses to function. This relates to corporate objectives and purpose. Determining and revising these objectives and directions is a prime consideration for the board of directors in assessing the risks that the corporation will take.

Systems View

From a systems viewpoint, corporate governance is an orderly arrangement of interdependent activities, related policies, and procedures that implement the various activities. Constraints on the system are either external or internal. The external ones are obvious—the societal response concerning expected welfare of the communities in which the corporation operates and the welfare of its customers and owners. Shaping these external constraints are the industry norms and accepted practices by which a company functions. A paradigm for this external environment is the private enterprise system in which the company operates competitively on an economic basis for survival and growth against competition. The internal constraints are also obvious. Essentially they are the policies, practices, precedents, style, and values established by the board and the management.

System Philosophy. The system's perspective also concerns the corporate frame of mind or philosophy around corporate governance. This has certain aspects. There is the hardware view of the enterprise concerning plant installations, capital requirements, types of equipment, locations of plants, and similar needs. There is the process view of the company in which a corporation's activities are considered as a going concern. Certain dynamic processes cause changes and produce conflicts to be resolved. In management context, the general system's philosophy deals with the four basic concepts of boundary, tension, equilibrium, and feedback. These four concepts have normal components of organization, interaction, interdependence, and integration of parts. The systems approach concerns itself with growth and stability in the system under a range of possible futures, unpredictable perturbations, and alternative policies.

Another pertinent philosophical notion is the open versus closed system viewpoint. An open corporate governance system would establish regular contact with the environment, and closed system would have little commerce across the corporate borders. Corporations are being required to open their governance system to recognize contact and responsibility with the environment in all respects. Communications and free flow of intersectorial activity take place when borders are open and interfaces are fluid. Corporations are no longer allowed to isolate themselves from society's interests and activities.

Corporate Subsystems

Corporate governance as an overall system has certain recognizable subsystems, sub-subsystems, and so on. A key organizational issue in each of these subsystems is the uncertainty inherent in it and its control. The arrangements of the subsystems are sometimes investigated as hierarchies; but because the arrangement often involves a nesting in the manner of Chinese boxes, with systems within each other, they may also be defined by recursion. One of the interesting discoveries made by the systems approach is the extent to which attempts to improve the performance of a subsystem by its own criteria (suboptimization) may act to the detriment of the total system, and even to the defeat of its objectives.

I have witnessed a board of directors' imposing a management information system on the corporation that was so sophisticated and beyond the capability and needs of the operating management that the entire governance system was jeopardized. Enamored boards with a desire to computerize their company have often overloaded the management with costly hardware and administrative costs.

The corporate governance system may be viewed to include the following key subsystems. The governance system can be compared to a trunk in the attic filled with picture frames of various sizes. Each one of the frames has a separate boundary, which overlaps the others in a jumbled fashion. The entire collection of frames is contained within the boundaries of the trunk. The subsystems in corporate governance are as follows:

1. *Command and control systems.* Structure and related authority, responsibility, and power delegation; management information; two-way communications and public relations; financial, accounting, and taxation; operational; procurement and inventory control; quality control and quality assurance; environmental assurance; and corporate conduct norms and ethical principles.
2. *Operations systems.* Production, marketing, sales and advertising, distribution, and personnel.
3. *Planning systems.* Strategic, organizational, financial, operational, resource, and forecasting.
4. *Resource utilization, development, and design.* Organizational and human services, management development and succession, motivation and incentives, logistics, research and development, and engineering.
5. *External relations.* With public relations, legal, organized labor, shareowners, financial community, and the customer-clients.

Systemic Issues

Installation or improvement of any one of the subsystems into the overall governance system has circumambient implications. The following ten issues are organizational implications that immediately come to mind.

1. *Organizational processes.* This concerns the control of organizational processes and the relations of any one of the subsystems to other management control systems. It impinges on organization structure and such matters as the functions of the corporate staff groups versus line groups, the multiple rules required, and whether line or staff management participate or take the primary initiative.

2. *Authority-responsibility system.* This concerns power and status in the hierarchy of any subsystem. For example, certain board powers are created by statute, charter, law, and public opinion. Specific board powers are reserved to stockholders; others are conferred on the board. In turn, the board reserves certain powers for itself, which are handled by the board's agent (chairman). Other powers are delegated to committees (such as an environmental audit committee). Specific powers conferred by law to the board may also be delegated (by the board) to the management through the CEO office. The CEO in turn reserves certain powers of authority for himself and delegates others to corporate officers. A matrix of subsystem powers should relate to this authority system of the corporation (both official and real).

3. *Geographical concentration of manufacturing plants.* This issue deals with the critical size necessary for the economic operation of manufacturing plants; geographical location with respect to service to the market; availability of materials, supplies, and labor; delivery, storage, and distribution systems; optimal process unit size with respect to risk of technological obsolescence;

political environment in communities; economic costs of manufacture in different locales; plant site risk exposure as to earthquake, explosion, fire, toxic, or other hazardous operations at the facility. The potential loss of life or investment, potential injuries, damage, or work stoppage are other considerations.

5. *Resource allocation.* Given a portfolio concept on corporate objectives with respect to hazardous activities, the following are significant considerations: allocation of capital, maintenance, effort, process control, and monitoring and management of human resources (in order to ensure environmental compliance and competent hazard management). Economic rationing or allocation of resources for environmental purposes becomes a trade-off versus other operational needs for such resources.

6. *Risk tolerance.* Beyond legal requirements, this is a matter of corporate philosophy as manifest in policy concerning the rationing of risk management costs versus benefits derived. The very nature of certain businesses is such that certain risk tolerance must be acknowledged by the board and the management. This means how much damage, injury, or loss of life, property, or income will be risked in the pursuit of a corporate strategic course. These rationing and trade-off decisions are matters for explicit consideration by the board and top management. The conflict essentially deals with the degree of uncertainty and its control.

Just where a corporation chooses to operate on the uncertainty continuum is a board policy question. The uncertainty continuum can run from areas of operation in which the consequences are certain, there is a probalistic risk, there is uncertainty, or there is ignorance of the risks involved.

Ignorance, in turn, normally divides into two dimensions. One area is where ignorance exists because of unknown factors after investigation or adequate attention. To get more abstract, there is also the area of unknown unknowns "unk unks," i.e., those unknowns that are not even suspected. This, of course, is an area calling for expert business risk or hazard assessment and an unrelenting professional effort at vigilance in regard to development progress and environmental hazard potentials.

7. *Decision process.* This concerns corporate policy for delegating certain authority for action and degrees of delegation thereof. These degrees can be granting independent authority, authority after notice to or advice from others, authority after approval by others, jointly shared authority, or no authority. Degrees of responsibility and authority that are integral with the normal anatomy of the authority responsibility system are a key part of any subsystem. (See chapter 9 for more explicit treatment of this delegation gradient.)

8. *Independent, disinterested audits and assessment.* This raises the question for need of an objective qualified outside disinterested-unaffiliated check (in the SEC definition sense) on the corporate governance system and the various subsystems. Normally, this is a board of directors' decision area to decide when or if an external, professionally recognized, third-party check

on the management performances and competence and the management's internal checking system is appropriate. The extent of any independent audit and/or assessment depends upon the nature of the company's business, a situational analysis of the corporation, and the public, regulatory, and legal framework.

Many companies have the problem of catch-up with the extent of the independent need for such audits, and perspective may be increased during the immediate future until the overall corporate governance system and the condition of the corporation are more at equilibrium with external and internal system requirements and normative objectives. A problem exists in the fact that systemic requirements are dynamic and usually have not reached a plateau.

9. *Social and psychological aspects of the organization.* This concerns organizational climate, management leadership, peer leadership, and process. A subordinate dimension of corporate governance, this envelope of aspects includes such abstract considerations as ideology, culture, values, biases, beliefs, ethics, probity (uprightness, honesty, principles, and ideals), and rectitude (moral integrity or quality of being correct in judgment or procedure). This value-laden overlay is established or tacitly accepted, explicitly or implicitly, by the board and top management. It involves respective attitudes, sense of social responsibility, degree of understanding, and tolerance of individual directors and top managers.

Comprehension of an open systems concepts for a corporation, with its board and management's relationship (linkages or interface) with the environment, deals with the very character of the corporation. This issue involves the education of the board, the management, and employees on the doctrines that underlie a comprehensive set of subsystems involved in corporate governance. Continued vigilance, as well as the ability and willingness to change to correct the present situation and cope with requirements in the future is needed.

10. *Types of control strategies.* Centralization and formalization are key issues. Whether an organization retains its present structural type or provides for separate containments in satellite subsidiaries, a holding company, or associated company pattern are determining to a control strategy. The three conventional dimensions of structure are complexity, formalization, and centralization. The factor of administrative intensity, might be added.

Complexity refers to the extent of differentiation within a given system (horizontal, vertical, spatial, or personal in nature). A number of hierarchical levels, number of functions, departments, jobs, number of operating sites, and degrees of personal expertise can be involved.

Formalization is the degree to which rules and procedures within a corporate system are specified and/or are adherred to as a strategy of control. It encompasses both the existence of rules on procedures (whether or not they are codified) and the degree of variation allowed therein.

A third dimension, centralization, can be defined as the locus of formal control or power within a system. It includes such factors as locus of decision-making authority, hierarchy of authority levels, autonomy, and participative decision making. Positioning of support or professional functional talent in the organizational structure is involved.

Administrative intensity is referred to as a supportive or administrative component. There is an optional measure of number of administrative personnel within a system. It can be expressed as a ratio of administrative personnel (indirect labor) to total production personnel (direct labor) or as a simple head count of administrative personnel. Other arbitrary criteria are often used in defining administrative intensity.

Note that there is a growing contemporary interest in technology as a determinant of organization structure. A linear relationship has been determined in certain industries between technical complexity and various measures of administrative intensity in vertical differentiation. A curvilinear relationship exists to elements such as span of control of first-line supervisors. Firms operating at the high range of technological complexity (for example, continuous processes as in a chemical plant) have an organic type of management system and structures, whereas those in the center range of technical complexity tend to be more fixed and mechanistic in structure.[5]

There are some relationships between success and appropriateness of an organization structure for a particular operations type of technology. This has been called the organizational technological imperative. However, this is a controversial thesis, with other research questioning technology's importance to structure. The size of a company has been demonstrated to have a much closer relationship to aspects of organizational structure than does the technological imperative.

The Scarabaeus Structure

Looking at the total governance system with its component subsystems is an organic view. Another way to perceive it is in a morphological context as in the following. The four levels in the relevance tree and the three zones of management in corporate governance overlay each other in the system sense and form an iconic diagram as shown in figure 13-3.[6] The diagram is shaped like the conventional representation of a stout-bodied beetle with its three separate armoured platelets (from the apex downward) of increasing size superimposed on the classical organizational pyramid.

The scarabaeus diagram graphically shapes the system aspects of corporate governance, together with the organizational aspects.[7] The top purposeful and normative levels relate to the director province and concerns of the corporation. The second largest plate of functions are the function-oriented components of the CEO and corporate staff units. The third and largest portion of the "sacred beetle" is analogous to the service (or product) profit centers of the enterprise.

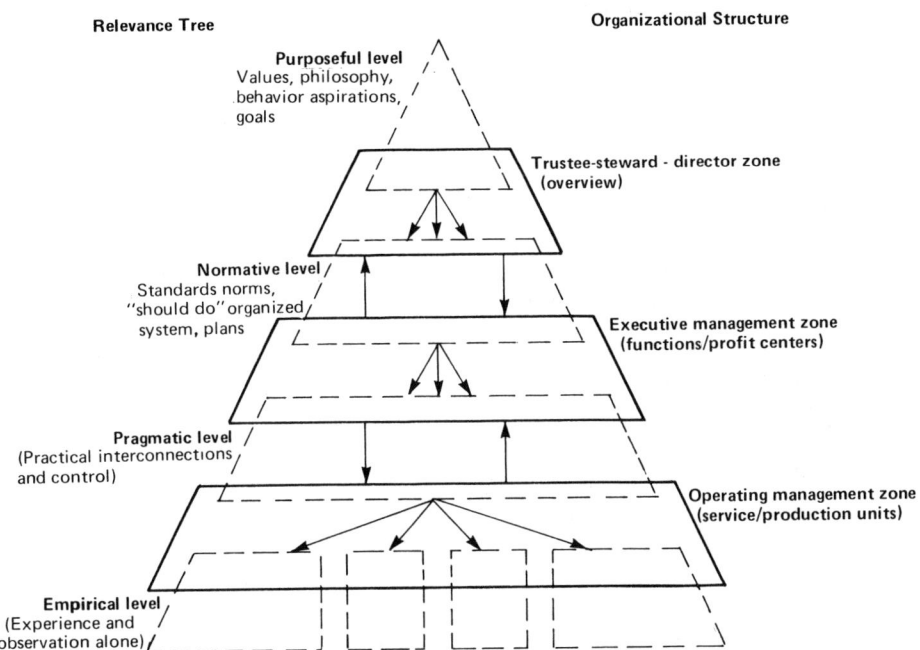

ICONIC DIAGRAM: Interdisciplinary System

Figure 13-3. Iconic Diagram: Interdisciplinary System

The ancient Egyptians regarded a scarabaeus as symbolic of resurrection and immortality, and the symbol was worn as an amulet to placate a god. The mythology connected with this symbol sets an ancient stage. It symbolizes the threads of concern that hold the modern system of governance together against the internal stress and external wear and tear on the fabric of our institutions that are under attack from many quarters. Some hope can be secured from the beliefs of the ancients as to the scarab symbol of corporate governance, if its immortality and fertility have any modern resurrection for our current boardrooms.

Adopted as the soul of man and reproduced in countless forms as a symbol of immortal life, the ancient scarab is an appropriate talisman for the modern "immortal" corporate institution. To carry along the allegorical play one more step, the scared scarab god, Khepri, was worshipped by the people in Buot, who considered the sacred sacrab also the god of transformation. This attribute is a fitting one for our modern corporate form. It was established initially for the purpose of generating goods and services and then evolved into a useful source of both social and economic growth and development for the benefit of man and society.

The forcefulness of the scarab allegory as a symbol of normative corporate governance can swing all the way from the talisman of self-generating life force imputed to a dung beetle to another of the Scarabaeidae family of stout-bodied beetles. The other is the water beetle with its unique philosophy of keeping going in spite of the aggravation it causes the human race. Thus an impertinent question before the boardroom might be somewhat inelegantly posed in this way: Are we governing as dung beetles or as water beetles? The insecticidal answer might be:

> The water beetle here shall teach
> A lesson far beyond your reach.
> She aggravates the human race
> By gliding on the water's face
> Assigning each to each its place.
> But if she ever stopped to think
> Of how she did it, she would sink.

Moral: Don't ask questions.[8]

Notes

1. C. William Verity, "New Job at the Top: Chief Governance Officer," *Financier* 2 (November 1978): 18-21.

2. For a good treatment of this subject, see Harold J. Leavitt, William R. Dill, and Henry B. Eyring, *The Organizational World* (New York: Harcourt Brace Jovanovich, 1973), esp. chap. 20.

3. Paul Tabori, *The Art of Folly* (New York: Chilton, 1961), p. 509.

4. Peter P. Schoderbek, *Management Systems* (New York: John Wiley, 1967), p. 4.

5. Jeffrey D. Ford and John W. Slocum, Jr., "Size, Technology, Environment and the Structure of Organizations," *Academy of Management Review* (October 1977): 561-575.

6. This model is an adaptation of the transdisciplinary university structure diagram discussed in Erich Jantsch, *Technological Planning and Social Futures* (London: Cassell/Associated Business Programmes, 1972), pp. 221, 237.

7. I am indebted to Derek Medford, director of the University of South Pacific's Centre for Applied Studies in Development, for pointing out the nature of the scarabaeous iconic design, with its pleasing shape and commonsensual relation to Jantsch's relevance trees (in ibid.).

8. From Willard R. Espy, *An Almanac of Words at Play* (New York: Clarkson Potter, 1975), p. 162. Reprinted with permission.

14 The Hidden Agenda

"Some boards look with disfavour on a full agenda on the grounds that the nature of the business to be discussed may be revealed to persons other than those who are permitted to attend the meeting. In such circumstances, important matters are introduced under the heading of 'other business.' Cases have not been unknown where managing directors favour an agenda of such insular proportions!"[1]

This quote serves as a reminder that boardroom agenda are often structured to avoid certain issues which could have a severe impact on a company. Sometimes such issues are skirted because of unwarranted optimism, unwillingness to face reality, unawareness or unpreparedness of the chief executive officer or the secretary, chairman, or legal counsel who may influence preparation of the agenda. To be complete about the realities of agenda drafting practice, perhaps one should also include situations which involve misconduct, nonfeasance, fraud or guile, or maybe just insecurity on the part of the chairman or chief executive officer.

Illiberal boardroom agenda can be either willful or naive. Advance docketing of agenda topics such as a stock split, acquisition, divestiture, merger, or reorganization could cause serious problems. Such topics are the unmentionables referred to in the foregoing quotation where insularity is favored. Legal, regulatory, and parliamentary procedures are available to cope with most willful omissions or obfuscations of a director's meeting agenda. But these items are often not easily identifiable to an outside director who is exposed only, say, four times a year to the workings of a company.

The artless agenda detached from the realities of the institution's problems and opportunities is a serious kind of insularity.

One way of looking at such insularity is to see the board agenda as a sort of "bill of fare" set forth on the company table as a menu for corporate existence. Survival, growth, and development of a corporation occur in a nonlinear series of stages. These range from progression to retrogression in an ambiance where the outcome is either certain, risky, or uncertain. The respective boardroom agenda should constitute a record of such corporate existence.

Beyond the certain-to-uncertain situations in which a corporation seeks a succession of stable states of growth, there are Gordian knots further along the certainty-uncertainty chain. Some may concern states of ignorance—for example, ignorance of the future, of existing circumstances and dilemmas, or of the unknown forces at work. All is not lost, however. As a sign in a Boston bar indicates, "One thing about ignorance, it can get you into some interesting arguments." Besides, there are also those unknowns that are not even suspected. Space experts have a buzzword for these: "Unk-unks," or unknown-unknowns. There is no way of putting them on the agenda.

The potential range and scope of agenda items are broad to be sure. As Thomas Mann once opined, "The actual enemy is the unknown." It is therefore the purpose of this discussion to suggest some current topics of concern, both known and unknown, to responsible but perhaps uninformed directors. These days it is easy to find oneself in unfamiliar director-trustee territory. The future will undoubtedly see many a director saddled with sophisticated stewardship situations without being completely at ease in regard to his or her director's obligations and exposures. Before addressing these latent issues for the board-room let's take a brief look at the estate of the directorate.

The Three Domains

During World War I, Lord John Fletcher Moulton, a high official in the British Munitions Ministry, articulated the "three great domains of human action."[2] First is the domain of "Positive Law," where law in all its various forms properly binds and constrains us. Second is the domain of "Free Choice" or "Absolute Freedom," where citizens can properly claim complete freedom of personal action.

Third is the domain of "Manners" or "Obedience to the Unenforceable." According to Moulton, this is the sphere where we do what we should do, though not obliged to do so by any law. It is an area where neither law nor free choice controls. Moulton believed that a nation's greatness, its civilization, rests in the extent of this third domain.

Many boards of directors are content to confine their activities, if possible, to the first domain of positive law. The free choice domain requires some individual director initiative—a rare trait these days with the liabilities and complexities involved in being an effective director.

The third and normative domain of Moulton's "obedience to the unenforceable" implies, first, that there exists an initiative in a boardroom context; and, second, that the chairman, the secretary of the board, the chief executive officer, the directors (both independent outsiders and executive insiders) obey their instincts in surfacing the core issues before the meeting, if such issues can be identified.

The problem comes, of course, in the obedience to intuitive and responsible concerns for board effectiveness when others do not share such concerns or have such instincts. The trade-offs involved risk the rupture of relationships with the chairman, other independent directors, or the chief executive—particularly if none of these persons shares the same apprehension or concern over board matters that are not on the agenda because of positive law or even free choice of the agenda maker.

Agenda Species

Former President Dwight D. Eisenhower at a Radio and TV Broadcasters Annual Dinner observed that "only two kinds of problems reach my desk. Those marked *urgent*, and those marked *important*. I spend so much time on the urgent, I never get to the important."

Things-to-be-done at a board meeting include certain stereotyped matters required by statute or bylaw, such as exercise or delegation of powers, reports on performance, declaration of dividends, alterations in capital structure, major organizational changes, and strategic directions or policies affecting the company. An understandable tendency is to minimize discussions of problems or threats unless the operating management is in a position to deal with them. Explicit use of the directors as a resource to management for exploring, solving, or coping with major problems is a relatively undeveloped role and a delicate process.

Needless to say, there are outstanding examples of companies where the board is involved in problem solving and where the solution is one which trespasses on the board's domain and becomes a board problem. For many companies, however, the management-board role relationship is so undefined or such a remote linkage exists that an agenda of seminal issues may remain hidden because of (a) lack of interest or inquisitiveness of directors, or (b) failure, inability, or neglect of the management or the chairman to recognize and surface the problem issues.

Construction, control, and issuance of board meeting agenda are as powerful a tool for corporate management as design and implementation of a management information system are to the executive level of an organization. Control of the matters that are either passed up the organization or called for from the topside can either make or break a company's performance in the long run. Control is the essence of good governance provided that plans, criteria, goals, and objectives are clear.

The art of agenda preparation is to preserve balance, perspective, and order amidst change, yet preserve change amidst order. Given the opportunity to set up an agenda constructively, it is helpful to recognize that there are at least four species of agenda.

The "trite-rite" agenda. Stereotyped patterns are required by law and bylaw for shareowners' meetings and some board meetings. These can be liturgy-like drills, easily executed to use up the available time so that, like

Ike, the meeting never gets into the important issues. One time-worn rite is use of a technique called "clarification." This means filling in the background with so much detail that the foreground goes underground.

One difference between agenda for shareowners' meetings and agenda for directors' meetings is the legal requirement that no substantive matters, if known in advance, can be brought up at the shareowners' meeting unless put on the agenda in advance. There is always the option, of course, of bringing up "new matters." Proxy votes cannot be properly submitted unless the agenda so indicates. While directors' meetings have certain legal constraints by the so-called positive law domain, the free choice option is usually available.

The legal framework surrounding a director's meeting agenda is a mix of laws and conventions. Most state statutes leave it up to the individual corporation's charter or bylaws as to the type of notice that is required before a directors' meeting is valid, or if notice is required at all.

As an example, Sections 56 and 58 of the Massachusetts General Laws (Chapter 156B) permit meetings to be held without notice provided the meeting dates are fixed beforehand; and even if the dates are not fixed beforehand, the notice need not specify the purpose of the meeting.

Similarly, Section 141 of the Delaware Corporation Law has no notice requirements at all. It permits further a quorum to be only one third of all the directors.

Thus it would appear under the cited cases that as long as the company's bylaws require some sort of notification (no matter how meager), compliance with that requirement would suffice for the purposes of the validity of the meeting.

It is important that directors understand the charter or bylaw requirements for meeting notice. If that notice is insufficient, the bylaws should be changed to ensure sufficient notice for each director to be present to protest (or approve) a proposed corporate action.

A typical company bylaw permits notification by telephone, cable, or radio, say, two days before the meeting. The notice need not specify the business to be transacted at the meeting. However, the board may appoint an executive committee to exercise all the powers vested in the board of directors and to hold meetings under whatever notice requirements it (the executive committee) determines to be appropriate. In the example of a company diversifying, a company with this type of bylaw could enter into a new business after giving only a day's telephone notice to a minority of the board of directors.

There are valid reasons to retain this kind of flexibility for quick action when necessary. It is important for a director to know the ease with which a corporation can take legally binding actions without full board participation.

It is interesting to compare the protections and notification requirements for stockholders' meetings. If the company is not public, the state statutes still ordinarily contain considerably more stringent notice requirements for stockholders' actions. If the company is public, Section 14 of the Securities

Exchange Act of 1934 prohibits any proxy solicitations to stockholders without considerable notice requirements, including identifying "clearly and impartially each matter or group of related matters intended to be acted upon, whether proposed by the management or by security holders" (Rule 14a-4(a)(3)).

The trouble with the "trite-rite" agenda is that its nature is such that usually no expectation exists or time is contemplated for other than perfunctory procedures. The American author Ambrose Bierce captured this type of agenda "boardom" in his 1906 definition of ritualism as "a Dutch Garden of God where He may walk in rectilinear freedom, keeping off the grass."[3]

The "vicarious authority" agenda. The form such an agenda will take depends greatly upon the size of a company, the nature of its business, and whether it is a private or public company.

In the case of a small private or public company, the agenda usually follows fairly simple lines. Routine matters are placed first, to be followed by matters brought forward from previous meetings, after which new business or business that requires full and detailed consideration would be noted.

In a larger business—either private or public—management control is usually delegated to executive and administrative officers or board committees. This delegation leaves the board ostensibly free to dwell mainly with statutory, strategic, or other important policy matters. In such settings, the delegation of powers of decision making and action is performed by other than the directors who bestow "vicarious authority" on the deputy executives or the commissioned committees.

Agenda for directors' meetings where such vicarious authority exists would normally include formal committee and officer reports on important matters—as far as they are known or predictable—that affect the performance of the corporation.

The problem with this idealized concept of agenda architecture is that for practical considerations the agenda is usually structured by the chairman or chief executive officer. The secretary and legal counsel of the company, of course, advise and help concoct the agenda. These individuals may or may not know what is on the "worry list" of each independent director if exposure to and empathy with these directors happen to be limited.

This relationship may be circumscribed by geography, disposition, personality, interest, perspective, competence, rapport, or other factors at play in the social or intellectual equations that link an outside director to any boardroom. Coping with this circumstance may require an extra effort in improving relationships and communications with each director in between formal meetings of the board.

The plenary agenda. The fully constituted agenda would provide for a relaxed period of exchange among directors and with management without fear of unwise tangling of director and executive roles. The period on the agenda for such communication would be after the required statutory matters are disposed of and would encourage meaningful director participation in helping formulate the company's stance on important matters. Some of this exchange can take place prior to board meeting at lunches or dinners provided the practice is not abused and cliques are prevented from forming.

Use of independent directors as a resource to the management and the board requires special competence and willingness of the independent directors to be available for such a process. There is an art in obtaining a sophisticated balance of tapping directors' wisdom before a policy decision without violating the requirement for an objective opinion by the director later when a corporate decision is called for. The political process versus the judicial process must be kept in mind in indulging in this use of independent directors as a competent resource in resolving a company problem.

One chairman I know uses the "British Question Period" procedure to safeguard against his board's harboring unasked questions. The British government considers one of its greatest democratic safeguards to be the question period which lasts for about an hour at the beginning of proceedings in the Commons on Mondays through Thursdays. Except for "private notice" questions of such an urgent character that normal advance notice is not given, two days' notice of a question is normally required.

Applied to a multibillion dollar corporation, this technique has proved beneficial, even exciting, for the board, the chairman, and the management over the past three years of its use. Directors submit questions in writing to the chairman, who arranges at a subsequent board meeting to provide an answer and appropriate discussion without divulging who raised the sometimes sticky question.

The omission agenda. Setting aside any hide-and-seek game playing with critical issues that should be aired in the boardroom but are not on the agenda for various reasons, the key issues are not really mysterious. Some of them are quiescent; others may be explosive. If the chief executive officer does not discover or reveal these issues or members of the board do not perceive them, then something may be wrong with the system, the CEO, or the perspective and effectiveness of the board.

Remedies include (a) the board's charging the management with seeking out these covert or unrecognized issues, (b) management's soliciting the board members' input on issues on their minds, or (c) outside help's educating the board on issues affecting the corporation. Such outsiders must be qualified to assess realistically a company's situation and to define external trends or events that might affect the company adversely or favorably in the future.

Complexities of our world could swamp boardrooms with all sorts of environmental, social, moral, ethical, and other value-laden issues. The specific impact caused by the expected actions of legislatures or regulatory agencies, shareowners, employees, and various activists' groups needs to be interpreted for each company and industry. Many of the issues never get put on the boardroom agenda. Of late, many are right on target and should be agenda items for a responsible board of directors, no matter how diverting and perturbing they may be to a board that is used to a stable environment in which to conduct the company's activities.

Which of these issues are hidden from boardroom review in a particular company situation and which should be placed on its future agenda depend, of course, on each company and each board setting. It is not a one-time problem. It is a continuing phenomenon. New issues will appear and can become malignant. Old issues may resolve themselves. Some issues will continue unsettled.

Similar to problems in mathematics, many boardroom issues can be resolved by means of common sense, axioms, and rules of inference. However, some boardroom issues may even fall into the "purgatory of perpetual undecidability." The director's quest should be to get these agenda topics out in the open to ensure a surprise-free board process.

Cache of Board Issues

More than a score and a half issues have surfaced in recent studies of corporations. These have been for-profit and not-for-profit institutions, including manufacturing and service organizations, educational institutions, governments at various levels, and in situations both domestic and international. Not all of these issues are pertinent or hidden from the agenda of responsible boardrooms. Depending on the maturity and sophistication of the board and the management, various of these core issues are recognized by responsible directorates and dealt with in some measure.

The following checklist of issues may or may not be on the hidden agenda of a typical board of directors. Most issues are obvious, but alas are too often neglected. The list implies no priority but a collection of some of the most topical. Try these out on a board, under "other business" if necessary. Best not surprise the chairman or chief executive officer, if, as a director, you wish to use this list effectively and constructively. Issues in this context are points for boardroom debate on which directors are likely to take either affirmative or negative positions.

Social responsibility corporate conduct. Could your company stand a social audit by an outside group, probably conducted as an adversary proceeding? Would the company pass with flying colors an ethics audit by an outside group? What have been the relationships with foreign government agents? Is the company accepting even tacitly the restraints of trade boycotts?[4]

Public owner interests. Can you identify where the company interests may conflict with public or owner interests now and in the future? Are there plans in hand to cope with this?[5]

Corporate Activism. Environmentalists, consumerists, and other well-meaning groups concerned with corporate conduct and employee well-being are gaining credibility and effectiveness. Are their objectives equitably recognized and addressed in situations where they reach into the zone of board decisions?

Business conflicts of interest. Interaction and interdependence of business-sector activities with those of the public sector are increasing. Is your board informed and can your board adequately decide when (a) the conduct of the company's business is perceived to be not in the public interest in a locale or market, (b) there are optional uses for corporate resources, (c) the key is reduction in labor content, (d) the activity involves production of military goods or services, (e) manufacture or sale of boycotted products or services is involved, (f) foreign investment in the United States or investment overseas is planned, and (g) public opinion or government jawboning is adverse?

Nature of the board. Is the composition of your current board of directors appropriate for being an effective board? Are the criteria for membership, performance, and board tenure realistic? Is the balance of inside and outside directors proper for the circumstances?

Corporate strategic objectives, goals. Are these explicit, comprehensive, and realistically monitored adequately at boardroom level? Are disaster plans in hand?[6]

Director executive linkages. Can you tally the significant other directorships held by all principals (executives and directors) and assess whether they have apparent or real insider or other conflicts? Are they partners of your audit or legal firms? Is the interface between the board and the chairman a proper professional one? How about stock ownership and trading activity by executives and directors? Are these responsibly handled and monitored?[7]

Boardroom dynamics. Are board meetings effective, meaningful, rewarding, and adequate for the matters at hand? Does the chairman handle peer relationships properly to elicit the best efforts from the board? Are committee appointments intelligent and unbiased?

Director liability. Has the general counsel been aggressive and professional in his explanation to the board of exposure and extent of liability? Does the company provide adequate protection, and is its premise of same insured? Kidnappings and ransom matters may raise other liability questions.

Separate chairman and CEO roles. Calls for board reform are increasingly vocal on the need to have a separate chairman to act as the board's agent dealing at arms' length with corporate responsibilities. Does your management-board complex warrant separation of these roles? Is the management succession issue out in the open, and is there an emergency plan in case the CEO position has to be filled in a hurry?[8]

Corporate information. Directors are beholden to management for information. The issue is either overload or screening. Is your board properly informed?

Whistle blowing. The issue concerns the disputable practice of someone (or some committee) in the corporation or on the board being able to call attention to an activity when it is seen as off the track and doing serious harm to the corporation, to individuals, or to society. A controversial concept, whistle blowing can be a lively topic for a plenary board meeting agenda, whether the practice is adopted or not.

Whether any of the foregoing agenda topics is hidden in a corporation is perhaps unimportant. What really is important is to set up a board process and agenda for uncovering such issues before they become troublesome. Some extra measures may have to be taken if the directors themselves and/or the management neglect or fail to perceive these and other future issues in time for the board to properly consider their impact on the corporation. Time is also required to devise strategies for coping with them.

A hidden agenda is a personal challenge to every chairman, chief executive officer, and director. Such issues should not be merely perceived or programmed as abstractions into board meetings. Computer experts make an interesting and pertinent distinction between two types of agenda as defined in computer usage. The computer dictionary defines an agenda as the set of control-language statements used to (a) prescribe a solution path or computer run procedure, or as (b) an ordered list of the major operations constituting a procedure for a solution or a computer run.

It is best to try to get any hidden agenda items out for boardroom contemplation and onto a solution path rather than allowing them to remain concealed. An equally unsatisfactory practice to concealment would be to merely run them through a trite-rite procedure with no solution attempted or contemplated.

Notes

1. Frank Shackleton, *The Chairman's Guide and Secretary's Companion* (London: Ward, Lock, 1955).
2. Lord John Fletcher Moulton, "Law and Manners" (speech presented at the Author's Club, London, 1914).
3. Ambrose Bierce, *The Devil's Dictionary* (New York: Dover Publications, Inc. 1958), pg. 115.
4. See my "Are Directors Boardworthy? A Report Card for Board Members," *Management Review* (September 1976): 14.
5. Ibid.
6. Ibid.
7. Ibid.
8. Ibid.

Index

Index

About the Author

Robert K. Mueller, chairman of the Board of Arthur D. Little, Inc., is also director of Arthur D. Little Limited (London).

Mueller's work at Arthur D. Little involves board of director, corporate governance and management aspects of multinational institutions: business development, new ventures, acquisitions, corporate organization, planning, and diversification in various industries and financial organizations.

Prior to joining Arthur D. Little in 1968, he was vice-president of Monsanto Company and a member of its board of directors and executive committee. Mueller also served as Shawinigan Resins Corporation's president and chairman of the board. During World War II, he was plant manager of the Longhorn Ordnance Works, following which he became general manager of Monsanto's Plastics Division in 1952, subsequently moving into corporate international activities.

He is a member of the board of directors and executive committee of Massachusetts Mutual Life Insurance Company, member of the board and executive committee of BayBanks, Inc., and member of the board of Mass-Mutual Income Investors, Inc. Other business and professional affiliations include technical and management associations, both here and abroad. He is vice-chancellor of the International Academy of Management (CIOS); a fellow of the Institute of Directors (London); a fellow of the American Association for the Advancement of Science; a life member of the American Management Associations; a member of the AMA International Council, the New York Academy of Sciences; and a trustee of The Cheswick Center (Boston).

Mueller received the B.S. degree in chemical engineering from Washington University and the M.S. degree in chemistry from the University of Michigan, and he completed the Advanced Management Program at the Harvard University Graduate School of Business Administration.

A well-known speaker in professional circles, he is the author of eight books on management and board of director matters, as well as numerous articles in scientific and business journals. In 1970, Mueller served as chairman of the faculty for a Management of Technology session at the Salzburg Seminars in American Studies and currently is a member of that organization's board of directors and executive committee.

Mueller is a vice-chairman of trustees of Colby-Sawyer College, New Hampshire. He was appointed visiting professor at Manhattan College, Bronx, New York, for 1976, and is a member of the board of visitors for the School of Management of Boston University.